AF600261

Time's Visible Surface

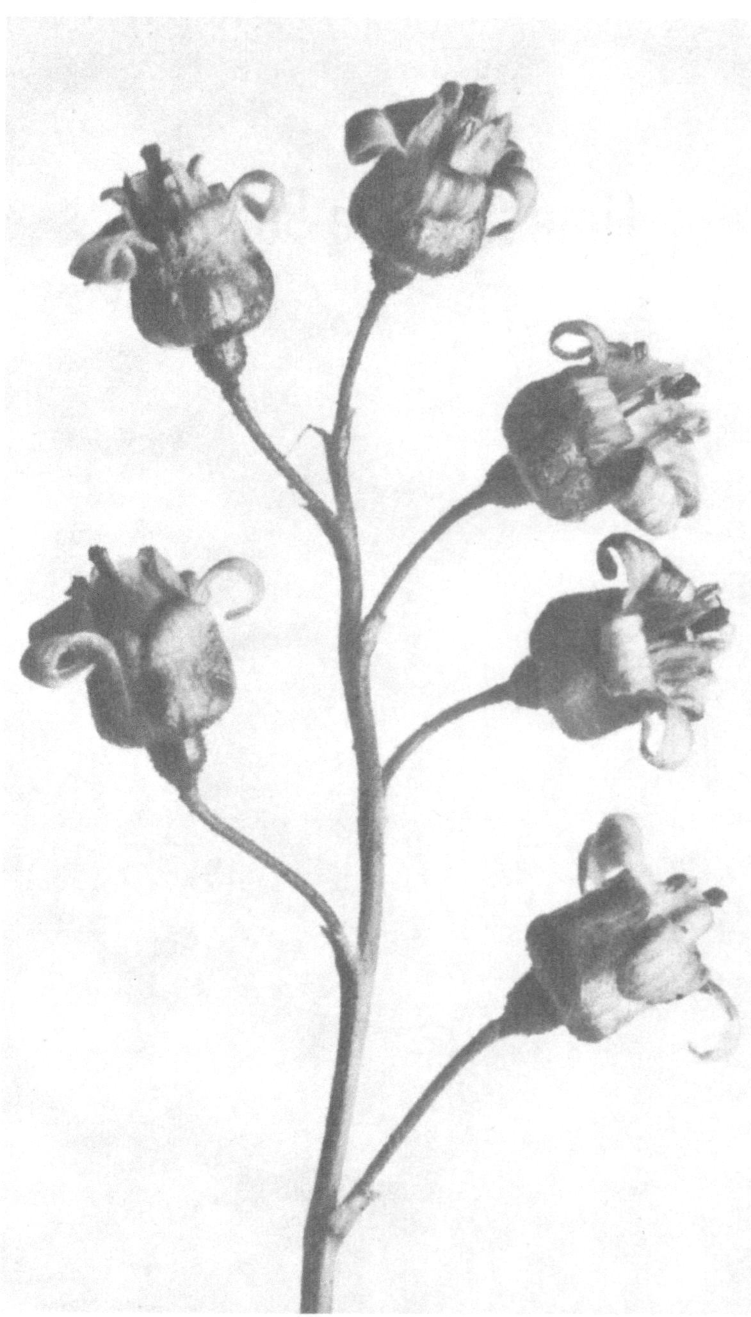

Ribes nigrum, common black currant. Raceme enlarged 4.5x.
From *Art Forms in the Plant World*, Karl Blossfeldt (Dover Publications, 1985)

Time's Visible Surface

Alois Riegl and the Discourse on History and Temporality in Fin-de-Siècle Vienna

MICHAEL GUBSER

Wayne State University Press
Detroit

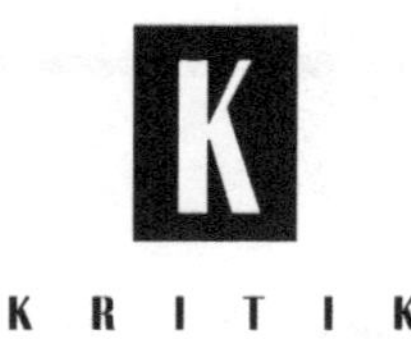

K R I T I K

German Literary Theory and Cultural Studies
Liliane Weissberg, Editor

A complete listing of the books in this series can be found online at http://wsupress.wayne.edu

Manufactured in the United States of America.
ISBN-13: 978-0-8143-3208-5 ISBN-10: 0-8143-3208-0

Library of Congress Cataloging-in-Publication Data
Gubser, Mike.
Time's visible surface : Alois Riegl and the discourse on history and temporality in fin-de-siecle Vienna / Michael Gubser.
p. cm. — (Kritik: German literary theory and cultural studies)
Includes bibliographical references and index.
ISBN 0-8143-3208-0 (cloth : alk. paper)
1. Riegl, Alois, 1858–1905—Criticism and interpretation. 2. Art—Historiography.
3. Art and history. 4. Space and time in art. 5. Aesthetics, Austrian—19th century.
I. Title: Alois Riegl and the discourse on history and temporality in fin-de-siecle Vienna. II. Title. III. Kritik (Detroit, Mich.)
N7483.R54G83 2006
707'.2'2—dc22
2005017433

∞ The paper used in this publication meets the minimum requirements of the American National Standard for Information Sciences—Permanence of Paper for Printed Library Materials, ANSI Z39.48-1984.

Dedicated to my mother,
father, and sister

Contents

Acknowledgments

WHILE WRITING THIS BOOK, I have incurred debts of gratitude to many people and organizations. Numerous libraries, archives, and universities assisted me in my research. In Austria, the Institut für Kunstgeschichte at the University of Vienna, where I received tremendous assistance from Professor Hans Aurenhammer, and the Forschungsstelle für österreichische Philosophie in Graz were open during the summer, helpful in their advice, and efficient in making resources available. St. Stephen's and St. Agnes School in Alexandria, Virginia, where I taught history between 1998 and 2001, generously provided me with an Association of Parents and Teachers Grant to help fund a research trip to Austria in the summer of 1999. And my colleagues in Virginia and at the Waring School in Beverly, Massachusetts, where I taught between 2001 and 2003, provided intellectual encouragement as I wrote my dissertation and then revised it into this book.

Of course, many of my debts are of a more personal nature. I do not know if I would have even embarked on the project had it not been for the support of several friends in Berkeley. Edouard Servan-Schreiber, Mike Signer, and Ania Wertz provided friendship and encouragement at a time when they were sorely needed. As I hunkered down to write in Virginia, Jeremy Baguyos, Jean Hunt, and Boyd White picked up where my Berkeley colleagues left off; they offered comradeship as well as countless worthy excuses for not working. This account of distraction would be incomplete without congratulating my high school students in

Virginia and Massachusetts for generating so much diversionary entertainment.

Four close friends deserve a special note of gratitude. With conversations in person and over the phone, Anthony Marasco and Emek Uçarer bore me through the difficult transition from graduate student to teacher. Chris Vitiello showed that neither time nor distance, both of which we crossed together in a car in summer 1998, could dim our friendship. And about Paolo Prandoni, who nearly flew from Europe at the drop of a hat to help me, I will simply say this: he was my best man formally in 2001, but informally he has been so for years.

Many people have read parts or all of the manuscript. Carl Schorske, David Luft, Margaret Olin, Diana Graham Reynolds, and Barry Smith offered valuable suggestions and encouragement. Don Puchala, Jennifer Ring, and Roger Coate, at the University of South Carolina, went out of their way to further my academic career. Despite my unorthodox path through graduate school, my committee members—Margaret Anderson, Kathleen James, and my advisor Martin Jay—have offered unwavering support as well as commentary and criticism throughout the writing process. I have long valued their intellectual advice, but over the last few years I have come to appreciate deeply the genuine concern, respect, and generosity they have extended to me on a personal as well as a professional level.

To my family, of course, I owe a far more heartfelt debt of gratitude than any acknowledgment can repay. It is trite but true to say that I could not have completed this book without their many forms of support. My mother, father, and sister, to whom this book is dedicated, held me together at times, even though I could not always do the same for them.

My final acknowledgment goes to Elisa Oh, whom I met almost a year after starting this project and married in 2001, a month after completing the dissertation that formed the basis of this book. She has accompanied me through much of the work. It is hard to imagine living with someone longer than I have lived with this project, but now that it is behind me, I look forward to a lifetime with her, full of many future projects and joys.

AUGUST 2003

Introduction:
Alois Riegl and Fin-de-Siècle Vienna

In a letter written to Jean-Baptiste Colbert congratulating France on its scientific advances, the philosopher Wilhelm Gottfried von Leibniz claimed that man's interest in "the secret of the heavens, the greatness of the earth, and time measurement" revealed that the human mind contained "something of the divine."[1] The great clockwork of the universe still puzzled and challenged modern thinkers even as inventions such as the telescope and timepiece helped to illuminate its mysteries. Time's lofty position in this seventeenth-century pantheon of wonders suggests something of its power to enthrall the intellect and inspire the poetic and philosophical imagination, a power that increased in subsequent centuries.

Since Leibniz's age, time has achieved a truly preeminent position in Western philosophical, cultural, and social consciousness. Modernity's emphasis on time and transience is by now proverbial.[2] As Charles Baudelaire famously remarked, "[M]odernity [is] the ephemeral, the fugitive, the contingent, the half of art whose other half is the eternal and the immutable."[3] What holds for art is true of modern society in general: the sense of temporal acceleration and historical fragmentation, of an ephemerality at once exhilarating and devastating, is so pervasive in the pronouncements of modern culture and society as to seem ubiquitous. In *All That Is Solid Melts into Air,* cultural critic Marshall

Berman divides the modern experience of transience into three historical phases: from the sixteenth century to the eighteenth, cultural and political elites began to remark on the quickening of change and innovation and the fragmentation of social life. Ernst Cassirer has argued that the Enlightenment sought to harness the rapid scientific and intellectual transformations of the era to an accelerated historical progress.[4] The revolutions of the late eighteenth and nineteenth centuries, Berman's second phase, disrupted the faith in an unbroken progress but made the awareness of temporal and historical transience even more acute and pervasive. By the twentieth century, Berman's third and final phase, the heightened time consciousness of modernity had expanded across the globe. The establishment of a universal standard time at the turn of the twentieth century emblematized the modern concern for punctuality and capped the nearly five hundred year rise of the clock to its preeminence in modern life.[5] This time consciousness has grown even more pronounced in recent years, as anticipation of the millennium and fears about Y2K intensified our fascination with temporal passage and breakdown.

Scholarly interest in the topic has paralleled this popular fascination. The modern philosophical, historical, and sociological literature on time is far too vast to summarize in any meaningful way here. Its explication has been one of the central concerns of modern Continental thought since Kant and Hegel incorporated time as a fundamental category in their philosophical systems. Their influential treatises made time and history central to all *Wissenschaften* in the nineteenth century. Evolutionary biology, historicist social science, and even architecture, with its stylistic revivals, offered distinctly historical approaches to the understanding of natural, cultural, and artistic phenomena. By the turn of the twentieth century, as the historical sciences faced a crisis of methodology and objectivity, many thinkers elevated time to a position of priority among philosophical concerns, analyzing *inter alia* the temporal constitution of being and the temporality of perception.

Twentieth-century interest in time emerged in part from this fascination with and crisis of history as the premier explanatory paradigm of the nineteenth-century humanities. Whether tacitly or openly, historical accounts make assumptions about the nature of time that are not based on purely documentary evidence. Among these assumptions, a strong sense of temporal continuity, mitigated in part by the analytic separation of present from past, informs the explanatory paradigms of most historical research. Historians elicit meaning from documents by placing them in context along a continuous timeline. Since the late nineteenth century, this model of continuous historical time has come under increasing scrutiny. Indeed, a recent outpouring of scholarship in the humanities has sought both to illuminate the assumptions about narrativity, temporality, and objectivity that structure historical practice and to uncover the origins of these concepts in the writings of the founders of modern disciplines.[6] It is in this spirit of reevaluating foundations that I investigate the work of the Austrian art historian Alois Riegl and the intellectual field from which he emerged. I hope to demonstrate that Riegl, like such contemporaries as Wilhelm Dilthey, Henri Bergson, and Edmund Husserl, took it as a priority to rethink the categories of time and history.

Alois Riegl is considered one of the foremost late-nineteenth-century architects of the modern discipline of art history. He helped to establish art history as an autonomous discipline by distinguishing its subject matter, thematic goals, and visual methods from the parent disciplines of history and aesthetics.[7] Riegl's scholarship was rooted in his historical training, and his work drew widely on developments within the nineteenth-century disciplines of history, philosophy, archaeology, aesthetics, and anthropology. In a century that privileged historical explanations for social and cultural phenomena, German scholarship witnessed an extraordinary flowering of historical thought as luminaries such as Wilhelm von Humboldt, Leopold von Ranke, and Johann Droysen established the historiographical paradigms within or against which many scholars continue to work today. Art history participated in these groundbreaking developments, and by the late nineteenth and early twentieth centuries it had emancipated itself from both an auxiliary historical status and purely aesthetic criteria of evaluation. Scholars from the German-speaking world, such as Jakub Burckhardt, Heinrich Wölfflin, and Riegl himself, took the lead in setting the goals and methods of the emerging discipline.

Riegl displayed a remarkable persistence in examining the relationship between history and art and the presumptions entailed in historical narrative and visual description. Despite this focus, his insights were achieved with little overt historiographical theorizing, and only rarely did he treat methodological concerns separately from the historical narratives they informed. Riegl's work is therefore deceptively straightforward and atheoretical in exposition; a first-time reader impressed by the richness of empirical description found in *Problems of Style,* Riegl's seminal history of ancient decorative form, might be hard-pressed to give a detailed account of its theoretical commitments. Due to this elusiveness, interpretations of Riegl vary wildly; he could be enlisted to support Wilhelm Worringer's cultural essentialist typologies, Erwin Panofsky's theories of artistic symbolism, Walter Benjamin's cultural Marxism, and, more recently, Paul Feyerabend's scientific relativism and Gilles Deleuze and Félix Guattari's analysis of capitalism.[8] His work was cited favorably by figures as diverse as Oswald Spengler and Georg Lukács, Karl Mannheim, Walter Gropius, Mikhail Bakhtin, and Hermann Bahr. Riegl provided the methodological basis for the New Vienna School of Art History founded in the 1930s by Hans Sedlmayr and Otto Pächt; the school's reputation suffered after Sedlmayr's notorious foray into Nazism, but its less tainted methods and writings are enjoying a resurgence of interest today.[9] And through his Austrian disciple Victor Lowenfeld, Riegl came to influence art education in America.[10] Nevertheless, despite a notable following among art historians and cultural theorists, only in the last decades of the twentieth century have Riegl's complex analyses emerged from the shadow of Wölfflin's more well-known classifications, which were *de rigueur* for introductory art history courses. This marginalization is partly due to the elusiveness of Riegl's ideas and the difficulty of his prose.[11] Riegl's theoretical reticence creates special problems for an analysis devoted to his theories of time and history. Unlike Wölfflin, Riegl was loath to structure historical discussions around straightforward expository categories. Even his distinctive and idiosyncratic conceptual terminology is hard to pin down; rather than delimit conceptual boundaries at the outset of an analysis, Riegl preferred to work out the manifold significance of concepts in the detailed narrative elaboration and description of exemplary artworks. Neologisms abound in his writing, often with only cursory definition. His famously elliptical notion of *Kunstwollen,* for example, first introduced in *Problems of Style* but used more fully in *Late Roman Art Industry,* invites radically divergent readings and provokes frequent interpretive dispute.

An example of Riegl's characteristic rhetorical tactics helps to illustrate these challenges. Wolfgang Kemp has noted that Riegl frequently employed binary oppositions as a "prestructured system of taxonomy" that channels "artistic volition." The opposing concepts of "optical or haptic, farsighted or nearsighted, isolating or bonding, subjective or objective, idealistic or naturalistic, crystalline or organic, space or demarcation" are only among the better-known examples of this strategy.[12] Riegl's seminal work *Problems of Style,* which capped the first phase of his scholarly career, is replete with dichotomies pitting natural mimesis against artistic convention, materialism against idealism. At times Riegl seemed to treat such binary categories as genuine oppositions, endpoints of a spectrum that distinguished one artwork from another according to mutually exclusive characteristics. At other moments, binary categories appeared as juxtapositions within works; they did not describe exclusive qualities, but, rather, historically coincident variables. Art historian Hans Sedlmayr noted this potential confusion when he cautioned, "With Riegl, there are generally two polar possibilities—conceptual pairs—but they must not be dichotomized."[13] Although Riegl's logic invites misreading, his art historical analyses consistently transcended the framework of categories he used to orient them. That many commentators on Riegl have fallen into the trap of adjudicating between oversimplified and reductive oppositions testifies to the maddening nature of his arguments, but it also misses the point of his work, namely, to trace the complex relationships and juxtapositions that characterize art history. In attempting to explore the theoretical underpinnings of Riegl's narratives, therefore, I admit to a degree of interpretive temerity, especially since the historiographical spirit of this book runs counter to Riegl's own practice of subordinating theory to historical example.

The aim of this book is to explicate Riegl's conception of history and temporality and to situate it within his late nineteenth-century Austrian intellectual context. Time is an extremely elusive concept, one that has pushed the analytic and imaginative faculties of many thinkers to the bounds of paradox.[14] In my work, I do not seek to advance a new theory of historical time, but try instead to illuminate Riegl's complex thoughts on the subject. Of course, interpretation does entail a degree of theorizing, which I try to manage by remaining close to Riegl's texts. I hope to demonstrate that Riegl's work represents, among other things, a sustained effort to grasp the nature of temporality in the visual relationship between history and art.

Although Riegl's explicit aim was to examine the relationship between art and history, this book shows that a multifaceted concept of time underlay his analyses. I should stress at the outset that the term "temporality" is my own, not Riegl's. It is therefore necessary to distinguish conceptually between the notions of history and temporality that inform my analysis. Conceptually, history designates the narrative organization of events and material evidence from the past. Each of history's many forms—circular, linear, teleological, evolutionary, sacred, national, universal—imposes a certain order and structure on the past, or, more precisely, on its evidence and traces. History is thus an overarching framework that embraces and organizes evidence from the past, indeed, as past. By contrast, time (or temporality) is a characteristic of material evidence itself. Riegl's empiricism frequently enlisted a chronological notion of time as date, the register of events stressed by the descriptive and empirical sciences in which he was schooled. Dating plots events along a historical yardstick as a succession of equable moments that suggest, in Hayden White's terms, the fullness of time even in the absence of events.[15] This chronological time established a measurable relationship among events and between the historian and the objects studied, gave the historian an accounting of the order of time, and positioned the historian within history. This accounting, however, evoked a continuous temporal passage or flux underlying the consecutive moments of history. This sense of temporality as historicity, as *durée,* infused Riegl's notion of art history, determining the event-horizon for human activity and constituting all human production as temporal. Temporality could not be discerned directly, but it could be recognized through the mediation of art; artworks rendered time in a perceptible "object," as objective temporality. I refer to this material historicity as temporality, a continuous time embraced by objects rather than a chronological history that embraces objects.

Another way to express the difference between history and time is in terms of the commitment to objectivity that stood at the center of the nineteenth-century historical profession. The notion of history that historicists, universal historians, and empirical historians alike espoused rested on the assumption that the events forming the material of historical study had an objective external existence. Documents and artifacts attested to the real existence of past events, and the historian had a duty to depict that past as objectively as possible. Riegl inherited this commitment to historical objectivity. In the late nineteenth century, however, the combined intellectual influence of perceptual psychology, phenomenology, and post-Kantian philosophy began to weaken the faith in external objectivity as the basis for scientific inquiry and produced a shift toward notions of objectivity based on perceptual construction or mental inexistence. In Husserlian vocabulary, the question of the external, or noumenal, reality of an object was "bracketed." Riegl stood at the cusp of this shift. In his work, a commitment to traditional notions of historical objectivity conflicted with the project of discerning the temporal constitution of art objects, a project that stressed the role of perception in constructing the objective coherence of both historical and physical continuity. Whereas history accepted the external objectivity of its phenomena as given, time as a concept presumed an interrelationship between subject and object. Riegl's work marked a shift away from nineteenth-century historicism to the twentieth-century concerns with historicity, temporality, and subjectivity.

Riegl's historical training at the University of Vienna emphasized empirical study, and his choice of art history as a sub-disciplinary specialization made available to him a set of tools for visual analysis that he used throughout his career. Along with other art historians of his and the preceding generation, Riegl renounced aesthetic evaluation as a goal for art history. Although he conceded that art historians had tastes of their own, he insisted that their scholarly duty was to acknowledge and overcome these preferences in order to grasp the artistry of a past era on its own terms.[16] The art historian's primary task was not to safeguard allegedly timeless standards of aesthetic quality but to trace the historical and cultural development of perceptual and visual form. Riegl synthesized aspects of empiricism and psychology into a proto-phenomenological approach to art history. Judith Ryan's work is especially helpful in comparing nineteenth-century positivism and phenomenology around questions of perception. In *The Vanishing Subject*, Ryan distinguishes between nineteenth-century experimentalists, who "explored in detail the functioning of sensory perception," and empiricists who were "primarily concerned to work out the philosophical premises for sense perceptions." The latter current gave rise to "a kind of protophenomenology that permeated the thought of most early psychologists."[17] Riegl's empiricism should be understood within this context. The term "phenomenology," of course, invokes the work of Edmund Husserl, like Riegl a student of the philosopher Franz Brentano. Husserl claimed that phenomenology represented a true positivism that did not rest solely on sensory, subjective, or psychological evidence, but instead investigated the objective and philosophical premises of sense perception.[18] Brentano, Husserl, and Riegl each strove to dismantle the strong divide between subject and object that characterized mid-century positivism.[19] Toward the end of the century, many thinkers had come to doubt certain core positivist tenets, including the faith in the ability of the senses to access the world directly. Friedrich Nietzsche, Henri Bergson, Hermann Cohen, and others challenged the power of rationality to grasp the world, positing instead the preeminence of will, creativity, or a priori knowledge. The Kantian philosopher Friedrich Lange, whose *Geschichte des Materialismus und Kritik seiner Bedeutung in der Gegenwart* (1866) may have informed Riegl's work, argued that psychology, not positivistic natural science, offered the closest approximations to reality.[20] In her intellectual biography of Riegl, Margaret Olin notes that these revisions of mid-century scientific thought "encourage[d] psychological interpretations of Kant's a priori elements: space and time."[21] Riegl's empiricism, with its interest in the categories of time and perception, revealed a similarly troubled reception of positivism. Artworks were, for Riegl, the material products of historical perception and creativity and thus provided detailed objective evidence for empirical historical study. At the same time, however, their historical value arose in part because of the subjective involvement of the viewer. Artworks were both past and present, subjective and objective fields of meaning.

On one level, the problem that motivated Riegl's work is familiar to historians in all ages: how can we grasp the cultural and intellectual dynamics of a bygone era from the documents it leaves behind without misreading that era according to our own cultural prejudices? Riegl's unique approach to this question was to conduct a kind of phenomenology of history and time through the study of art. According to Husserl, phenomenology proposed a method for bracketing assumptions in order to arrive at the pure sensory data of perception; this data, he argued, could then be submitted to a descriptive analysis that outlined the objective contents of perception and provided an empirical basis for scientific investigation. Riegl's use of close description in order to uncover the immanent historicity of artworks fit into this proto-phenomenological mold. Indeed, one problem entailed in interpreting the past grows out of the fundamental difficulty of analyzing foreign notions of time from within our own historically conditioned temporal assumptions. Historians often assume a unified, continuous historical timeline when evaluating works of the past even though historical study quickly reveals that there is no single cross-cultural notion of history or temporality. All cultures have their own determinations of time, often presented in terms of religious or mythological narrative; they are not all structured around the clear notions of origin, direction, and continuity familiar in the West. Some cultures think in terms of variable subdivisions of time; others, such as modern Western cultures, use equable hours. History can be cyclical or linear. The list of characteristics could go on and on, offering ever more detailed temporal distinctions and contradictions. The point, however, is that whereas modern science encourages us to believe in a universal and objective chronometry, historical study reminds us of the radical cultural relativity and variety of temporal perception. In studying the past, it is extremely difficult for a scholar from an era that embraces one construction of time to grasp the temporalities of other eras and cultures without translating them into more familiar but also anachronistic terms. Riegl believed that art provided us with a way out of this historiographical dilemma. Artworks not only represented cultural and historical values but also depicted the movements of history and time in material form. In Riegl's formalism, art embodied the temporality of perception; it enacted and reenacted, as vision objectified in form, the perceptual relationship between man and the world in a past era, as well as the ever-changing perceptual relationship between past and present. To a trained eye, an artwork provided the formal and material clues of its own temporal constitution. In viewing artworks properly, the art historian could witness alternate temporal forms even from within his own historical framework.

The underlying aim of Riegl's scholarship, as I attempt to show, was to discern the movements of history and the perceptual forms of the past by investigating the visual matrices of artworks. His work sought to elucidate the historical premises of artistic creation and judgment. The significance of his narrative accounts, therefore, was not exhausted in detailed chronological descriptions of artworks. Although scrupulous description was a prominent feature of his work, Riegl was convinced that an empirical analysis of artworks could reveal both the perceptual characteristics of cultural periods and the physical traces of history. As historical evidence, art and artifacts held the past in a visible, material presence; a sequence of artworks from successive periods could illustrate the process of historical development. Art history, which grappled with the relationship between the synchronic art object (materially present for observation) and the diachronic development of visual forms, allowed Riegl to clarify the nature of historical time itself.

Among his contemporaries, Riegl was not alone in his investigations of the complexities of history and time. His work drew on the influences of his professors in Vienna and on scholarly debates across a number of disciplines. Given the prevalence of historicist thought in German universities, this involvement should hardly be surprising. Historicism, which Friedrich Meinecke described in 1936 as "one of the greatest intellectual revolutions that Western thought has experienced,"[22] encompasses a great variety of historiographical theories and practices prevalent in the German-speaking world from the late eighteenth to the early twentieth centuries; its unifying theme was the understanding of all social and political phenomena in terms of historical context and development rather than abstract, timeless logic or natural law.[23] Riegl worked at a time when mid-century historicist assumptions were facing stringent philosophical and methodological challenges, a period that scholars have described in terms of a crisis of historical consciousness. Figures such as Friedrich Nietzsche and Wilhelm Dilthey, and, after World War I, Ernst Troeltsch, Martin Heidegger, and Hans-Georg Gadamer, stood among the most prominent theorists to cast doubt on the epistemological underpinnings of historicism. Numerous works have traced the breakdown of historicism from its high point in the early to mid-nineteenth century, exemplified in very different ways by the works of Hegel, Ranke, and Droysen, through its professionalization among university historians and then its collapse as a unified set of assumptions around the turn of the century.[24] Friedrich Nietzsche's famous assault, "The Uses and Abuses of History for Life" (1873), influenced scores of followers in Austria, Germany, and elsewhere by contrasting a vibrant concept of life to a culture of dry historical fact and research. The tremendous success of the natural sciences in defining methodological rigor, and the concomitant fashion for positivism in the human sciences of the mid-century, also raised skepticism about the epistemological soundness of historicist thought. With his *Einleitung in der Geisteswissenschaften,* Wilhelm Dilthey produced the most renowned attempt at a critique of historical reason, an enterprise that he hoped would save historical thinking by providing it with a secure epistemological foundation distinct from the methods of natural science. Dilthey's concern for the status of history as a paradigm was shared by Neo-Kantians such as Hermann Cohen, Wilhelm Windelband, and Heinrich Rickert as well as non-German thinkers such as Henri Bergson and Benedetto Croce.

Ironically, the crisis of history provides an object lesson in the pitfalls of success, for it was generated in part by the ubiquitous acceptance of the fundamental historicist claim that all human phenomena should be understood in historical terms. As Theodore Ziolkowski notes, in the late nineteenth century a thoroughgoing professionalization of historicism followed naturally on the widespread acceptance of its basic assumption. This apparent victory for the historicist paradigm, however, produced some acute uncertainties.

> The recognition of the historicity of all human life and institutions led gradually to a profound skepticism regarding the possibility of any historical certainty or of any meaning in history. If all historical being is relative, then how can we continue to believe in the priority of Christianity and the Western values that had formerly provided the center of meaning for Western civilization? . . . At the same time, the new techniques of documentary analysis and archival research, which after Ranke produced the monumental compilations of the nineteenth century, led historians increasingly away from writing presentations for a general educated public, as had been the practice from classical antiquity down to the late eighteenth century, and into creating ever more highly specialized monographs instead. As professional historiography grew in sophistication, becoming at the same time and in every country more nationalistic in thrust and factual in substance, it lost the audience that from Sallust to the present had been drawn to history for its philosophical—that is to say, ethical—implications.[25]

The price of successfully conquering the humanistic disciplines was paid in the increasing specialization and fragmentation of the historical field. For if each phenomenon had its own distinct history, as historicism suggested, then each demanded its own specialized sub-discipline, method, and scholarly language. Context ceased to function as a unifying framework across the historical field; instead, unity was only to be found within disciplines in the evolution of distinctive forms and methods. With history as the ascendant mode of explanation, the humanities offered to the general public not a consolidated edifice of knowledge but a fragmented field of specializations devoid of any clear unifying or overarching meaning.

By the early twentieth century, the cumulative weight of these challenges to historicism, combined with the shock of cataclysms such as World War I and the Russian Revolution, led to the appearance of highly publicized works of grand narrative history such as Oswald Spengler's *The Decline of the West* (vol. 1, 1918), H. G. Wells's *The Outline of History* (1918–1919), and Arnold Toynbee's *Study of History* (1939). These volumes differed from their historicist predecessors in their implication that historical writing, in Theodor Lessing's term, involved "*giving* meaning to the meaningless" (emphasis mine).[26] Whereas nineteenth-century historians demanded that scholars seek to bridge the temporal gulf between themselves and their objects of study in order to reveal objective qualities of the past—that is, assume a recoverable continuity between past and present—early twentieth-century historians came to doubt the transparency of evidence, the possibility of recovering the objective past, and the belief that meaning emerges from history; they accepted instead that historical thought required, to some degree, the imposition of order and meaning on otherwise disorganized facts. These twentieth-century histories replaced the objectivist itinerary of the nineteenth-century discipline with more subjectivist programs. From the 1920s onward, this tradition gave way to an investigation of the philosophical preconditions for historical thinking. In the works of Edmund Husserl, Martin Heidegger, and Hans-Georg Gadamer, temporality and history became categories of experience that were irreducible to simple fact or chronology; time and historicity were constitutive features of meaning and experience, not discontinuities to be bridged or overcome.

Riegl's work was situated in the midst of this turn-of-the-century crisis of historical thought. While he retained a faith in the objectivist commitments of nineteenth-century historiography and believed that the proper scrutiny of material evidence could reveal traces of the past, he also acknowledged a subjective role in the creation of historical meaning. Indeed, his work on the *Denkmalpflege* argued that the art historical value of a monument emerged only in the tension between past and present, between objective features and subjective valuation.[27] Elsewhere, following Nietzsche, Riegl warned that an overweening historicism could stifle creativity.[28] Instead of accepting the historicist presumption that an artwork's meaning emerged from an unmediated material past, Riegl broached the question of art's problematic historicity by asking how artworks came to have historical value in the relationship between past and present. Moreover, Riegl advocated a broad vision of historical context and insisted on situating artistic developments within wider cultural trends, indeed ultimately within an overarching worldview that encompassed politics and economics as well as culture. At the same time, however, he remained a staunch proponent of disciplinary specialization; artworks demonstrated an autonomous human creative will and required an independent set of rigorous visual and historical methods of analysis. Thus, Riegl offered a complex response to the crisis of history around the turn of the century: his art history at once demonstrated nineteenth-century historicist convictions and foreshadowed the early twentieth-century shift toward subjectivism and concern for temporality.

Although historicism has garnered tremendous scholarly attention, Austrian contributions to nineteenth-century debates about philosophy of history and historiography have been largely ignored and at times dismissed outright. Heinrich Ritter von Srbik, for example, characterized the Austrian historical profession's lack of theoretical and methodological sophistication in the following terms: "the indigenous German-Austrian historiography . . . tended toward as objective a presentation as possible, tried to approach an unpolitical, strictly factual research ideal or devoted itself to a complete positivism that distanced itself from philosophy."[29] Some commentators, linking this atheoretical bent with a reluctance to probe recent Austrian history, have suggested that Austrian historians buried themselves in empirical facts and premodern eras to avoid confronting national, social, and international crises that would have demonstrated weakness and demanded political response." With an almost feverish forgetfulness, the Vienna historical school threw itself upon the German Middle Ages and on documentary criticism," lamented W. Bauer.[30] Historians in the Dual Monarchy, according to Alphons Lhotsky, merely depicted how the crises rampant in contemporary society had developed, but were reluctant to consider their broader historical implications or ways to work through them.[31] The myopic pursuit of empirical research provided escape from the suggestions of Austrian decline implicit within historicist theories of national development.

A burgeoning, more recent literature on the intellectual and cultural world of turn-of-the-century Austria, especially fin-de-siècle Vienna, has reinforced this view. Until the mid-1960s, most studies of Austrian culture tended to be monographic works about individual figures such as Freud or Wittgenstein, footnotes to political analyses of Habsburg decline, or chapters in broader histories of German culture. Some of these works, especially the numerous memoirs and histories written by Austrians, evoked the distinctive atmosphere of turn-of-the-century Austria as a kind of lost world.[32] Diverse in style and characterization, these reminiscences prefigured the full-blown analyses of fin-de-siècle Austria and Vienna that emerged in the English-language historical literature of the 1970s.[33] Everyone who writes in the field of Austrian cultural history owes a debt to Carl Schorske's now-classic *Fin-de-Siècle Vienna,* which, alongside the work of Allan Janik, Stephen Toulmin, and William Johnston, defined the fin-de-siècle Vienna paradigm of modernist innovation.[34] Although Schorske claimed that he had no intention of providing a thorough survey of Austrian fin-de-siècle modernism, Janik is correct to note that *Fin-de-Siècle Vienna* did offer a characterization of the Austrian cultural context, whether or not its author so intended.[35] Even if Schorske's aim was simply to trace the failure of liberalism or the rise of antihistoricism in Austria, as he purports, his performance was convincing enough to establish a contextualist paradigm for Austrian cultural and intellectual history.

These scholars of Austrian culture tend to make three fundamental presumptions about the fin-de-siècle period. First, most studies accept that fin-de-siècle Austria, and especially Vienna, had clearly demarcated temporal and geographical boundaries. Metropolitan, ethnic, and state borders are taken as markers of cultural as well as political jurisdiction. Accepting the intimate connection between culture and politics that Schorske proposed, most studies trust the sufficiency of firm dates set by political events to delimit their accounts of cultural development. These boundaries effectively reinforce the view that political context shaped cultural and intellectual developments, thus affirming what Schorske believed: that no scholar who investigates Austrian high culture "fails to be impressed by the sturdy integration of its components."[36] This connection, however, hinges on the dates used to mark the rise of Austrian modernism. The Austrian fin-de-siècle period is said to have begun in 1890 or 1873 or even 1867 and ended in 1914 or 1918, depending upon the themes an author chooses to highlight. This inexactitude in dating suggests the tenuousness of the periodization such boundaries establish. Schorske, for example, offers a carefully orchestrated account of turn-of-the-century Viennese culture beginning around the 1890s and centered on the year 1900, one that relies on both textual evidence and psychoanalytic and aesthetic tropes to link the rise of Austrian cultural modernism with the failure of political liberalism. If cultural modernism, however, can be traced to earlier decades, during or even before the liberal era, then the boundaries of the Austrian fin-de-siècle period become less clear and the links between political events and cultural achievements more complex and indirect.[37]

A second fundamental presumption of the literature follows on the first: that cultural achievements can be subsumed under singular explanatory hypotheses often tied to social and political context. These "theses that were would-be paradigms,"[38] to use Janik's apt phrase, include Schorske's "failure of liberalism," Johnston's "therapeutic nihilism," Le Rider's "crises of identity," and Janik's own "critical modernism" or "problems of identity and communication."[39] Numerous monographic studies of particular schools of thought offer their own tradition's achievement as an archetype of Austrian intellectual qualities; logical positivism, empiricism, aestheticism, psychologism—all become *Austrian* schools rooted in distinctively Austrian ways of thinking.[40] Studies of supposedly prototypical thinkers have shown the same tendency to collapse cultural context into the works of a single figure.[41] All of these studies posit an intimate connection between a thinker's immediate social milieu and his intellectual output. Indeed, cultural context is often seen as not simply one factor among many but as *the* crucial factor determining a thinker's accomplishments. Such accounts evince a certain nostalgia for the old Habsburg Empire, which, for all its turmoil and inefficiencies, embraced so many competing nationalities and produced such cultural efflorescence.[42]

The final presumption of much fin-de-siècle literature is that Austrian culture tended toward antihistoricism. Schorske, in fact, claimed as his central theme in *Fin-de-Siècle Vienna* the "historical genesis of modern cultural consciousness, with its deliberate rejection of history";[43] his work traced the rise of psychologism, aestheticism, and populism as explicitly antihistorical responses to the failure of liberalism.[44] Faced with political and social turmoil and a nineteenth-century history of decline, so the argument runs, the Austrian cultural elite turned away from history and sought alternate fields of inquiry that might explain contemporary problems, suggest redemptive solutions, or provide escapes from the social world.[45] Even in those accounts where antihistorical thinking is less explicit, it often remains a tacit assumption.

Scholars such as Johnston and to some extent Janik and Toulmin stress the tendency of Austrian modernists to reject historical explanations of social, psychological, and artistic phenomena as inadequate.[46] Johnston's compendious *The Austrian Mind,* for example, almost entirely ignores historical and historiographical works.[47] Even surveys of Austrian historiography stress the empirical, atheoretical bent of the historical discipline in Austria at a time when German scholars engaged in heated debates about historicism.[48] Austrian scholars, we are led to believe, studiously avoided questioning the historiographical assumptions of their disciplines.

Since the 1980s, several scholars have begun to challenge this antihistoricist thesis, although they rarely confront Schorske directly. Scholars of particular fields of cultural activity have attacked the presumption by arguing that it fails to explain developments within their disciplines.[49] James Shedel, for example, noting the metaphoricity connecting the Secessionist vegetal style with the flow of time, stressed the historical and temporal consciousness of Austrian art movements.[50] John Boyer issued a similar critique in his studies of Christian Socialism; populism was not politics in a new key, but a self-conscious transposition of the old.[51] Janik suggests that Austrian philosophy transformed history into a method for uncovering disciplinary presuppositions, a claim illustrated in the work of Brentano and Riegl. Alfred Pfabigan argues that Freudian psychoanalysis reflects a complex absorption and reworking of the Western cultural tradition, which Freud cherished throughout his career, rather than a rejection of history as Schorske implies.[52] And Herbert Spiegelberg contested Janik's characterization of Wittgenstein as an antihistorical thinker by situating him within Brentano's proto-phenomenological circle; Wittgensteinian experience, Spiegelberg contends, consisted of fluid continua, not discrete moments.[53] Nevertheless, this scholarship has yet to create a systematic counterargument capable of replacing the still powerful antihistoricist paradigm. Revisions and exceptions notwithstanding, the claim that Austrian fin-de-siècle thought was distinctively antihistorical still prevails as a standard characterization in the literature.

This book challenges the characterization of Austrian modernist culture as antihistorical in two ways. First, it seeks to illuminate the notions of history and temporality that animated Riegl's work, a theme that few commentators have stressed in their analyses. Although there has been a recent upsurge of interest in Riegl, commentators have tended to focus on his theories of representation by stressing the historical development of visual forms and analyzing the perceptual apparatus of cultures that produced them.[54] Questions about the cultural and representational implications of artworks were central to Riegl's concerns and crucial for understanding his impact on the modern art historical discipline. Indeed, Riegl devoted much of his writing to the analysis of this or that art object in terms of its representational tactics, cultural significance, and historical influence. Nevertheless, an emphasis on formal representation should not crowd out other questions equally fundamental to Riegl's thinking. Although he did not broach the topic of time directly, Riegl embedded a distinct notion of temporality within discussions of the visual representation and cultural perception of specific eras. Why do human beings represent images? What are the preconditions for representation? What is the nature of the object represented, and how is it perceived by a viewer? Time and history had a direct bearing on Riegl's responses to all these questions. It is my contention that the temporal-historical framework that informed Riegl's art history was not simply an assumed premise, but was itself a phenomenon under active scrutiny. Indeed Riegl's oeuvre can be read as a sustained effort to illuminate the nature of historical time through the study of art and artifacts—to treat art as time's visible surface.

Second, I aim to show that Riegl's examination of history and time was not anomalous among Austrian scholars. Many Austrian thinkers, even as they reacted against the perceived speculative excesses of historicist accounts, retained history as a framework for making sense of social phenomena by reformulating the methods and categories of historical research to emphasize their own empirical preoccupations. Aestheticism, psychologism, and empiricism should not be viewed in opposition to historical thought, as Schorske and others suggest; often these modes of thought subsumed forms of historical thinking within their own methodologies. Many of Riegl's teachers and colleagues—the philosophers Franz Brentano, Alexius Meinong, and Robert Zimmermann, the historians Theodor von Sickel and Max Büdinger, and the art historians Franz Wickhoff and Moritz Thausing—pondered the problems entailed in empirical research and historical method; their concerns, sometimes explicitly, often implicitly, raised questions about the nature of time and history and their status as objects of study. Thus, Riegl's interest in history was not an isolated idiosyncrasy; his professors were actively engaged in transforming the categories of historical research emanating from German universities to the north into terms that could be applied to their empirical concerns. These efforts stretched the boundaries of empiricism beyond the pale of sensory verification and into a region that I have loosely called proto-phenomenological. My work thus challenges the notion of an antihistorical Austrian intellectual milieu, although it does not purport to subsume Austrian thought on history or temporality under yet another single explanatory rubric.

My concentration on Riegl's professors and colleagues—his academic field—invokes the work of the French sociologist Pierre Bourdieu. Bourdieu defined an "academic field" as a "force-field as well as a field of struggles which aim at transforming or maintaining the established relation of forces: each of the agents commits the force (the capital) that he has acquired through previous struggles to strategies that depend for their general direction on his position in the power struggle, that is, on his specific capital."[55] Riegl was pioneering within the Austrian academic field in that he applied cultural and intellectual capital gained through his historical training to the promotion of an autonomous art historical discipline (a new "position" within the field, to use Bourdieuian terms) with its own standards, methods, and objects of study distinct from those of the historical profession from which it emerged. At the same time, however, many of Riegl's concerns and insights reflected themes and convictions shared by colleagues in various academic disciplines. Riegl's approach to temporality offered a unique perspective on a topic familiar within the Austrian philosophical and historical establishment. His work was embedded in a broad field of intellectual discourse on themes of history and temporality that engaged many of his professorial cohorts.

In concentrating on Riegl's academic field, I largely neglect the broader philosophical influences that affected his thinking. Nevertheless, in this introduction, I would like to indicate the more prominent philosophical traditions that may have contributed to his interest in time. I do so in part to stress that Austrian intellectual achievements did not occur in a cultural vacuum, sealed off from European intellectual trends, as the historical set piece of fin-de-siècle Vienna suggests. Attempts to claim Riegl for one tradition or another have been confounded by his generally lax attitude toward citation, which makes it difficult to document his reception of contemporary philosophical trends.[56] Scholars have frequently attempted to situate Riegl's art history within the rich tradition of aesthetic philosophy that emerged from the romantic movement. Moreover, much of Riegl's historical vision seems to reflect Hegelian philosophy, and several scholars have linked him with that embattled tradition. Riegl's teleology, his stress on the unified, internal, and purposive development of art, his notion of art as mind overcoming material, and even his emphasis on the role of the viewer in art all have a distinctly Hegelian resonance. Wolfgang Kemp fits Riegl squarely within a late nineteenth-century Hegelian revival;[57] Michael Podro incorporates him within a Hegelian critical tradition of art history that spanned the nineteenth and early twentieth centuries;[58] and Michael Ann Holly posits a clear tradition linking Kant and Hegel with Riegl and Panofsky.[59]

Others, however, just as firmly reject this influence, arguing that Hegel enjoyed scant support in Austria. Brentano's and Zimmermann's influential attacks on Hegel's thought lend credence this claim, especially given their influence at the University of Vienna. A recent commentator, Diana Graham Reynolds, discounts Hegel's influence on Riegl and instead connects him with Schopenhauer's and Nietzsche's philosophies of will. Early exposure to Nietzsche and Schopenhauer may have provided Riegl with a framework for considering questions of history in terms of will, becoming, and time. In pointing out his involvement with the *Leseverein der deutschen Studenten Wiens*, Reynolds demonstrates his exposure to the early Nietzsche reception in Austria that William McGrath chronicled.[60] Riegl's attacks on nineteenth-century historical scholarship reflected the influence of Nietzsche's famous essay, "The Use and Abuse of History," which members of the *Leseverein* read. Lambert Wiesing and Francesco dal Co also connect Riegl with Schopenhauer when they describe his *Kunstwollen* as an art historical will-to-form.[61]

There was yet a third philosophical tradition whose influence on nineteenth-century Austrian culture has been well documented. Leibniz's vision of a stable and harmonious universe of self-sufficient monads is often connected with an anti-idealist, empirical tradition that inspired a host of thinkers in Austria.[62] Riegl was certainly exposed to Leibniz through Robert Zimmermann, one of the philosopher's most prolific nineteenth-century publicists.[63] Nevertheless, the historiographical and temporal implications of Leibniz's thought were by no means clear. Leibniz's monadology seemed to construct a formal system of ideal synchronic harmony, immutable and timeless. The early nineteenth-century Austrian philosopher, Bernard Bolzano, however, whose influence on Brentano and Zimmermann is well established, revised the Leibnizian system to incorporate development and progress as crucial aspects of the divine creation.[64] The sense of an artwork as a monad or self-sufficient creation, the rendering of preestablished harmony in terms of developmental formalism, and a stress on empiricism were all components of Riegl's thought that can be traced back to a vibrant Leibnizian tradition in Austria.

Riegl's histories of perception can be read as tracing the continuous recession of the vantage point from which the world comes into meaningful focus, a visual analogue to the universalizing rational project celebrated by Hegel and derided by Nietzsche. This program seems especially pronounced in Riegl's model of the world historical shift from an ancient tactile to a modern optical reception of objects, a theory argued most clearly in *Late Roman Art Industry* and *The Group Portraiture of Holland*.[65] On closer inspection, however, a far more complicated history of perception emerges, one with abrupt convolutions and disjunctures that refuse to admit any single unifying metahistorical narrative. Riegl's analysis of the discontinuous nature of perception imprinted a fractured structure onto his history of art and undercuts the temptation to seek a universal and totalizing development that reconciles art's varied manifestations in a harmonizing historical continuity. It is this uneven Riegl, an isolated scholar whose intellectual convictions warred with his nineteenth-century sensibilities, whom Walter Benjamin found so methodologically, perhaps even personally, appealing.

A quiet and reserved man, Riegl left behind few personal documents. Born in Linz in 1858, the son of an official in the tobacco business, he lived only until the age of forty-seven.[66] In 1875, he moved to Vienna and enrolled in the university, where his academic career exposed him to many late nineteenth-century intellectual currents prevalent in the humanities and social sciences. Although Riegl at first honored the wishes of his late father by registering at the faculty of law, in 1877 he enrolled in the philosophical faculty and dedicated himself to the study of philosophy, history, and art history. He took courses in the historical faculty before being accepted in 1881 as a fellow at the Institute for Austrian Historical Research, which, under the leadership of Theodor von Sickel, emphasized the auxiliary disciplines (paleography, sphragistics, numismatics, and chronology) and their application to the empirical analysis of source documents. At the Institute, Riegl studied historical method under Sickel and art history with Rudolf von Eitelberger, Moritz Thausing, and Franz Wickhoff. His empirical leanings were reinforced by philosophy courses he attended with the influential Franz Brentano and his student, Alexius Meinong.

Riegl received his diploma in 1883 with a thesis concerning the Romanistic architecture of the Salzburg archdiocese. By December of the same year, he had set to work on his dissertation. Between 1882 and 1884, with support from the state education ministry, he was able to conduct research in northern Italy and Bavaria, the results of which were set down in an essay entitled "Die Bauzeit der Schottenkirche St. Jakob zu Regensburg und die Vita Marians Scoti." Upon receiving his doctorate in 1884, Riegl accepted a half-year fellowship in Rome before starting work as an apprentice at the new Austrian Museum of Art and Industry. Riegl's lifelong ties to Austrian museums and his involvement in cataloging and curating collections reinforced the inclination to close empirical observation and careful description of art objects that characterized his training and work. By 1887, he had become curator for the textile collection at the Austrian Museum, an appointment that provided the material for his first book, *Altorientalische Teppiche,* published in 1891. Also in 1887, he accepted a fellowship that allowed him a three-month sojourn in Rome, where he worked on the essay that became his *Habilitationsschrift,* "Die mittelalterliche Kalenderillustration." He became a lecturer (*Privatdozent*) in art history at the University of Vienna in 1889 and was promoted to *Extraordinarius* in 1895 and *Ordinarius ad personam* in 1897. In 1901, Riegl was appointed head of an Art Conservation Commission charged with evaluating the worth of architectural monuments in Vienna. His untimely death in 1905 cut short this documentation effort. Riegl's published writings include several seminal volumes (most notably *Problems of Style, Late Roman Art Industry,* and *The Group Portraiture of Holland*), numerous essays printed in newspapers and journals, and several posthumous collections of lectures and essays. His unpublished writings consist mostly of lecture notes, carefully written out, for seminars at the University of Vienna, some speeches, and occasional letters addressed to teachers or colleagues. Although Riegl was, by all accounts, a very shy and withdrawn figure, his lectures attracted students, and his writings have garnered considerable attention since his death.[67]

My explication of Riegl's approach to questions of historical time has three main sections. In the first chapter, I introduce the concept time as it appeared in Riegl's early writing. Although Riegl's method of studying history evolved over time, his interest in historiography remained consistent throughout his career. The first chapter focuses around a close analysis of "Die mittelalterliche Kalenderillustration," published in 1889 in the *Mitteilungen des Instituts für oesterreichische Geschichtsforschung,* the journal of the institute where he studied history, art history, and empirical methods. The seventy-four-page article, his second on the topic of calendars, announced Riegl's interest in historical time in several ways.[68] Most straightforwardly, it was concerned to date and locate calendar illustrations chronologically through close empirical analysis. As a basic facet of his training, the empirical concern for dating was not, in Riegl's view, an end in itself, but a method that helped discern the visual clues of temporal change. After pinpointing an art object chronologically, he could compare its characteristics with those of artworks from earlier and later epochs; in this way, he used empirical analysis to designate the characteristics of cultural epochs. Furthermore, he could link these periods together in order to trace the contours of a formal historical development, a preoccupation that shaped his work through *Problems of Style,* published in 1893. Through the careful observation, description, and sequencing of artworks, Riegl discerned subtle patterns of formal transformation—a kind of formal micrologic—that allowed him to follow historical change visually. Time and history thereby became gradually observable, crystallized in the visible form of artworks as a kind of geometry of formal development, a logic connecting formal visual relationships with temporal movement, contiguity with continuity. The artistic genre that Riegl chose to study in his *Habilitationsschrift*—calendar illustration—was not accidental. He investigated the instruments and images of time measurement in order to gain access to the historical perception and representation of time. In his introduction to *Thinking with History,* Carl Schorske writes that "[v]irtually the only stable center of the historian's armamentarium is the simple calendar that determines what came before something, what came after."[69] Riegl's essay challenges the apparent stability of this measuring device. His early attempts to render history phenomenologically emerged in the tension between time as a formal phenomenon and as an object of human perception—between time as an object measured and an object represented.

In part 1 of this book, I situate Riegl's notions of history and temporality within an intellectual discourse active in Austria between the mid-nineteenth century and World War I. Riegl's ideas drew on those of many of his teachers, and I will highlight and analyze these influences and trace their effects on emerging models of time and history, as well as on various aspects of Riegl's thinking. A key figure in these debates was Franz Brentano, the German theologian-cum-philosopher whose work contained numerous essays and précis outlining a proto-phenomenological conception of time. Alexius Meinong, Edmund Husserl, and Alois Riegl, all Brentano's students, inherited their teacher's preoccupation with time, although they substantially revised his views. Another figure of critical importance in Riegl's intellectual development, Theodor von Sickel, an expert on early medieval history trained at the Ecole des Chartres, actively promoted an empirical historical methodology at the Institute for Austrian Historical Research where Riegl trained. Sickel's work on historical methodology influenced scores of students eager to ground their historical studies in empirically verified facts. Influences on Riegl also included the speculative *Universalgeschichte* of Max Büdinger, a student of Ranke who taught in the historical faculty of the University of Vienna, and the philosophy of Robert Zimmermann, who was known for his work in psychology, aesthetics, and propaedeutics. Finally, Riegl's art history professors and colleagues, Moritz Thausing and Franz Wickhoff, encouraged their students to examine artworks for the stylistic clues of chronology, the visual forms characteristic of specific cultures, and the evidence of microprocesses of formal development. Thausing's exacting empiricism and attempts to promote a scientific art history and Wickhoff's work on late Roman art left their clear mark on Riegl. His art history emerged from the juxtaposition and piecemeal synthesis of proto-phenomenological theories of time, empirico-historical methodologies, and scientific notions of art history. Chapters 2 through 7 serve not only to trace these pedagogical influences on Riegl's work, but also to demonstrate the existence of an active discourse on time and history in Austria. Although this discourse had characteristics that distinguished it from German historicist and philosophical debates, it was neither univocal nor utterly distinct from and opposed to wider European historiographical currents.

In part 2 of this book, using as landmarks several of Riegl's major art historical texts, I analyze the notion of temporality and its relationship to artistic form and historical development in Riegl's mature work. The main texts considered in this section are his essay "The Modern Cult of Monuments" ("Der moderne Denkmalkultus") and the books *Problems of Style* (*Stilfragen*), *Late Roman Art Industry* (*Spätrömische Kunstindustrie*), and *The Group Portraiture of Holland* (*Das holländische Gruppenporträt*).[70] "The Modern Cult of Monuments," written toward the end of Riegl's life, outlined a theory of the temporality inherent in the relationship between art objects and observers. It capped more than a decade of work on the nature of temporality in art and offers probably Riegl's most explicit statement on the subject of time. In *Problems of Style,* Riegl presented visual evidence for the claim that a continuous and universal process of historical development unified ancient decorative art; he aimed to demonstrate a unitary and autonomous history of decoration. His later works, by contrast, focused on more isolated analyses of specific periods in art history, notably late Roman and early modern Dutch art. Riegl often chose periods considered hybrid, transitional, or decadent by other nineteenth-century art historians, understudied periods that were either deemed aesthetically unremarkable or did not fit into clear artistic categories and types. He believed that these periods exemplified the nature of historical change in art more clearly than periods of apparent cultural efflorescence; moreover, they allowed him to challenge conventional aesthetic hierarchies based on classical models of beauty. Whether through broad narratives that presented history on a grand scale or in narrower period studies of transitional eras, Riegl's interest in historical development, and for the formal tensions and temporal imperatives that fueled artistic innovation, persisted throughout his works. Chapters 8 through 12 present my main theoretical analysis of the relationship among time, history, and art in Riegl's work. By treating his art history as a consistent interrogation of the categories of temporality and history, by analyzing Riegl's view of artworks as visible surfaces registering the movements of historical time, and by demonstrating that his preoccupation with history and time was not unique among Austrian thinkers, this book revises one of the standard characterizations of Austrian modernism.

1

History, Temporality, and the Calendar

"Here we are in fine condition to keep a record of past events!" scoffed Michel Montaigne in the 1580s. Only a few years after the Gregorian calendar reform, farmers still adhered to their own cycles of sowing and reaping. Neither they nor the astrologers had yet managed to devise a time ordinance that correlated precisely with the heavens or enjoyed universal acceptance. "We have no other way of computing time but by years," Montaigne remarked. "The world has been using this measure for many centuries; and yet it is a measure that we have still not succeeded in fixing, and such that we are every day in doubt what form other nations have variously given it and in what sense they used it."[1] This uncertainty must have seemed all the more intriguing to Montaigne because of the tremendous efforts made by chronologists to overcome it. With roots in ancient and medieval scholarship, the modern discipline of chronology dates at least as far back as Montaigne's contemporary, Joseph Justus Scaliger, whose multivolume *De emendatione temporum,* published in 1583, correlated solar and lunar cycles of time measurement.[2] Rejecting Montaigne's skepticism, early modern scholars such as Scaliger and Archbishop Ussher sought to coordinate the calendars of diverse historical cultures in order to establish a universal scale for organizing the history of time measurement.

Interest in chronology burgeoned again in the nineteenth century, when it was enlisted as an auxiliary discipline to support the historical sciences. Among its numerous practitioners, Berlin professor Ludwig Ideler declared it his intent to make chronology available as a "Hülfswissenschaft der Geschichte" by analyzing the time measurement systems of numerous world cultures. In his *Handbuch der mathematischen und technischen Chronologie,* which Riegl cited in his early articles, Ideler offered a comprehensive survey of ancient chronology. "Time is nothing objective and does not exist outside us," he wrote, "rather, it is something subjective, namely the mode of presentation or thought through which we order things that follow one another."[3] With this statement, Ideler claimed chronology for the *Geisteswissenschaften,* even though the field relied heavily on natural sciences such as astronomy. Its position at the cusp of the natural and human sciences made chronology a particularly fruitful field of inquiry for historians who sought the legitimacy of scientific methods for their discipline. Several of Riegl's historical predecessors shared an active interest in chronology. Max Büdinger, for example, studied in Berlin under August Böckh, a colleague of Ranke and Ideler who commented on drafts of the *Handbuch* and spent his last years in a focused study of chronology.[4] Büdinger may have passed on his teacher's interest in time measurement and universal history to his student Riegl. A more certain agent of transmission can be found in Theodor von Sickel, whose work on calendars Riegl cited in an early essay.[5] Sickel directed a seminar on chronology at the Institute for Austrian Historical Research and contributed an article on medieval calendars to its journal. The historical analysis of datelines and indictions, which formed one component of Sickel's diplomatic method, demanded a chronological knowledge of various ancient and medieval forms of time measurement. Indeed, Riegl's early writing inclined toward chronology not simply as a tool for studying documents but as a field worthy of historical investigation in its own right. Exploiting his training in art history, Riegl's *Habilitationsschrift* carried on his predecessors' commitment to chronology by using medieval calendar illustrations to analyze the technical development of time measurement as well as changing conceptions of time and its subdivisions.

In this chapter, I examine Riegl's writings on time measurement and calendar illustration in order to outline his early theories on the relationship between history, time, and art. Riegl's early work, the often overlooked manuscripts that preceded the publication of *Problems of Style* in 1893, announced many methodological and substantive themes that preoccupied him throughout his scholarly career. These writings reveal his efforts to situate himself within the field of history, as organized at the University of Vienna, and its subfield, art history. Shaped by the mutual antagonisms of the traditional historical faculty and the upstart Institute for Austrian Historical Research, the study of history at the University of Vienna offered competing visions of the discipline's scope, purpose, and methods.[6] In his own work, Riegl combined aspects of Büdinger's *Universalhistorie* with the Institute's stress on empirical documentary research. Unfortunately, Riegl's oeuvre provides few clues to the sources of his early ideas. As noted previously, in neither his *Nachlaß*, which consists mainly of lecture notes and occasional letters written to colleagues, nor his published work did Riegl volunteer his sources; he credited those whom he cited directly but incorporated many themes without specifying their origin. Despite these difficulties, the early essays can help us reconstruct Riegl's intellectual development and offer the first outline of themes that emerged in his later work.

Riegl demonstrated his early interest in temporality in two essays, "Die Holzkalender des Mittelalters und der Renaissance" (1888) and his 1889 *Habilitationsschrift*, "Die mittelalterliche Kalenderillustration." Published in the *Mitteilungen des Instituts für österreichische Geschichtsforschung*, both works reflected Riegl's Institute training, with its stress on empirical strategies. These essays are among the only works in Riegl's oeuvre in which the artifacts under investigation are themselves devices that measure time. As such, they provide a unique insight into his views on the relationship between visual representation and historical temporality. My discussion concentrates on his *Habilitationsschrift* because it is the historically and theoretically richer essay of the two.

In "Die mittelalterliche Kalenderillustration," Riegl traced the shift from an ancient, pre-Christian form of lunar time measurement to a Christian solar annum that eventually dominated in the Middle Ages.[7] He situated his analysis of specific examples of calendar art within a "conception" [*Begriff*] of the calendar as a tradition with fixed characteristics. A calendar, Riegl noted, oriented human activity within the framework of temporal experience; it was designed for a specific purpose [*Bestimmung*] and around a particular natural basis [*Grundlage*].

"The purpose [of the calendar] was always to serve as an instrument through which men would establish a correspondence between rural or domestic, political or sacred functions and their respective days, months, or years."[8] A calendar addressed a human need: the regulation of tasks according to a framework of days, months, and years. This framework required visual articulation in order to be useful, and thus the need for temporal orientation called forth the representative capabilities of primordial man. In Riegl's later writings, visual representation *tout court* responded to an anthropological need for orientation within a threatening world.

To fulfill this purpose, prehistoric time reckoning demanded a stable natural reference point. For this service, men turned to the heavens. "The basis of the calendar is astronomical nature," Riegl wrote. "[I]t is indeed so simple and unchanging that since the earliest historical times it has remained essentially the same."[9] The heavens satisfied two conditions that assured their primacy as the standard reference for time measurement. "First, [the stable reference] couldn't be subject to rough and obvious fluctuations, and second it had to be . . . simultaneously and distinctly visible to all."[10] The heavens offered a stable set of universal and perceptible relationships, a fixed visual matrix for marking moments and durations in the life of primordial man. Turning to a visual field to articulate a non-visual sense of time, Riegl's primordial men engaged in a nascent act of representation. This correlation was not based on mimesis; throughout his career, Riegl insisted that nature offered a set of correlates, relationships, and motivations for art, but did not provide raw material for mimetic reproduction. Instead, representation, in its primordial form, involved the correlation of the non-visible with the visible, an act whose primary function was to designate, articulate, measure, perceive.

Riegl's historical account of calendar art rested on an anthropology of the calendar as a conceptual tradition rooted in a specific human need and a perceptual relationship between man and nature. As a device for fixing, measuring, and articulating time, the calendar correlated the anthropological need for temporal orientation with a stable and universal heavenly reference; calendars connected man with nature through the perception of time. These conceptual "pretexts for artistic expression"—human need and natural order—anchored the whole history of calendar art.[11] The calendar was thus transhistorical in a conceptual sense. In each historical epoch, artists strove to make calendars that adapted inherited meanings and visual forms to contemporary circumstances. Each period oriented itself toward the heavens according to the knowledge and technology of its day. Nevertheless, in its constant correlation of anthropological needs with heavenly reference, calendar art formed a conceptually unified and transhistorical tradition.

Indeed, still today the connection between time and the heavens seems panglobal, so fundamental to cultures that we might consider it, in Hayden White's term, a metacode, a "human universal on the basis of which transcultural messages about the nature of a shared reality can be transmitted."[12] White argues that narrative itself is a metacode, compelling not because of any unique ability to frame, link, or confer meaning upon events (many forms of representation can organize fictional or historical data), but because of its capacity to represent, or more properly to reenact, the intrinsic temporal nature of reality. Whereas events themselves cannot be presented, but only represented, temporality is something that both reality and narrative, presentation and representation, share. White paraphrases Paul Ricoeur when he states that narrative allows man to endow time with meaning, to allegorize the tragedy of temporal experience.[13] No mere representation of historical reality, narrative reenacts history's fundamental temporality.

Riegl was a dedicated practitioner of the narrative historical form. His accounts of formal historical imperatives in the visual arts appeared in volume after volume, seminar after seminar; the thick descriptions of *Problems of Style*, *Late Roman Art Industry*, and *The Group Portraiture of Holland* allowed the reader to witness the emergence of visual form in narrative historical trajectories. Riegl's art histories, however, were built around material objects, not dates or events. A calendar illustration is not an event in the same way that, say, the Battle of Crécy or the fall of Rome was because it remains present in a visual and material sense; an illustration or artifact persists materially through time and thus establishes a different relationship with the historical interpreter from that of bygone events. While the *production* of a calendar can be properly called a historical event, recoverable only in representation, the historical meaning of a calendar illustration is tied to both creation and reception, original moment and durable presence; history "attaches," in a sense, to the calendar not simply as date of origin but also in the temporal duration of presence, persistence, aging. Chronology, therefore, addressed only one aspect of the material temporality of artworks and artifacts: their value as registers of date and origin. As a historian, dedicated to the strenuous empirical methods of the profession, Riegl sought to base historical claims on this kind of chronological evidence and documentation. However, as an analyst of artistic meaning, he went beyond the indexical value of artifacts by "reading" or "interpreting" the historical significations contained in the visual form of artworks; his work stretched the bounds of empiricism beyond the limits of sensory perception toward a more hermeneutic approach by "reading out" broad cultural and theoretical significations from artifacts. Tracing the development of visual signification in material objects, not creating chronologies of artworks, was the fundamental aim of Riegl's art history.

If narrative was Riegl's chosen representational code, diachronic temporality was its presumptive core. Riegl sought not only to legitimize the anthropological and objective claims of his menological conception on the basis of evidence from the ancient and medieval world; this he could have done synchronically by compiling charts of calendars without tracing their temporal development in narrative form. Instead, he insisted on demonstrating the existence of historical continuity by tracing the design of integral artistic motifs across various manifestations over many centuries. Riegl's account posited a clear subject—calendar art as an anthropological need given objective representation—that exhibited a continuous progression of historical instantiations. His emplotment techniques can be read as equally comic and tragic, depending upon the temporal horizons an analyst imposes.[14] Riegl's narratives focused on the gradual but successful emergence of distinctive artistic forms—the medieval calendar, the Greek tendril, late Roman bounded space—from historical predecessors. Whether one sees in this narrative the provenance of the new or the decay and transformation of the old depends on the reader's inclination. As Riegl presented it, the dialectic struggle between a formal motivic inheritance and a set of contemporary needs fueled art historical innovation.

"Die mittelalterliche Kalenderillustration" opens with a kind of just-so story about the primordial development of the calendar. Lacking documentary evidence about the origins of prehistoric time measurement, Riegl relied on extrapolation from anthropological premises, a procedure whose necessity and epistemological soundness he did not question.[15] The first stage in the development of the calendar, he claimed, involved the designation of discrete temporal subdivisions that reflected religious, agricultural, and celestial patterns. A "primitive time reckoning" used the sun and the moon as the most visible reference points in the heavens.[16] "As a rule," Riegl wrote, "one can assume that primitive nature religions had a cult of the large stars: the sun and moon."[17] The cycle of the sun across the sky came to designate the day and night, the cycle of the moon the month. Riegl argued that agricultural peoples must have soon become aware that crops followed a pattern whose regularity coincided with less obvious movements of the sun; from this observation they developed a third unit of time: the year. The exact measurement of a year, however, was more difficult to pin down than that of the day or month. Though prehistoric men knew that the sun's annual cycle consisted of approximately twelve lunar orbits, the correspondence between solar and lunar years was inexact; whereas the new solar year lasted approximately 365 days, the traditional lunar year numbered only 354 days, leaving an eleven-day deficit that "must have led to a complete displacement of the seasons after a few years."[18] The attempt to fix this discrepancy fueled conflict and innovation among the caretakers of ancient time measurement.

Social stratification within primordial human society complicated efforts at calibrating the solar year. The calendar, according to Riegl, served two crucial but distinct social functions: designating the dates for festivals and religious observances, and regulating the agricultural season. These functions frequently worked at cross-purposes. In early religions, festivals were tied to the worship of stars and other natural phenomena; resistance to any kind of menological innovation, therefore, came from "cultic" and religious authorities. The Latin word *Cultus* has a triple significance here that offers clues about conflicts occasioned by competing systems of time measurement. Etymologically linked to the concept of tilling and agriculture, the term *cult* reinforces the importance of the sun and moon for a farmer's growing cycle. Moreover, it denotes a system of religious worship focused around a ritual object, in this case the great stars, especially the moon. Because the menstrual cycle was easier to observe and depict than the solar annum, "[t]ime reckoning according to lunar months . . . was, so to speak, written in the stars."[19] The term *cult* also describes the religious group that follows such worship, a group usually defined by strict ritual practices, exclusive indoctrination, and a priestly and political hierarchy. The cult of the great stars was structured around an exclusive and privileged ritual hierarchy of priests, political leaders, and other vested interests. "Various political and religious customs and functions are connected with the lunar calendar," Riegl wrote, "as we can observe even in historical times with the Greeks and Germans."[20] This hierarchy controlled the ordinance of time, so that lunar time reckoning had a social and political as well as natural basis.

However, the solar year as a unit of measure also enjoyed the support of an important though subordinate constituency. Developed as a means for marking agricultural seasons, the solar year was "by far the most important measure of time for agricultural people"[21] because it overcame the lunar calendar's eleven-day shortfall. Before the solar calendar could vie with its lunar counterpart, however, it had to be precisely demarcated. Greater exactitude was achieved, Riegl argued, by charting the solar path against a backdrop of fixed stars. Early advocates of the solar annum defined their system by marking a reference star—a "fixed point"[22] along the solar orbit—and tallying the days between the sun's initial passby and its return to the same location. This act of designation, of pointing, singled out from amidst a firmament of lights a star or cluster of stars to serve as a locus of orientation and thereby imposed a sequence on the otherwise unordered celestial lights. This point marked a moment of passage; it became the visual indicator of a temporal event. This primordial act of designation, for Riegl, marked a further advance in the development of a representative system for temporality; it established the heavens as a visual landscape that charted the routes of celestial objects and correlated their spatial movements with temporal passage. Through these acts of designation and mapping, the vital movement of time was made manifest in the formal relationships of visual objects. Time was established (*establir* [OFr]); literally, it was made to stand still so that it could be seen.

Advocates of the now precisely calibrated solar year entered a phase of protracted struggle with the political and religious supervisors of the older lunar calendar.

> If men were . . . determined to know the length of the solar year more exactly, it would have been easiest to abandon the old lunar months, and to divide the solar year . . . into a number of conventional parts all of equal length. However, tradition stood opposed to this. The month was the oldest, the customary measure of time, and enjoyed as such great esteem everywhere. . . . Thus the difficulty of simply relinquishing

> lunar months and advancing to a more rational division within the boundaries of the solar year.[23]

For a period of time the two calendars coexisted: a farmer's calendar, such as the one produced by Hesiod, based on observations of stars whose rising and setting foretold seasonal changes, and an official calendar based on lunar cycles that catalogued festivals and political events.[24] The work of reconciling the two calendar systems ultimately stimulated further representational innovation. Those attempting to establish conventional divisions for the solar year, Riegl argued, made every possible effort to accommodate themselves to the lunar months that enjoyed official sanction. Over time, their efforts at compromise produced the zodiac, the twelve constellations through which the sun passed on its annual orbit. That the number of zodiac signs was twelve demonstrated that advocates of the solar year did not derive their subdivisions from an "objective" observation of the firmament, but instead combined an awareness of the stars in the sun's path with a concession to the traditional order of the lunar year. A duodecimal subdivision prevented opposition from being mounted on the grounds that the solar year was merely convention. The zodiac legitimized the solar year by linking its divisions with both the heavens and tradition.

The distinction between a form of lunar time measurement favored by elites and a solar calendar with broad support among farmers hints at the well-known division between high culture or *Kultur*, centered around a mandarin cult of ritual, and material culture or *Zivilisation*, encompassing the practices, products, and needs of social life in agricultural societies.[25] Under the influence of Winckelmann's classical aesthetic, late eighteenth- and nineteenth-century art historians focused their attentions on the refined products of high culture by celebrating the aesthetic pinnacles of antiquity.[26] Riegl's effort to undermine this hierarchy in his history of calendar art presaged a career spent attacking the distinction between high and low art. He treated the decorative arts and handicrafts with the same scholarly care traditionally reserved for the canonical masterworks. The distinction between high and low art, he contended, was scientifically baseless, a reflection of lax modern linguistic usage [*Sprachgebrauch*], not historical fact. Ancient artworks such as the Parthenon or Greek vases combined both practical and aesthetic functions and displayed both figural and decorative elements.[27] Artistic masterworks and artifactual handicrafts expressed the cultural spirit of an era; both were equally valuable to the art historian. Indeed, Riegl's choice of calendar art as the topic of his *Habilitationsschrift* illustrated this quiet, scholarly irreverence. The explicit utility of the visual images on calendars, which gave even illiterate viewers access to their temporal services,[28] disqualified calendar art from the category of the pure aesthetic that came to characterize high art.

I have already noted that the visual representation of the solar year began with the designation of a star to stand as a marker within the otherwise undifferentiated celestial band of the solar orbit. This star set the boundary of the solar year and gave it a point of reference. Following on this achievement, early observers of the heavens subdivided the orbital band into twelve even and distinct clusters, each a separate visual form made up of individual stars. As constellations, these formal clusters could be correlated with sublunary creatures whose shapes they resembled, a step that illustrated a further advance of the nascent representational impulse: "As concerns the constellations of the zodiac cycle, the imagination of the ancients knew how to discover within each single group or constellation of stars specific resemblances with definite earthly beings and creatures, and then name the star-pictures after them."[29] This process of correlation established the animal symbology of the zodiac, naturalized the constellations, and made them recognizable to men. Zodiac images maintained their natural affiliation [*natürliche Verbindung*] in two ways: they were composed of individual stars whose collective form and objectivity they retained; and they corresponded with natural earthly objects (animals or human activities) whose images were dignified in calendar reproductions as representations of the months.[30] Thus Riegl's description of the development of primordial time measurement can be broken down into a sequence of distinct representational acts: an initial designation that marks the boundaries of a cycle within a larger undifferentiated field; the subdivision of that cycle into discrete clusters; the formation of those clusters into recognizable shapes and relationships; and the correlation of those shapes with familiar earthly forms. The final naturalization, an act that Riegl credited to the "phantasie" of the ancients,[31] was a representational choice motivated by political and social exigencies, not by a desire to mimic nature.

I want to highlight the notion of a constellation in Riegl's anthropology of representation. The term denotes a group of objects (stars) set perceptually into a relationship with each other. While Riegl used the term without much clarification (sometimes interchanging *Constellation* and *Sternenbilder*), Walter Benjamin later invoked it to explain and illustrate his epistemology in *The Origin of German Tragic Drama.* Benjamin's notion of constellation echoes Riegl's in important ways. For Riegl, a constellation prepared separate stars for associative forms and meanings. Similarly, for Benjamin, constellations, like ideas, served to configure objects in such a way that their nonsubjective, redemptive significance emerged. Benjamin asserted that "[i]deas are to objects as constellations are to stars."

> [P]henomena are not incorporated in ideas. . . . Ideas are, rather, their objective, virtual arrangement, their objective interpretation. . . . Whereas phenomena determine the scope and content of the concepts which encompass them, by their existence, by what they have in common, and by their differences, their relationship to ideas is the opposite of this inasmuch as the idea, the objective interpretation of the phenomena—or rather their elements—determines their relationship to each other. Ideas are timeless constellations, and by virtue of the elements being seen as points in such constellations, phenomena are subdivided and at the same time redeemed.[32]

For Benjamin, ideas at once preserved and redeemed phenomena by releasing them from the imperious, reductive grasp of conceptual knowledge. To be sure, Riegl did not propose such a fine distinction between idea and concept or such a redemptive notion of constellation. Nevertheless, his use of the term *constellation* to denote a presemiotic arrangement of stars that at once preserved stellar autonomy and established stellar interrelationships bore notable similarities to Benjamin's later use of the term as an epistemological analogy.

In the context of his essay on medieval calendar art, Riegl used the term *constellation* to describe a stage in the representational transfiguration of the heavens. A constellation fixed a set of stars into a basic order that, as yet devoid of significance, could be correlated with familiar earthly beings and forms [*irdischen Wesen und Gebilden*] and so acquire visual meaning. A presemiotic structure, the constellation itself did not confer meaning upon its component stars; instead, it gave perceptual form to the objects it comprised by grouping them so as to distinguish each cluster from the others and prepare the formal whole for conceptual correlation and meaning conferral. A constellation oriented otherwise distinct component stars within a formal field by arranging single elements collectively into shapes and relationships. Established in a conventionalized gesture, constellations nonetheless retained as primary phenomena the natural objects they encompassed. A constellation was, in effect, a skeleton awaiting the flesh of a familiar image. The subsequent conferral of meaning—of correlating celestial with terrestrial forms—established the zodiac as a recognizable representation of time. For Benjamin as for Riegl, representational significance was based on a prior geometry of relations among constellary subphenomena—stars. In this stellar geometry Riegl sought to unearth the phenomenological riches of representative art, and Benjamin sought to illustrate its redemptive possibility. As Lambert Wiesing notes: "Riegl arrived at the assumption—which he certainly held as unproblematic—that the relations of a work are a perceptible phenomenon and not, on the contrary, a product of interpretation."[33] This priority of perceptual form over meaning, illustrated in the work of the constellation, informed Riegl's ideas on representation in the essay on calendars; time measurement and calendar illustration became meaningful subjects of history on the basis of an evolving presemiotic relationship between the celestial firmament and human needs. It is easy to see that this evolution was temporal in nature; that is, even in Riegl's prehistoric *Urzeit,* temporal representation had a history.

The transformation of constellations into a cycle of zodiac signs served two functions crucial to the history of the calendar. First, it facilitated a gradual accommodation between the solar and lunar models of time measurement. Riegl maintained that the use of the solar calendar increased by degrees as ancient patriarchal relations weakened. Acceptance was never complete or unproblematic—indeed, Riegl traced the juxtaposition of lunar and solar images through the Renaissance[34]—but sufficient correlation between the two systems permitted their gradual reconciliation in a single universal time reckoning. Second, the equation of constellations with zodiac signs set up a catalogue of visual images for representing heliocentric time, images that formed a traditional canon for artists to draw on and reproduce. "Due to its concrete interconnected images, the zodiac signs were also utilized in the visual arts, and thus became the first and most natural representations of the twelve months of the solar year."[35] In this regard, visual art stood as a privileged point of access for the investigation of temporality because it offered material images of the human perception of time. Art made historical time visible; it crystallized temporality within a conventionalized lexicon of visual forms that retained within themselves the contours and demarcations of their objective origins. Art, therefore, was representational and indexical; it both recorded and registered its time. Indeed, time was art's fundamental subject. Other disciplines, Riegl believed, could not hope to attain such direct access to the phenomenon of time because their subject matters did not visually externalize temporality in such an immediate way.

Riegl's anthropology was admittedly speculative; although he insisted on the necessity of the cultural developments he had traced, he conceded that they could not be established historically [*geschichtlich*] owing to a lack of empirical evidence. Despite his training under Theodor von Sickel, who required historical claims to withstand rigorous empirical verification; despite his disdain for purely speculative aesthetics and his attempts to ground art history in meticulous observation; and despite the vivid detail and exact description for which he became famous, Riegl preserved a role for something akin to phenomenological intuition at the very core of his art historical approach. This impulse was built into his practice of reading art history as a canvas whose movements and relations were visible in art objects. For Riegl, the necessity of art history was predicated upon the visible legibility of artworks, and his anthropology of the origin of calendar images grew out of visible markers in calendar illustrations.

Though Riegl and Husserl, both students of Brentano, never cited each other's work, Husserl's phenomenology can help us clarify the notion of speculative history that underpinned Riegl's anthropology. In his well-known essay "The Origin of Geometry" (1936), Husserl outlined a program for a historical method that he contrasted with conventional paradigms in the humanities:

> [I]n the so-called descriptive sciences the theoretical interest, classifying and describing, remains within the sphere of sense intuition, which for it represents self-evidence. . . . All merely factual history remains incomprehensible because, always merely drawing its conclusions naively and straightforwardly from facts, it never makes thematic the general

> ground of meaning upon which all such conclusions rest, has never investigated the immense structural a priori which is proper to it.[36]

Husserl called for a historical program of "explication," of the active reconstruction of "ideal objects" that constitute the origin and transhistorical meaning of intellectual traditions such as geometry. The aim of phenomenological history, Husserl insisted, was to grasp "the vital movement of the coexistence and the interweaving of original formations and sedimentations of meaning,"[37] a formula that recalls Riegl's negotiation between tradition and innovation. Rejecting the distinction between epistemological inquiry and descriptive history, Husserl argued that historical investigation should seek to elucidate the essential inheritance orienting a tradition from its inception. He called this meaning-origin the "ideal object" of a tradition and argued that it was contained as sedimented signification in all historical instantiations of that tradition, much as Riegl's calendar conception informed all historical calendars. That the ideal object of geometry was first established through human activity, within the horizons of the life-world (language, space, time),[38] was just as indisputable to Husserl as the fact that its actual historical invention could never be factually verified. Neither certitude negated the historicity or the *aeterna veritas* of that ideal object.[39] Thus, Husserl's program cannot be classified as either idealism or empiricism in any conventional sense.

Riegl grappled with concepts akin to Husserl, although he did so, paradoxically, within the characteristically descriptive science of art history. He adopted a similar program of explication to illuminate the vital movement of time within primordial representation. In "The Origin of Geometry," Husserl incorporated time as a facet of the human life-world, the horizon of human activities and traditions. For Riegl, time was itself an ideal meaning-object; it was both subject to history and its precondition. Insofar as Riegl's oeuvre extended the concepts of early phenomenology to a domain—descriptive history—for which they might seem ill-suited, it represented an implicit challenge to the historicist cult of the empirically verifiable fact. The fundamental conception and significance of a tradition such as calendar art—its essence or ideal origin, Husserl might say—could not be elucidated by empirical methodologies that restricted themselves exclusively to sensory verification. This was a limitation of Theodor von Sickel's historical methodology and an error of historicists who sought the primordial origins of traditions in empirically documented facts. The temporal significance of artworks could be discerned only through an art history that privileged a proto-phenomenological approach to the descriptive analysis of perception and form. Like Husserl from within the field of philosophy, Riegl illustrated the ways in which a complex empirical history might aspire to a kind of phenomenological insight.

As if to defend his anthropological speculations in "Die mittelalterliche Kalenderillustration," Riegl expressed general skepticism about any attempt to establish a factual origin for the calendar art tradition on the basis of meager archaeological evidence. He dismissed as far-fetched attempts to attribute the origins of the zodiac to the Chinese and "mythischen Atlantiker."[40] And although he acknowledged that a case could be made for crediting the Chaldaeans with the original zodiac, Riegl doubted that even this attribution could be definitively verified. The question of the historical origin of calendar art eluded empirical analysis altogether; the scientific art historian could begin definitively only with the classical era, by which time the tradition of calendar art was already well established and underway. Without evidence, a scholar justifiably relied on anthropological insight; one could only undertake pure empirical analysis where sufficient evidence permitted it.

Of course, Riegl's calendar essay was not devoid of empirical evidence or argument. After presenting his speculative anthropology of the primordial origins of art, Riegl investigated the historical development of calendar art by considering exemplars from successive eras, beginning with the classical age. As in much of his work anticipating *Problems of Style*, Riegl's analysis of Greek and Roman calendar illustration sought to demonstrate empirically a strong historical continuity in the progression of art. Thus, although Riegl recognized Greek and Roman calendar art as falling into distinct *Stilperioden* (periods of style), he insisted that "the culture of Roman imperial times is a continuation of Hellenistic culture," that they shared a common inheritance and tradition.[41] Riegl began his historical discussion in "Die mittelalterliche Kalenderillustration" by considering an Athenian festival calendar relief on the Hellenistic *Panagra Gorgiopiko* from the second or first century BCE, a work that stood as the earliest surviving example of calendar art. On this calendar, he found the empirical evidence to affirm his introductory claims; the lunar calendar consisted of the two elements that characterized his tradition: "the connection on the one hand with the starry heavens as its basis, and on the other hand with human change, whose regulation is its ultimate purpose."[42] The *Gorgiopiko* calendar, moreover, contained an incipient version of the zodiac signs that later became conventional.[43]

Margaret Olin remarks notes that it was on the *Panagra Gorgiopiko* that Riegl first noticed isolated images of contemporary life.[44] Whereas most of the monthly images corresponded to Greek folk festivals, Riegl observed that three figures—the vintner, the plower, and the sower—remained ambiguous in their symbology and did not clearly refer to ancient rituals. He suggested two possible explanations for this anomaly. First, he concurred with other contemporary scholars that perhaps festivals connected with these activities were tied to the annual seasons and thus did not fall consistently within a particular month as religious festivals did. That the seasonal unit of measurement was connected exclusively with the solar year reinforced the view that the festivals in question were popular celebrations and not the official religious fêtes recorded on the lunar calendar. Riegl's second and more remarkable explanation accounted for the ambiguity of the three images of plowing, sowing, and wine-making in terms of the "artistic spirit of the Athenians."

> After all it appears peculiar that no relevant festivals were created for these very crucial activities. And it appears that the Athenian artistic spirit, even in these advanced times, resisted creating representations of the profane occupations of everyday life in their naked reality. . . . Thus the Hellenes transformed human activities into a cult of divinity, and this spirit helps us to clarify why the Attic artist, when he represents the activities which men tend chiefly to undertake in a given season, does not do so straightforwardly as they are, but endows them with a religious solemnity that it confers on the visual sensibilities of the masses.[45]

Greek artistic representation, Riegl claimed, was a gesture of respect that conferred a kind of divinity on the object represented. The connection between time-reckoning and religious signification on Greek calendars necessitated the exclusion of lowly images from the catalogue of zodiac symbols. Images of calendar art had to satisfy religious *and* agricultural needs; whereas animal images could function in that dual capacity, images of mere agricultural tasks were considered too mundane to serve as religious material. That profane tasks did appear as images on the *Gorgiopiko* calendar, therefore, demonstrated to Riegl the weakening of Hellenic cultural norms during the Hellenistic period; that those icons remained ambiguous in their signification (did they symbolize seasonal or monthly activities?) revealed that Greek artistic norms still maintained some influence. The often incongruous juxtaposition of cultural content and traditional forms on Hellenistic images indicated a transitional moment in the history of calendar art.[46]

Another way to understand Riegl's history of Greek zodiac illustration is to follow the transformation of images from symbolic representation in the Hellenic period toward a more allegorical set of associations during the Hellenistic and Roman eras. Walter Benjamin distinguished between symbolic representation, which posits an essential connection between image and object, and allegorical representation, which accepts a more ephemeral, inexact, and contingent relationship. Symbols establish conceptual links between objects that seal out the ravages of time; in so doing, they express microcosmic claims to eternal significance. Allegory, by contrast, registers the passage of time in open-ended associations that generate transitory meanings and possibilities through the juxtaposition of images, even as they mark the ultimate meaninglessness of objects. According to Riegl's analysis, Hellenic artists posited an essential link between depictions and the activities depicted; calendar images became icons, symbols connecting sacred and earthly time. Hellenic zodiac emblems symbolized at least three distinct phenomena: a month within the annual cycle; the religious festivals that took place during that month; and the practical activities associated with the month. Because time was closely tied to religious observances and because representation in some sense sanctified the object depicted, mundane objects and activities were deemed unfit to carry religious weight and were excluded from depiction. This prohibition was gradually relaxed during Hellenistic times, when an image designated a time period and depicted its characteristic activities without necessarily representing an essential connection—homologous, theophanous, or otherwise—among these phenomena. Hellenistic representation thus became more open to the rhythm of human time and the various activities associated with it. Moreover, the weakening of the Greek cult of the symbol permitted the development of more abstract representations of time [*abstracte Zeitbegriffe*] in the Hellenistic era.[47]

Freed from the obligation to represent religious festivals, Hellenistic artists drew on a wider repertoire of images, including those of everyday life, to allegorize the annual cycle. The *Panagra Gorgiopiko* calendar, situated in the midst of this transition, became the site of juxtapositions of a traditional formal inheritance and contemporary scenes.

Riegl carried these themes forward into his discussion of late Roman calendar art. Drawing on the "fixed canon of calendar illustration,"[48] Roman artists maintained a correlation between images and activities, but they did not presume the direct symbolism of one by the other. Thus, they could adapt their subject matter more freely than their Hellenic or even Hellenistic predecessors. Nevertheless, Roman artists continued to transform traditional images through gradual adjustment to changing historical realities, a process that enabled pre-Christian images to survive in the Christian era: "As long as the things of the cult [*Dinge des Cultus*] did not immediately come into question, the relationship of early Christian artists to heathen antiquity was entirely naive. In Rome, particularly in the decorative arts, no one marked any essential difference between heathen and Christian."[49] As long as traditional symbols did not challenge the new Christian ethos, they were retained in Roman calendars as personifications of time, though they lost earlier pagan religious connotations. These calendar images grew more abstracted from their original sources as late Roman authorities abandoned Greek religious festivals. In place of the old Greek celebrations, imperfectly correlated to zodiac images, late Roman officials substituted new festivals and holy days appropriate to the ascendant Christian culture. These changes, displayed on the late Roman Filocalus Calendar (designed by the papal curia Furius Dionysius Filocalus), allowed calendar artists to retain zodiac images from Greek calendars only in personifications that designated months as abstract temporal units; images transplanted from Hellenic sources no longer designated in symbolic fashion the Roman festivals or activities that filled those months.[50] This weakening of symbolic expectations enabled calendar artists to adopt and incorporate direct representations of everyday life into their catalogue of images: "In the figures of the Filocalian cycle of months, we therefore have an oscillation between older references to cultural traditions and relations and the newer references to a direct concern with human everyday life, both of which figure in the cycle of months."[51] Paradoxically, the increased abstraction of temporal images, divorced from their original associations and inherited denotations, allowed for an expanded subject matter in Roman art and released profane activity from its representational exclusion. This emancipation signaled a crucial historical watershed in Riegl's account, for it established "a process that continued into the early Middle Ages, and makes the whole development of art from Alexander the Great until the Renaissance appear unified."[52] Riegl described this trend as the emancipation of the profane life of men and the natural life of animals for symbolic use in artistic representation.[53]

"The art of the early Middle Ages," Riegl insisted, "was a continuation of late Roman antiquity just as the latter can be called a continuation of Hellenistic culture and art."[54] Though stylistically distinct, Roman art and medieval art were linked by a formal continuity that manifested itself in two ways: in some medieval manuscripts, ancient forms retained their traditional significations undisturbed by medieval conditions; in others, content and form were adjusted to accommodate medieval religious and agricultural circumstances. While the medieval perpetuation of tradition was evident in those calendars that directly adopted ancient forms, the connection between antiquity and the Middle Ages was less clear in the more adaptive calendars. These works, in which artists "pour[ed] a new content into the emptied forms,"[55] demonstrated the existence of a distinct medieval aesthetic in embryonic form, one "that steadily found its emergence from an inner necessity."[56] Riegl noted, however, that even as medieval calendar artists strove to develop a contemporary aesthetic style, their work retained the original conceptual framework and vestiges of ancient forms: "Since Hellenistic times, two elements have been combined in the calendar and its illustration; one element—the astronomical—determined from within each group what texts and images from antiquity would be incorporated unchanged and passed on; whereas the second element—that which connects with the regulation of the living everyday activities of men—tended much more to indicate that certain changes and transformations of time were unavoidable."[57] The attitude of medieval calendar artists toward the ancient tradition was one of neither unquestioning adherence nor outright dismissal. While the calendar's unchanging astronomical reference inclined artists to draw on a catalogue of ready-made images, the injunction to accommodate contemporary needs encouraged them to experiment with newer forms. In its conception, the calendar demanded *both* adherence to the past and regular innovation; it pulled in two directions, retaining an inherited set of images while striving toward novel forms. The calendar art tradition was not therefore built out of unquestioned acceptance of the inherited past, but instead from adaptation and accommodation between past and present. In this way, each calendar exhibited its own formal temporal imperatives that linked the past with the present and future.

The inherent temporality of calendar art, reaching backward and forward in time, facilitated the adjustment of pagan images to a Christian worldview. That the transition to Christianity was monumental, Riegl had little doubt; but that it was a clean and sudden break with the pre-Christian past, he just as strongly disputed. "At last, one no longer conceives of Christianity as a power directly inimical to the continuation and transmission of ancient art,"[58] Riegl affirmed. Manuscripts, miniature paintings, and calendar art all showed ancient forms persisting as models for Carolingian artists.[59] A distinctly medieval art developed only through the gradual, centuries-long adaptation and resignification of a pre-Christian catalogue of images: "Between the fifth century and the Carolingian period, an unbroken tradition must have been available which guarded the form of the old Roman calendar until the moment when it was decided to adopt this form for the calendar of Christian festivals; as references to everything about the old heathen cults grew distant, the new content of the festival catalogue could be inserted into the emptied forms."[60]

The process of adjusting ancient images to medieval circumstances became necessary for poets earlier than for visual artists.[61] Indeed, the transition to distinct medieval visual forms occurred only as artists were called upon to illustrate contemporary verse.[62] This unevenness among genres was thematized in Riegl's 1901 volume, *Late Roman Art Industry*, where he remarked that poetry and religion were closely linked in their preponderant concern for content. Visual art, by contrast, dealt more with the "how" of form and style than with the "what" of content.[63] The visual language of form was less semantically tied to the contemporary world than the words employed by poets. Poetry therefore had to respond more immediately to cultural shifts than did visual art, which could follow in more gradual transition. Moreover, visual artists benefited from the accretions of signification offered by a formal tradition, whereas the same quality often muddled a poet's attempt to communicate. "Carolingian poetry showed the same character as the visual arts of its time to the extent that its form displayed the closest connections with antiquity. However, in the visual arts, form is the determinant component, and beside it meaning, even if a new content asserts itself, recedes completely; poetry by contrast is forced to give expression to its own era, with its altered ideas and goals, as well as the various national peculiarities of its guardians."[64]

Though visual art was primarily formal and poetry semantic, Riegl found parallels between the two media; in an 1890–1891 seminar he argued that *Ornamentik,* rhetoric, and poetics served similar theoretical functions within their respective fields of art: "Thus poetics, for example, deals with the laws which govern the art of poetry, those the poet has to follow to . . . produce an artwork. The same type of laws also exist for *Ornamentik* or the art of decoration. There are universal laws of symmetry and proportion, then specific laws for decoration. . . . Grasped in this sense, we would understand by the designation *'Ornamentik'* the theory of decoration."[65] Although Riegl declared this theory the domain of aesthetics and did not elaborate on it, he clearly believed that the laws of decorative art were revealed in the ever-changing forms of appearance [*werkselnden Erscheinungsformen*], which he *did* propose to investigate as an unbroken causal chain [*ununterbrochenen Causalzusammenhang*]. Historical continuity, therefore, was more than a mere methodological presumption; Riegl's seminar on *Ornamentik* sought to establish the existence of an organic and continuous history of decoration, one that could be verified by empirical evidence.[66] Historical continuity, Riegl believed, was an order elicited from, not imposed on, art forms. Just as each medieval poem contained an implicit history and theory of the poetic form, artworks contained their own inherent temporal and historical frameworks.[67]

Even as Carolingian calendar verses retained formal traces of their ancient predecessors, they revealed tendencies characteristic of a later medieval style that reflected the quotidian social events of the day. Riegl described Carolingian calendar poems as embodying a further step in the developmental history of representation that he had traced from prehistoric times. Roman calendar images, we recall, whether traditional or contemporary, were understood to personify or emblematize temporal units in an allegorical fashion. Not directly symbolic of events but not yet wholly abstracted from the months depicted, late Roman images stood transitionally between Greek symbolism and medieval narrative abstraction. Carolingian art revealed a weakening of this tendency toward personification. Carolingian poets as well turned away from rich allegories to a style that favored "simple and straightforward narrative."[68] Their reliance on mundane images could on one level seem deceptively representational, almost a return to the Greek symbolic connections between events and images. Riegl cited as exemplary an anonymous Salzburg poet who depicted recognizable images of everyday life during a particular month. However, Carolingian calendar verses, according to Riegl, did not aim to directly link temporal units and life events; instead, they sought to depict visually the abstract, narrative, teleological time of the human world *as such* within a Christian age. "For the poet, the individual figure is therefore no more a personification than is the individual figure in the later images of months: indeed they represent nothing other than man himself, who devotes himself to a particular task in a given season."[69] Gradually the visual arts followed suit. To represent the spring and summer months, for example, early medieval artists rejected ancient forms and adopted contemporary images of life and work that anticipated the representational patterns of the later Middle Ages.[70] However, several months presented no clear human activity; according to Riegl, in these months men were mere passive inhabitants of the natural world. "March and April presented tremendous difficulties. . . . Passive events transpire in nature, and man has no active part in them."[71] Lacking clear candidates for depiction, medieval artists resorted to images borrowed from the inherited formal canon of calendar art, acknowledging thereby a continuing debt to ancient tradition.

Riegl culminated his discussion of the tradition of calendar art by considering two tenth-century medieval calendars: the Wandalbert-Martyrolog der Regina, modeled on the Filocalus calendar, and the calendar of St. Mesmin. As with his analyses of earlier calendars, the discussion focused on close descriptions of monthly images. Applying strict empirical techniques, Riegl described the handwriting of the Wandalbert-Martyrolog, its decorations, and dedication,[72] determining that the calendar was representative of both its medieval period and an ongoing tradition dating from antiquity. Close empirical observation of images indicated to Riegl that even the contemporary illustrations that replaced older forms, often revealed traces of a traditional inheritance.

> On the right side of our June image a crab is depicted, stylized like a cockchafer, which demonstrates that men did not think of the zodiac image as in any way naturalistic representation; instead they strove to copy the ancient literature on

> the stars, even though these models were sometimes badly corrupted. How could it be explained otherwise that the scorpion is presented in a fairly naturalistic pose with its tail, while the well-known crab went without a tail? The explanation lies in the fact that Scorpio needed its tail because of stars which men had designated as tail-stars, whereas the crab's lack of any tail-stars did not present a problem because they were not necessary.[73]

New images, Riegl claimed, in an argument that became central to *Problems of Style,* evolved not as an impulse toward naturalization but as a formal revision and adaptation of images from the traditional artistic lexicon. The move toward greater correspondence with contemporary needs thus maintained essential aspects of the ancient menological conception. In the second of the two high medieval calendars, the late tenth-century calendar of St. Mesmin, Riegl found a cycle of images that he considered "the true product of the medieval spirit."[74] Although a few of the images, notably April with its garland of flowers, obviously referred to the ancient canon, most monthly images broke with the symbolic universe of late Roman personification and bore only subtle formal reminders of their distant source. Emptied of traditional symbolic content, the transformed forms took on a new significance pertinent to medieval life.[75]

Riegl concluded "Die mittelalterliche Kalenderillustration" by surveying calendar art from the tenth and eleventh centuries. Devoting separate sections to art from various cultures of western Europe and the Byzantine world, he emphasized again the omnipresent turn away from abstract personifications of time toward representations of daily activities associated with the contemporary period—toward things that took place in a *particular* time[76] and revealed "the connection between time reckoning and earthly human life."[77] This change in representational goals was, he contended, continuous with the past, and reaffirmed the existence of a tradition of calendar art stretching from ancient Greek times (and by anthropological extrapolation to prehistory before it) through the Middle Ages.

> Thus we have worked to establish in the iconography of the months a connected development from Hellenistic times until the eleventh century: partly by conjecture because of a

> lack of sources, but not without fixed reference points of transmission between Hellenistic and late Roman artistic practice, not without resistance but then ultimately clearly realized between late Roman antiquity and the Romanesque Middle Ages; this provides fresh proof that the culture and artistic era that commenced in Alexander the Great's time . . . continued in the Middle Ages as a living, organic connection.[78]

Riegl's art history progressed through a continuous interaction of inherited forms and contemporary innovations. Indeed, the initial conceptual dichotomy between tradition and innovation, exemplified in the competing prehistoric demands of political and sacerdotal elites on the one hand and agricultural interests on the other, merged in Riegl's historical analysis into a fruitful negotiation and integration.

Riegl stressed the unique and innovative departures of medieval calendar art by emphasizing its break with the past:

> If we now take note of the unqualified respect for those things that antiquity had passed down, that prevailed not only in the time around 900 but lasted unweakened and powerful over centuries, then we need to ask ourselves: why did men decide so early to break with the traditional and sacred paths in the relatively minor domain of calendar illustration and go their own way.[79]

Riegl answered this question by noting that the calendar regulated a domain of practical activities that required artists to heed contemporary relevance, not simply reproduce antiquated forms: "We have . . . already seen in the history of calendar illustration during Hellenistic and Roman times the inner connections that the calendar and its decoration had to daily life; and to express these connections the medieval monk could just as little use the conceptions of the old Roman farmer from the Campagna, as this farmer could have used the Greek circle of twelve gods in his time."[80] Changing social needs forced calendar images to evolve.[81] Just as the "Hellenic spirit" embraced symbolic form as its representative style of calendar art, the "medieval spirit" used a narrative style to link temporal abstraction and depictions of human daily life.[82]

Although Riegl concluded his essay by highlighting the emergence of a distinctly medieval art as the "product of a medieval spirit,"[83] this emphasis should not overwhelm the main thesis of "Die mittelalterliche Kalenderillustration": that a continuous tradition linked ancient and medieval calendar art. Cultural distinctiveness and traditional continuity were not mutually exclusive. After all, even profound medieval innovations in calendar images could be connected to the ancient world through a set of continuous transitions. The medieval calendar rejected images handed down by Hellenistic and Roman calendar artists that no longer reflected daily medieval life, and yet traces of these ancient images remained in altered form. Medieval innovation, moreover, was predicated on the retention of the essential anthropological and objective referents of calendar art, namely, a concern for daily human needs and the orientation of these needs around celestial points. This basic conception remained even as the visual forms changed. The relationship can be stated even more strongly: maintaining the calendar's essential tradition actively demanded formal innovation. Medieval artists reshaped and transformed the ancient heritage to reflect contemporary life; they adapted the tradition "in order to pour in a new content that corresponded to their own, recent time."[84] Innovation for Riegl came to mean variation within a tradition, variation that preserved the tradition's basic conception. Even radical artistic innovation maintained its connection with the past by adapting and revising traditional forms.[85]

Riegl's stress on innovation within tradition had direct contemporary relevance, for it shaped his evaluation of modern artists, such as Gustav Klimt and Adolf Loos, who worked during his lifetime. Modernists tended to demand that art break from traditional forms and create works that reflected the realities of contemporary life. Riegl's response to this attitude could be seen as both conservative and sympathetic. Although his vision of history emphasized the continuing debt owed by all innovative works to the artistic inheritance from the past, he recognized the imperative for artworks to speak to the needs and experiences of their contemporary audiences, to reflect the "spirit" of their age.

Riegl predicated his history of calendar art on a model of continuous temporality and at the same time attempted to show that this continuity manifested itself within artworks. This apparent tautology—artworks both contained and were contained by time—was a paradox similar to that which Ricoeur identified in Husserl:[86] the unity of time contains all objects, including artworks; yet art allows man to grasp time by incorporating its continuity as formalized signification. Time and art mutually encompassed each other in Riegl's thought. Contained and container, overarching unity and discrete chronological datum, an artwork exhibited time formally by giving temporality a visible image or surface. In "Die mittelalterliche Kalenderillustration," a continuous temporality and a progressive history were assumed as preconditions for the investigation of calendar art; the calendar, after all, represented time, which supposedly existed independently of it. During the 1890s, Riegl gradually came to recognize and confront the subtle tautological implications of this early assumption. Subsequent chapters of this book will examine his attempts to express the relationship among history, time, and art.

"Die mittelalterliche Kalenderillustration" laid the basis for Riegl's future work by announcing both his interest in historical time and his proto-phenomenological approach to investigating it. Its themes, moreover, reflected the prevalence of a discourse on time, empiricism, and history in late nineteenth-century Austria. In the following section, I will explore these themes in the work of Riegl's teachers and colleagues.

1

Wellenberg und Wellenthal: History and Time in Fin-de-Siècle Austrian Thought

Both Alois Riegl and his colleague Franz Wickhoff used the metaphor of waves (*Wellenspiel, Wellenthal, Wellenberg*) to describe the movements of art history.[1] The towering stylistic influences of one artistic era often subside in the next; they submerge into the undercurrents of history only to resurface later in new and unexpected crests. The metaphor provides an apt description of the convergence, transformation, and adaptation of ideas that characterized the interdisciplinary discourse on time and history in nineteenth-century Vienna. Part 1 of this book (chapters 2 through 7) highlights the intellectual influences on and context of Riegl's development of a scientific art history and a model of temporality to underpin it. Many of Riegl's ideas came from professors working in fields outside his own—from history, philosophy, archaeology, philology. These contributions were often indirect, as Riegl adapted and transformed their applications in his work. Nevertheless, a survey of the work of Riegl's teachers and mentors uncovers many themes central to his scholarship.

In his first year at the University of Vienna, Riegl enrolled in an ethics course taught by the philosopher Franz Brentano.[2] The lectures introduced Riegl to a philosophical empiricism that complemented the empirical methodologies he studied with the historians Max Büdinger and Theodor von Sickel. Brentano hoped to establish philosophy as a truly scientific enterprise by grounding it in the empirical observation and description of psychological data. He presented his methodological program as a descriptive psychology: only after perceptual reality had been carefully observed, only after its objects had been identified and described, would general laws and patterns emerge. The analytic description of psychological objects in terms of their component parts and modes laid the basis for scientific theories of philosophy and psychology.

In various forms, Riegl encountered a similar emphasis on description, observation, and perceptual psychology throughout his university education. Brentano's descriptive taxonomy of psychological modes had strong affinities with the historical and art historical methods of many of

Riegl's mentors. Brentano and Sickel, Moritz Thausing and Robert Zimmermann—each sought to establish their disciplines on a so-called scientific basis that rejected the idealism of Kant and Hegel, the speculative philosophical underpinnings of historicism, and the timeless standards of classical aesthetics. Instead, Riegl's teachers drew heavily on the philosophical systems of Aristotle, Descartes, and Leibniz, whose attempts to provide logical and analytic foundations for empirical science considerably influenced eighteenth- and nineteenth-century Austrian thought.[3] Riegl's teachers developed empirical methods for investigating their objects of study and the modes of perception appropriate to their respective disciplines. In philosophy, history, and art history, psychological and perceptual considerations received new attention as scholars questioned the relationship between objectivity and subjective perception. Perception, many thinkers came to believe, did not merely receive objective data; it participated in constructing that objectivity. In grappling with this awareness, Austrian thinkers struggled to develop a "flexible positivism" that remained scientific and empirical without degenerating into an oversimplified, positivistic view of reality experienced unproblematically through the senses.[4] Riegl's own work emerged in this context.

However, while Riegl and his mentors stressed empiricism, they did not let analytic methodologies overtake the synthetic aims of their enterprises. Although they denounced philosophical idealism and German historicism as overly speculative, Austrian empiricists believed that a valid historical and philosophical science needed to propose general theories of objectivity, perception, and historical development. A discipline that failed to produce such insights only ensured its inability to compete with the seductions of idealism. In recognizing that their scientific enterprises culminated in synthetic meta-theories of history, art history, and philosophy, Austrian empiricists accepted that not all phenomena were available for immediate sensory perception and scrutiny. They had to find ways to address the connections among sensory phenomena and preconditions for empirical observation, relationships that were not themselves empirically verifiable. They had, in other words, to find ways to gain empirical access to the unobservable. Although such requirements demanded speculative leaps from sensory data to broader synthetic theories, many Austrian thinkers hoped to anchor their theories as firmly as possible in the ground of scientific evidence and procedure. In this regard, Riegl and others maintained an ideal of the scientific and empirical verification of knowledge even while they attempted to expand its methods and extend its insights.

During the nineteenth century, aesthetics was one of the fields transformed by a burgeoning empiricist interest in perception.[5] Many commentators trace the development of nineteenth-century formalist and empiricist aesthetics back to the philosopher Alexander Baumgarten's *Aesthetica,* published in 1750.[6] Baumgarten's aesthetics eschewed the realm of pure conceptual thought and reclaimed for philosophical inquiry the somatic domain of sensation and perception. Aesthetics grasped reason within matter and thus required its own form of logic, distinct from purely conceptual analysis. Following Baumgarten, Immanuel Kant's investigation of perceptual judgment in the Third Critique (1790), with its notion of the "purposeless purposiveness" of formal beauty, reoriented the study of aesthetics away from objective theories of absolute beauty and toward a stress on artistic perception as a relationship between artworks and a community of judging observers.[7] His *Critique of Pure Reason* (1781) had already insisted that time and space were a priori mental categories structuring our perception of reality, rather than pure correlates of external reality as such. This insight that the observation and study of reality had to take perception as its fundamental object laid the groundwork for the dominant aesthetic trends of the nineteenth century: Schopenhauer's theory of will and perception; art history's rejection of absolute notions of beauty; and an empiricist aesthetics that sought to uncover the psychological and physiological rules of formal beauty. No longer, it was believed, should aesthetic value be measured against a timeless absolute; instead, theorists of art investigated the relative and changeable nature of beauty. Time and history entered these considerations as constitutive features of the perception of form.

Drawing on the research of physiologists such as Xavier Bichat, Franz Josef Gall, and Josef Gaspar Spurzheim, the philosopher Arthur Schopenhauer came to understand life primarily in terms of physiological processes that could be studied empirically. Among the many systems and functions into which life could be parceled, visual perception was one of the most complex and crucial, for it stood as the very basis of human awareness. "What is *knowledge?*" Schopenhauer asked in *The World as Will and Representation.* "It is above all else and essentially *representation*. What is *representation?* A very complicated *physiological* occurrence in an animal's brain, whose result is the consciousness of a *picture or image* at that very spot."[8] The objectification of vision, its reduction to physiological processes and localization in the eye and mind of the observer, helped to achieve the state of will-less contemplation that Schopenhauer sought, for it transformed perception into a set of physical acts that could be dispassionately observed and analyzed. A host of scientists during the first half of the century, notably Johannes Müller in his *Handbuch der Physiologie des Menschen* (1833), had inspired Schopenhauer by enlisting new theories of color and light to posit wholly physiological theories of human sight.[9] These doctrines confounded traditional notions of an objective external reality available to an abstract viewer by training the "objectivity" of science on the apparatus of sight itself in order to discern the processes involved in representation. In this regard, objectivity referred to that which could be scientifically verified, that which the senses perceived, not an external reality that ultimately remained an article of faith.

A thinker equal to Kant in his influence on nineteenth-century Austrian psychology and aesthetics, Johann Friedrich Herbart has been largely overlooked by twentieth-century scholars outside of pedagogical circles.[10] His theory of human consciousness affected the development of formalist aesthetics and perceptual psychology throughout the German-speaking world. In *Psychologie als Wissenschaft,* Herbart proposed a model of the mind as a manifold of continuously interacting ideas (*Vorstellungen*) that merged and submerged, fused and split apart. External forms, perceived through the senses, triggered presentations in the mind, reinforcing some ideas while suppressing others in a constantly shifting relationship between mind and senses.[11] The mind for Herbart did not comprise separate ideas or Kantian faculties that independently shaped the data of the senses. Instead, it consisted of nothing but pure perception confronting the world through the senses. All ideas and sensations took the form of interacting presentations, and new sensory data either intensified or inhibited already existing mental forms. Central to this model of mental activity as a continuous interplay of phenomenal presentations was the notion that past experiences were stored as presentations in the mind, often below the threshold of awareness yet available for recovery when a new presentation recalled a similar experience. In this way, mental life became intelligible through an association of past and present experiences, a fusion of new and old ideas.

Herbart's stimulus-response psychology, with its associative interplay of pure forms in the mind,[12] prompted scientists such as Hermann Helmholtz, Gustav Fechner, Hermann Lotze, and Wilhelm Wundt to seek the psychological and physiological rules that governed mental activity and aesthetic perception. Their attempts to demonstrate these laws through laboratory experiments and inductive analysis further localized and objectified perception.[13] Robert Zimmermann, one of Riegl's teachers, sought to expand Herbart's ideas into a full-blown science of aesthetics that could provide the framework for later empirical investigations. His *Aesthetik* presented a comprehensive and systematic account of the history of aesthetic thought followed by a detailed organon describing the formalist properties of aesthetic types. These innovations, both empirical and theoretical, encouraged numerous artists and scholars, including Adolf Hildebrand, Conrad Fiedler, Heinrich Wölfflin, and Robert Vischer, to examine the precise relationship between aesthetics and perception. Toward the end of the century, Theodor Lipps's scientific theory of empathy enjoyed a prominent following that included the architect Henry van de Velde, the architectural theorist Richard Streiter, and the notorious art historian Wilhelm Worringer. Riegl's work also needs to be understood against the backdrop of this Herbartian tradition.

Moreover, Riegl's background suggests that the Austrian break with historicism and philosophical idealism was not as pronounced as commentators on Austrian historiography have suggested.[14] Although Riegl's commitment to empiricism provided the basis for a critical reception/rejection of idealism the impact of Ranke and Hegel (both of whom had empiricist moments in their thought) is also evident throughout Riegl's oeuvre. A student of the Rankean universal historian Max Büdinger, Riegl dedicated himself to the construction of a scientific art history that achieved universal-historical insights. He presented each of his historical *topoi*—late Roman art, Dutch art—as component parts of an all-encompassing whole defined in terms of the historical development of style, form, and perception. His oeuvre comprised analyses of the successive relationships among historical artworks and periods, each of which gained their ultimate significance from their position in a patently speculative, universal-historical system. Riegl's hope, like that of his colleagues in philosophy or history, was to construct that speculative system on an empirical foundation. However, the ability of empiricism to ground a stable scientific and philosophical system was much less certain than mid-century positivists might have hoped. Riegl was well aware of the limits of an empiricism that stressed pure sensory perception with its fleeting moments and ephemeral impressions. He had inherited this awareness from teachers such as Brentano, whose doctrine of intentionality was crucial in weakening the strong empiricist distinction between subject and object. Nevertheless, like Brentano, Riegl was committed to retaining empirical foundations for the human sciences even as he revised the emphasis on pure sense perception and subject-object dualism. Empiricism provided the foundation for a universal art historical system that extended beyond the limits of strict sensory verification.[16]

In light of these empiricist and universalist commitments, Riegl directed his career toward combating aesthetic absolutism, whether it took the form of an ideal that measured all art against the classical standards of ancient Greece and the Renaissance or a teleology that saw modern aesthetic taste as the pinnacle and goal of art historical development. He shared with Wickhoff and Thausing the conviction that all art was equally worthy of historical investigation. Not only were absolute categories of beauty empirically baseless and inappropriate to scientific historical discourse therefore Riegl's conception of art also grew beyond the narrow definitions of high *Kultur*, with its celebration of traditional masterworks, to encompass decoration, artifacts, and a variety of products of material *Zivilization*. The hierarchy of high and low art was, in Riegl's view, simply unscientific. If in practice Riegl concentrated his analyses more on the so-called decorative arts than on items of practical use, this was because decoration exemplified in its purest form the creative impulse that he believed shaped all artistic production. The scientific art historian, Riegl declared, "sought in artworks not that which corresponded to modern tastes, but tried instead to read out of artworks the *Kunstwollen* which brought them forth and shaped them as they are and not otherwise."[15] At the same time, however, Riegl maintained the firm conviction that art history revealed a framework of universal interconnections. In *The Group Portraiture of Holland*, for example, he used insights from Wickhoff's and his own earlier work on late Roman art to trace a universal-historical shift from ancient objective to modern subjective depiction, from art that stood apart from the viewer as an object to art that was shaped by the viewer's perceptions: "In this regard, we can recognize two extreme viewpoints in the history of mankind: at first the conception that every subject was at once an object and that therefore only objects existed; today the opposite applies: there are absolutely no objects and only a singular subject exists. The history of classical antiquity, the Christian Middle Ages, the Renaissance, and Baroque art allow us to follow step by step the transition from the former to the latter conception."[16] Although Riegl rejected the timeless universal standards of classical aesthetics, he embraced, in more systematic form, his teacher Büdinger's model of a single, universal history. The notion of temporal continuity that underpinned this universal history became, therefore, the linchpin of Riegl's conceptual system.

Riegl's interest in the temporal and historical components of aesthetic perception was not an isolated phenomenon. For many of his mentors, the problem of time exemplified the quandaries of dealing in a scientific fashion with a phenomenon that was not available for immediate sensory perception. Acknowledged as a basic constituent of perception and experience, time could be witnessed only indirectly, and only insofar as its effects could be traced visibly and then described. In seeking to understand the temporal constitution of perception, empiricists had to abandon the search for direct sensory data fundamental to most notions of empirical verification. The step from a descriptive account of the effects of temporal change to a fuller theory of time drew several of Riegl's teachers into a historical and philosophical discussion on the temporality of man's perceptual relationship with his world.

During his student days at the University of Vienna, Riegl encountered myriad, often conflicting opinions about the relationship between history, psychology, and empiricism. Although Austrian thinkers shared a social and political environment that affected their ideas, Austrian universities were not homogeneous intellectual atmospheres. Indeed, to survey Austrian thought on time and history would be beyond the scope this book; instead, I focus on a specific discourse of history and temporality that took place largely at the University of Vienna, the flagship institution of Austria's university system. Despite (and at times because of) direct imperial oversight, the University of Vienna boasted a diverse and vibrant academic culture during the late nineteenth century, and its reputation rivaled that of many German academic centers. Although

Sickel and Brentano complained of Ultramontanism at the university and both faced impediments to academic advancement, the institution's scholars benefited from Count Leo Thun's mid-century reforms and a state commitment to academic freedom.[17] Its students also flourished under a program of *Lehr-und-Lern Freiheit* that encouraged them to attend lectures in various faculties and departments before specializing.[18] The university attracted scholars from regions throughout the multinational empire and the German-speaking world. Several of Riegl's teachers were born and educated outside Austria; they researched in Italy and France and often embraced methodologies prevalent among English and French scholars rather than native German and Austrian trends.

Chapters 2 through 7 analyze the work of those scholars with whom Riegl himself studied. The writings of Franz Brentano and Robert Zimmermann, Theodor von Sickel and Max Büdinger, Moritz Thausing and Franz Wickhoff represent several disciplines within the humanities. Although most were quite influential in their own right, as a group they formed neither a school nor a movement; indeed, their work varied enormously in topic and method. And although some shared a collegial or pedagogical acquaintanceship, others were associated only by common employment in the historical and philosophical faculties of the University of Vienna during the 1870s and 1880s. By discussing aspects their works, I hope to establish the prevalence of a lively discourse on historiography and temporality at the university, a discourse that Riegl entered and elaborated. Indeed, Riegl combined facets of each of his teachers' thought in his art historical program. That these disparate figures all highlighted questions of history and temporality illustrates the extent and significance of historiographical debate within the intellectual concerns of modernist Vienna.

2

Franz Brentano and the In-existence of Time

There was much to attract Riegl to the lectures of Franz Brentano, the renowned philosopher and religious iconoclast recently transplanted from Würzburg to Vienna. In 1874, on the heels of his appointment as professor of philosophy at the University of Vienna, Brentano published *Psychology from an Empirical Standpoint,* the work that established his international reputation as a philosopher and spokesman for empirical psychology. The book advanced Brentano's two most famous and influential doctrines: the method of inner perception and the theory of intentionality, or the mental in-existence of objects. These ideas had a monumental influence on contemporary Austrian philosophy and subsequent European thought.

Brentano (1838–1917) faced both tremendous success and persistent controversy during his career.[1] By the time he habilitated at Würzburg in 1866, he was already known in the German academic community as an outspoken Aristotelian and a sharp critic of idealist trends in German philosophy.[2] In the public disputation that accompanied his habilitation, he defended a set of propositions regarding philosophical inquiry, the most famous of which—*Vera philosophiae methodus nulla alia nisi scientiae naturalis est* (The true method of philosophy is none other than that of the natural sciences)—announced his empiricist allegiances and guided his subsequent work. Brentano immediately took up a post as docent in the philosophical faculty of the University of Würzburg, and in 1867 his second book on Aristotle's psychology appeared in print.[3]

After receiving his doctorate in 1862, Brentano studied theology, spent a short time in residence at a Dominican monastery, and, in 1864, was ordained a Catholic priest. Catholicism remained a central intellectual and personal commitment throughout his career. Edmund Husserl once remarked of his teacher: "I never heard Brentano speak of Catholicism itself in other than tones of great respect."[4] By 1873, however, Brentano had abandoned both the priesthood and his position as *professor extraordinarius* in Würzburg due to conflicts over the Pius IX's declaration of papal infallibility, which Brentano rejected as contradicting the Gospels, Catholic faith, and Church history. So vehement was his condemnation of Vatican policy that one student, Georg von Hertling, later chancellor of Germany, compared Brentano to Martin Luther.[5] Biographers have made much of the intellectual and emotional doubts that led to Brentano's break with the Church, and most agree that his quarrels were not limited to the 1871 declaration. Antos Rancurello suggests that Brentano's religious crisis had already begun by spring 1870, prior to the July declaration of infallibility.[6] He argues that by 1870 Brentano had started to doubt the validity of Church teachings on faith because they seemed to lack the certainty of inner evidence. Brentano's writings on the existence of God testify to his great efforts at reconciling his philosophical commitments with his religious convictions.[7] Although they often led him into conflict with Catholic authorities, science and philosophy reinforced his personal faith by demonstrating empirically the glory of creation. Attached to an ideal of pure Catholic faith, Brentano rejected both Bismarck's anti-Catholic policies and his former professor Ignaz von Döllinger's attempts to recruit him for the Old Catholic movement.[8]

In 1874, the renegade Brentano was named *professor ordinarius* at the University of Vienna, an appointment made possible by the Austrian May Laws of 1868, which established secular control of education, and by the 1870 termination of the controversial Concordat with the Catholic Church. Disputes related to Brentano's faith, however, continued to dog him throughout his years in Austria. As an erstwhile priest out of step with the Church hierarchy, and a German transplant to Vienna, Brentano encountered many critics among the Austrian clergy and the predominantly Catholic faculty. Attacks against him grew more strident when, in 1880, he decided to marry. When opponents called attention to Austrian court cases that denied marriage to former priests, Brentano took the dramatic step of resigning his professorship, acquiring Saxon citizenship, and participating in a civil ceremony in Leipzig.[9] Despite promises from the Austrian government that he would be reappointed professor soon after his marriage, Brentano could only secure a post as *Privatdozent* at the University of Vienna; his repeated attempts to get his full professorship restored were blocked. Growing disgust over this delay, combined with the death of his wife in 1893, prompted his decision to leave Austria in 1894.[10]

Brentano remains something of a shadow figure in the history of European Continental thought.[11] Although his influence on twentieth-century philosophy and cognitive psychology is often acknowledged, his legacy is given short shrift in many histories of philosophical thought. Diverse and sometimes antagonistic philosophical movements claim him as a predecessor and seek to enlist him in partisan fashion for one philosophical camp or another. Logical positivists, for example, claim Brentano as a founding member, although they distance themselves from his purported psychologism. Phenomenologists celebrate his doctrine of intentionality, although they too attack its psychologistic inclinations.[12] A more distant but nonetheless crucial successor, Martin Heidegger credited Brentano with leading him to both philosophy and the question of Being.[13] Freud as well was sufficiently impressed with Brentano's reputation to enroll in two of his courses in 1875, and several commentators have noted the mark that Brentano left on the young medical student.[14] However, the full scope of his impact on broader intellectual developments within and outside Austria has only rarely been assessed. Even more uncommon are considerations of his impact outside the fields of philosophy and psychology.[15]

Brentano's most famous volume, *Psychology from an Empirical Standpoint*, declared his methodological and philosophical commitment to psychology as an exact science and outlined a system of empirical psychology applicable to philosophical study. In that work, Brentano sought to establish the distinctive epistemological priority of psychology by designating inner perception as an empirical method of verification. Knowledge of physical phenomena, Brentano believed, could be secured only by understanding the mental states that apprehend them; this understanding could only be achieved through a method called inner perception. Brentano's inner perception worked by way of indirection; it must be distinguished from inner observation, or introspection, which gazes directly at a mental state as if it were an external object. The ultimate "objects" of inner perception, however, are mental states that can not be isolated from the acts of perceiving and observing.

> Inner perception, and not introspection, i.e., inner observation, constitutes this primary and essential source of psychology. . . . We can observe objects which, as they say, are perceived externally. In observation, we direct our full attention to a phenomenon in order to apprehend it accurately. But with objects of inner perception this is absolutely impossible. . . . It is only while our attention is turned toward a different object that we are able to perceive, incidentally, the mental processes which are directed toward that object. Thus, the observation of physical phenomena in external perception, while offering a basis for knowledge of nature, can at the same time become a means of attaining knowledge of the mind. Indeed, turning one's attention to physical phenomena in our imagination is, if not the only source of our knowledge of laws governing the mind, at least the immediate and principal source.[16]

The phenomena of inner perception are not directly observed; one cannot designate them in the same way that one can a physical object selected for scientific scrutiny. Inner perception, however, *is* tied up with observation. Only by observing an external object can one come to recognize the indirect perception of mental states. A philosopher-psychologist (in Brentano's term, a psychognost) trained himself to notice these oblique awarenesses, which accompany observation and consciousness of the external world.

"Psychognosy," Brentano declared, "is pure psychology," and it "belongs to the exact sciences."[17] In *Descriptive Psychology*, the posthumously published third volume of the *Psychology from an Empirical Standpoint*, Brentano detailed the method of inner perception in a succession of procedures.[18] The psychognost, he wrote, must first experience a wealth of facts about human consciousness; he must notice the component parts that make up the unity of these experiences; he must fix those components in memory so that they become elements of knowledge that can be communicated and compared; he must then generalize inductively from the facts of consciousness in order to discern laws of consciousness; and finally he must deduce or intuit from these general laws to distinguish among the types and components of mental acts. Through sedulous adherence to these steps, the philosopher could systematically explain the processes of mental acts. Indeed, only by establishing such a systematic method of inner perception, Brentano argued, could psychology be set on a truly scientific basis.

Brentano rejected the distinction between pure consciousness and the objects it perceived, arguing instead that consciousness was "always and everywhere a certain kind of relation, relating a subject to an object,"[19] an act rather than an entity. In *Psychology from an Empirical Standpoint*, he advanced his highly influential notion of intentionality to describe this relationship between mind and object: "Every mental phenomenon is characterized by what the Scholastics of the Middle Ages called the intentional (or mental) inexistence of an object, and what we might call, though not wholly unambiguously, reference to a content, direction, or toward an object (which is not to be understood here as meaning a thing), or immanent objectivity. Every mental phenomenon includes something as object within itself, although they do not all do so in the same way."[20] According to the doctrine of intentionality, thought does not exist independently of the objects it considers; instead it is always directed toward its object. Thus, the doctrine of intentionality effectively weakens the distinction between subject and object by joining them in a permanent dependence. Drawing on the Aristotelian theory that objects impressed their form on the mind through the senses, Brentano argued that there was a correspondence between the sensed thing and the thought thing, that the objects of consciousness were themselves in-dwelling forms. Much as a "piece of wax takes on the form of a seal,"[21] the mind takes in the intelligible form of sensed objects. Consciousness was always consciousness of something, a relationship, an act, not an object distinct unto itself. But this object of consciousness was not to be understood as a physical object distinct from the perceiving mind. Instead, Brentano's psychology emphasized the analysis of mentally immanent forms and objects, forms intrinsic to the mind in its relationship to the world. By apprehending intentional objects, the mind indirectly became aware of its own activity, its own involvement in an objective world, for the recognition of objective in-existence was itself a product of the mind grasping its own active worldliness.[22]

It is important to stress that the objects of inner perception did not necessarily have to correspond directly with a sensed external reality for them to provide a basis for scientific philosophical inquiry. Brentano's empiricism did not propose an untroubled acceptance of the external world whose immediacy and availability to consciousness Kant had done so much to question. Nevertheless, during at least the first part of his career, Brentano did indeed attempt to combine a psychology emphasizing intentional objects with an ontology that accepted the correspondence of sense and reality, mental and external objectivity, in a divinely created world.[23] From the time of his earliest works on Aristotle, Brentano's ontology of the multifarious unity of divine creation mirrored his psychology, which, like Herbart's psychology, presented the mind as a unity made up of interrelating parts, acts, and objects. In this mereological model of both ontology and psychology, time occupied a unique and problematic position.[24] Was time an external object that could be directly grasped by the senses, or was it an intentional form, indirectly perceived and intuited? In his first published work, *On the Several Senses of Being in Aristotle,* which set out to classify the categories in which being presented itself, time and place were considered absolute accidents of being, categories of containment. "There are two measures through which all finite things are measured and determined from outside, viz. time and place."[25] These coordinates were the parameters of being, not, as Kant would have it, the mental preconditions for experience. Brentano invoked Aristotle's *Physics* to underscore this point: "So it is necessary that all the things in time should be contained by time, just like other things which also are contained 'in anything,' e.g., the things 'in place' by place."[26] Time was a correlate that marked one boundary of Being. In this early conception, time was effectively spatialized, and one could move across its extent as one moved from point to point on a map. Late in his career, however, Brentano came to reject Aristotle's correlation of temporal and spatial measure.

> Aristotle gives the following explanation of time: it is the number of the movement of the uppermost celestial sphere in so far as this supplies the measure of the earlier and later for all other change and perseverance. If one sets aside the

> errors attached to this definition as a result of its connection to the pre-Copernican astronomy, then it asserts nothing other than that the question of "When?" is customarily answered by determinations which relate to the changing state of the heavenly bodies. . . . Aristotle has not so much defined the essence of space and time as named that to which, because we presuppose it as sufficiently familiar in its spatial and temporal determinations, further relative spatial and temporal determinations are referred.[27]

Like Henri Bergson, Brentano disputed the tendency to mistake time for the spatial correlates of its measure, an identification that ignored the unique qualities of temporal phenomena. "When" could not simply be reduced to "where."

During his last decades, Brentano devoted increasing attention to the philosophical problem of temporality, dictating numerous manuscripts that remained unpublished in his lifetime. Disputing both the Kantian view that time was a mental category through which experience was filtered and the Aristotelian claim that time was an objective framework within which experience became manifest, Brentano developed a theory of time as a mode of the presentation of objects:

> When that which was first of all given as present appears as more and more past it is not other objects which are accepted as existing, but the same objects which are accepted in a different way, with a different modus of acceptance. This modus, however, is not something unitary: in reflection of the continuity of temporal intuition it is a continuum of modi, first of all of presentation and then also of acceptance. That which is past is after all not presented as equally past, but as more or less past.[28]

Brentano did not consider time to be an independent phenomenon, a quality of or framework for external objects; instead, he proposed a doctrine of time as the mode of presentation of in-dwelling objects. Time, he argued, could only be viewed indirectly in the presentation of other phenomena, not as an object with its own autonomous existence. Time could be neither isolated nor observed; it had to be intuited from the perception and consciousness of objects. As a mode of the intentional presentation of objects, time had only an oblique and mediate existence.[29] An investigation of time, therefore, required the psychognost to adopt a flexible empiricism that did not restrict itself to exclusively sensory verification. Brentano claimed that time constituted all objects in presentation, but that it had to be intuited from the inner perception of intentional objects. Every experience, even the briefest and most isolated, contained an intuition of time; Brentano called this essential quality of temporal extension *proterosis,* and considered it a basic attribute, the "boundary," of all perception. "No intuition," he wrote in 1914, "is entirely free of the concept of that which is continuous."[30] Through the association of successive past, present, and future temporal presentations, one could gain an intuitive awareness of a longer temporal continuity that encompassed and unified experience, an awareness that Brentano termed *proteraesthesis.* Proterosis was to proteraesthesis as part to whole; the continuity of experience derived from the temporal extension of its smallest units. Brentano's mereology of temporal presentation was thus closely tied to his distinctive method of inner perception and his models of psychology and ontology.

Direct concern for time as a philosophical topic was only one way in which temporality and historiography entered into Brentano's consideration. In his early works, those with which Riegl was probably most familiar, time appeared as an ancillary concern in investigations of other phenomena (fulfilling, perhaps, the belief that time could only be perceived indirectly). Before and even during his tenure in Vienna, in fact, Brentano's interest in philosophical history overshadowed his concern for temporality and continuity as such. As early as the 1860s, for example, Brentano compiled notes for a proposed history of philosophy divided into eras—ancient, medieval, and modern.[31] A theory of the historical phases of philosophical tradition informed several of Brentano's essays, including his inaugural lecture at the University of Vienna, "Über die Gründe der Entmutigung auf philosophischem Gebiet." "The history of every science," he wrote, "must develop in such a way that an incomplete understanding in the beginning expands more and more through the addition of newly discovered truths and thus grows to become a consummate science. A science does not begin anew in each mind. It endures as a tradition, a trove of knowledge, through which later periods take possession of the inheritance of earlier times."[32]

In *The Four Phases of Philosophy,* Brentano characterized the history of philosophy as a cyclical rise and decline; periods of pure theoretical insight and interest gave way to phases of dogmatism, skepticism, and finally mysticism before philosophy was reborn to a new theoretical clarity.[33] In Brentano's view, modern idealism represented the final phase of decline into speculative mysticism; he looked to positivist and empiricist philosophers such as Auguste Comte and John Stuart Mill for philosophical rejuvenation.

In a fragment written in the late 1880s, Brentano insisted that only disciplinary specialists should write the history of philosophy: "Not every philologist will undertake to explain a Euclid or an Archimedes, but only those who are also mathematicians. And not every historian will venture successfully to write a history of chemistry or physics, but only those who are natural scientists. By the same token, research on the history of philosophy demands a philosopher."[34] The most recent historians of philosophy failed precisely because they were not "men of science." Even those scholars who had studied philosophy tended to ignore their training when they embarked on historical research.[35] As a result, their methods often produced violations of the "logical rule," and hence the "rule of historical research," that the plausibility of purported facts must be taken into account before they are asserted as true.[36]

Brentano admitted that philosophers were generally taken up with philosophical studies that prevented them from turning their attentions to history. However, history did play an important role in his philosophical procedures. Throughout his oeuvre, Brentano used historical surveys to outline the parameters and assumptions of philosophical concepts. In *Psychology from an Empirical Standpoint,* as part of his attempt to establish a psychological method, he noted that "history provides many facts which are important to psychologists. . . . [T]he course of world history considered in and for itself, the succession of phenomena which are exhibited in the masses, progress and retrogression, the rise and fall of nations, can often render great service to those who want to investigate the general laws of man's mental nature."[37] Critical, historical surveys of viewpoints on a particular issue, he argued, could outline the "*aporiai*"—the uncertainties as well as the boundaries—of a particular topic. This aporetic procedure, which Brentano adopted from Aristotle, "exhibit[ed] all the various conceivable assumptions, indicat[ed] for each of them the characteristic difficulties, and in particular [gave] a dialectical and critical survey of all the opposing views."[38] Such a survey was valuable scientifically because all viewpoints contained aspects of the truth: "I believe that it is evident why psychologists in particular can derive even greater profit from the conflicting opinions of others than investigators in any other field. There is some truth, some experiential basis, underlying each of these opinions even though it may be viewed one-sidedly or interpreted erroneously."[39] History expressed psychological and philosophical truths for those who could discern the objective clues within its record of collective experience. Much as psychognosy demanded the systematic analysis of mental objects, history offered a varied set of insights whose truths could be discerned and evaluated through careful descriptive and analytic procedures. Historical surveys mapped (but did not exhaust) human psychological forms.

While history could provide an index of human conceptual possibilities, however, it could not offer moral or philosophical prescriptions. "The concept of the good must be abstracted from inner intuition or perception";[40] it did not arise from historical circumstance. In a seminar on ethics that he taught numerous times between 1875 and 1894, Brentano insisted that history was morally ambiguous. Historical surveys could outline an issue and recall past solutions, but history could not dictate ethical values. Disputing the historicist notion that history could be understood as a progressive revelation of ethical truth, Brentano argued instead that ethics was based on apodictic judgments rooted in inner perception and experience.[41] The mind apprehended phenomena in three ways: in presentations whereby the subject became conscious of an objective perception; in judgments that affirmed or rejected the existence of a presented object; and through interest that attached either positive or negative value to the object.[42] Echoing the Cartesian notion of clear and evident judgment, Brentano based his ethics on the immediate, apodictic apprehension of the "rightness" or "wrongness" of interest in a perceived object. This verdict, he maintained, was rooted in the clear intuition of perceptual evidence; positive ethical judgments combined the "subjective" certainty of the "rightness" of something with the "objective" affirmation of its truth and existence. The source of these judgments was a sudden intuitive awareness of "loving correctly"; the worth of an object, Brentano claimed, "becomes obvious at a single stroke, so to speak, and without any induction from a particular case."[43] Thus, ethics was not historically bound; by using an intuition similar to that employed in judging truth, the mind determined whether an object was good or bad according to its evident correctness or incorrectness. Further ethical principles could be derived from this fundamental intuition according to a logic of compatibility. Ultimately then, Brentano believed that "evident judgment,"[44] not history, served as the empirical basis for a logical extrapolation of ethics.

Brentano had not yet formalized his theory of time as a mode of presentation in the ethics lectures that Riegl attended, and his logic of ethical judgments suggested that ethics escaped the perceptual qualifications of time. Whereas inner perception was temporally constituted in presentation, the apodictic judgments abstracted from it had synchronic and categorical immediacy. However, despite the implication that ethics transcended time, Brentano's notes from later versions of the seminar revealed a close connection between temporality and objectivity:

> Everything that is is simultaneously with everything else that is. The only difference is temporal; among the things that are present, one is beginning while another is continuing and a third is ending. In other words, it is either the beginning or the end of a temporal episode that connects what has already taken place with what will come out of it. Precise observation discloses that we are dealing in every case with continuous temporal change, even in the cases where we are speaking of "unchanging continuity."[45]

In this sense time seems to describe the continuity of episodic disclosures within an otherwise simultaneous field. That is, temporality designates the continuous variation of ontologically and psychologically simultaneous laws, judgments, and objects; it emerges in the *perception* of continuous change and difference that qualifies the higher synchronic unity of creation.

This model of time, combining a belief in both temporal continuity and ontological simultaneity, informed Brentano's vision of history. Although he did not share historicist or idealist notions of history fulfilling a greater inevitability, he did insist that historical indeterminacy was logically absurd. The fact that things persist and endure through time demonstrated to Brentano that random chance did not govern the world; "at every single moment during the existence of something arising by chance, an abrupt alteration between existing and not existing is at least as probable as its enduring."[46] The observable fact of persistence alone, therefore, demonstrated the implausibility of theories of random chance and the likelihood that relations among objects share a temporal and historical continuity.

On this point as on many others, Brentano owed a debt to Descartes. An admiration for the Cartesian system, with its emphasis on the certainty of inner perception, apodictic logic, and clear and evident ideas, runs throughout Brentano's work. The influence of Descartes's Third Meditation is clear in the argument for the certainty of temporal continuity from the evidence of objective perseverance. "[F]rom the fact that I was in existence a short time ago," wrote Descartes,

> it does not follow that I must be in existence now, unless some cause at this instant, so to speak, produces me anew, that is to say, conserves me. It is as a matter of fact perfectly clear and evident to all those who consider with attention the nature of time, that, in order to be conserved in each moment in which it endures, a substance has need of the same power and action as would be necessary to produce and create it anew, supposing it did not yet exist.[47]

Descartes believed that this sustaining power was God, and he concluded from the evidence of temporal persistence and continuity that a perfect, eternal deity must logically exist or else all objects would wink in and out of existence randomly. Descartes's emphasis on self-evidence, his affirmation of causality and continuity, and his conviction of God's benevolent intervention and sustenance found a congenial audience in Brentano. Nevertheless, by the turn-of-the-century, Brentano had found reason to criticize Cartesian theories of time for failing to specify the ways in which time was attributed to substance and the "inner differences [between] being past, being present, and being future."[48] Although these criticisms signaled important revisions of his own earlier theories, Brentano never lost his admiration for the Cartesian quest for logical certainty and inner evidence.[49]

Like Descartes, Brentano, the erstwhile priest, insisted on the logical certainty of God's existence.[50] From his earliest writings on Aristotle through his late works, Brentano considered being to be the creation and manifestation of the divine, an infinite variety existing in simultaneous spatial and temporal extension. As an emanation of divine unity, earthly temporality, continuous and unceasing, reflected the unity and eternity of creation; as a mode of human perception, temporality accounted for the coming-into-being and receding-from-being that characterized worldly experience. Temporality and simultaneity could coexist only in the eye of God. In his recent work on Brentano's philosophical legacy, Barry Smith tries to account for Brentano's temporal paradoxes in the following terms: "there is only one temporal determination which all things share in common. Thus it is as if, with each successive instant of time, an entire new complement of worldly furniture comes into being to replace the old."[51] This interpretation of Brentano's philosophy of time privileges synchronic unity and simultaneity; it proposes a model of temporality as successive but disjunctive present moments. Smith qualifies this notion of an apparently disconnected succession by acknowledging that a "pre- (or constantly re-) established harmony [links] the microcosmos of perception and the macrocosmos of qualitatively extended things" in Brentano's thought; a *concursus dei* sustains the present as a "continuous [rather than successive] process of recreation."[52] As I have argued above, however, Brentano insisted that temporal extension—*proterosis*—characterized every human perception and every present moment, and that this quality *inherently* linked present perceptions with past and future presents in the continuous *proteraesthesis* of all experience. Unlike Descartes, Brentano did not fall back on an exclusively divine guarantor of continuity. His modal theory of time preserved both continuity *and* simultaneity by arguing that past, present, and future were qualifying modes of the inherently continuous presentation of objects, which themselves remained one and the same. In even the briefest presentation, objective inner perception secured the continuous simultaneity of past, present, and future, for the mind always grasped its objects as temporally constituted.

Brentano's philosophy presented temporal continuity as an expression of the multiplicitous unity of the world of creation. Time expressed the striving of our world toward what in Brentano's view was the ultimate end of all beings: the divine. Temporality reflected the intuited desire of multiplicitous beings for progressive redemption, for the unity of the divine, and it affirmed the existence of that unity. In

Aristotelian terms, time was the *entelechy* of being toward divinity, of multiplicity toward unity, of continuous extension toward eternal simultaneity. In this sense, Brentano displayed what Roger Bauer identified as the catholic or "creationist" empiricism of the Austrian literati, a tendency to focus on the empirical world as an expression of the divine.[53] But unlike Bauer's literati, who fell prey to a kind of fatalism when faced with a reality dispersed into particles, Brentano maintained an irrepressible optimism about the redemptive possibilities of empirical science and philosophy.

Riegl was exposed to Brentano's ideas not only in the seminar on the foundation and construction of ethics that he attended in 1875, but also in a colloquium on Kant's *Prolegomena* taught by Brentano's student Alexius Meinong. Along with philosophers such as Henri Bergson and William James, Meinong recognized that any thorough psychological investigation had to account for the nature of temporal perception. His 1899 essay "Über Gegenstände höherer Ordnung und deren Verhältniss zur inneren Wahrnehmung" and the 1906 volume *Über die Erfahrungsgrundlagen unseres Wissens* included considerations of time that drew on Brentano's thought.[54] How could we perceive objects that were temporally extended, Meinong asked, when our immediate perception was always limited to the moment? How, for example, was a melody, composed of a succession of distinct notes sounded over time, grasped as a whole in the momentary act of perception? For Meinong even more than for Brentano, explanations of time revolved around problems of perception; although he did not deny the reality of the external world, the correspondence between temporal perception and external reality seemed to trouble him little. Meinong asserted that temporal objects could only be apprehended when the temporal process was complete, when for example the last note of a melody had sounded. In his model, the perception of temporality existed as the boundary of memory, which alone could grasp continuity as a synthetic whole. Thus, his philosophy of time was based on a kind of arithmetic of parts, in which perceptions distributed over multiple moments were added up to form a temporally extended whole once the "object" had been perceived in full. The act of perception itself had no duration, no inherent temporality; with the aid of memory, it merely grasped a temporal object as whole and complete. Numerous analysts have rejected this approach as atomistic and oversimplified, arguing that the experience of time is not analytically constructed but is instead *given* in the act of perception.[55]

Brentano's work privileged empiricism but rejected both atomism and an oversimplified reliance on the senses. His concern for time within the framework of philosophical psychology was shared by many subsequent thinkers, including James and Bergson, Husserl and Meinong. Whereas certain forms of empiricism tended to reduce epistemology to immediate sensory perceptions, these thinkers, to a greater or lesser extent, preserved a role for intuition at the heart of their empirical programs. Although they disagreed over the precise nature of temporal perception, both logical positivists and phenomenologists recognized the cardinal importance of temporality in any philosophical or psychological system. Time, indeed, became a quintessential test case for phenomenologists and positivists alike, challenging them to expand the methodological premises of mid-century empiricism.

3

Theodor von Sickel and the Institute for Austrian Historical Research

In 1881, Riegl enrolled at the Institut für österreichische Geschichtsforschung, where he trained in the empiricist, documentary criticism pioneered by its chair, the historian Theodor von Sickel (1826–1908). Sickel was more of a methodologist than a theoretician; he offered methodological seminars and practica that were closely tied to the investigation of specific historical topics and the redaction of document collections. His essays and edited volumes of manuscripts highlight practical concerns raised in relation to historical research and documentation. Unlike Brentano, Sickel largely ignored the philosophical and conceptual implications of his methodological practices. His preference for empirically documented historical narrative with little overt theoretical elaboration lingered on in Riegl's art histories.

Raised in Protestant Saxony and educated at the theological and philosophical faculties of Halle and Berlin, Sickel pursued an interest in early medieval Burgundy by enrolling in the Special School for Paleography and Diplomatics at the Ecole des Chartes in Paris.[1] There he studied from 1847 through the early 1850s, when, on a temporary research stopover in Vienna, he impressed Albert Jäger, the director of the newly founded Institute for Austrian Historical Research, with his advanced knowledge of paleography, diplomatics, and chronology. The Institute's founders considered these auxiliary disciplines essential to their mandate of establishing scientific documentary criticism as the basis of historical study, and in 1856 Sickel was hired as a docent. Promoted to professor and then, from 1869 to 1891, director of the Institute, Sickel championed a rigorous, empirical method of documentary analysis called diplomatics as the basis for scientific historiography. Under Sickel's stewardship, Riegl, Wickhoff, Thausing, and others adapted his strict empiricist methodologies to their own work.

Established in the early 1850s as part of Education Minister Leo Thun's educational reform program, the Institute for Austrian Historical Research promoted a supra-national agenda that emphasized the research and writing of histories that celebrated Austria as an organic unit.[2] This mandate was expressed by Johann Alexander von Helfert, an undersecretary in Thun's education ministry, in his essay *Über Nationalgeschichte und den gegenwärtigen Stand ihrer Pflege in Österreich* (1853). Helfert called for institutional promotion of the study of Austrian transnational history in order to foster social and cultural unity: "Austrian national history is for us the history of the Austrian collective state and collective peoples, which appears organically through the intricate linking together of members who were by descent, education, and manners of different tribes, each of whom lives within the region of the Empire, in some places separate and to a large extent distinct, elsewhere mixed and mingled with others."[3] Writing in the aftermath of the 1848 revolutions, Helfert recognized how politically fraught and ideologically charged the term "nation" had become. He proposed a political rather than an ethnographic definition of the term, claiming that the nation comprised all those who lived within the state borders of Habsburg territory. "National history," he wrote, "is the history of people who share a common territorial and political unit, who are bound together by the same authority, a people protected by the same laws."[4] Helfert attacked romantic and idealist approaches to history and instead tied the fate of the nationalist historical program to the development of scientific and empirical methodologies. He described what he saw as the gradual evolution of historical knowledge from "romantic magic" through a "twilight [*halbdunkel*]" of "heroic shapes [*athletischen Gestalten*]" to increasingly clear and scientific insight.[5] Since the eighteenth century, however, historical knowledge had languished in such a state of disrepair that "few know it, fewer understand it, and even fewer make use of it." The institutionalization of historical study, Helfert believed, could rescue it from the "dust of forgetfulness," not in the form of "booty, for romantic play," but as a rigorous and scientific discipline that promoted state unity.[6]

From its inception, the Institute adopted Helfert's program and sought to modernize the study of history by applying "scientific" research methods. Its first statutes, written by Jäger in 1853, stressed the training in scientific and empirical documentary criticism.

> The school has a two-fold task that is flexible only in its accommodation to the number and level of the students. The school
> a) acquaints young men with the scholarly material (with the archival and bibliographic sources) and with the auxiliary disciplines necessary to understand those sources, and
> b) makes them further acquainted with the principles and methods of scientific/critical historical research, and through these, leads them to pursue new research and generate new results.[7]

A Benedictine monk and professor of Austrian history, Jäger lacked the methodological sophistication necessary to carry out this program fully.[8] The hiring of Sickel, therefore, helped to fulfill the methodological intentions of the Institute's founders. Although Jäger shared Sickel's desire for autonomous and scientific historical study, political, religious, and even methodological differences gradually distanced the two men. Sickel's political inclinations leaned toward a moderate German nationalism;[9] he favored gradual liberal reform tied with German unification along ***kleindeutsch*** lines. This attitude alone could bring him into conflict with Jäger and other Austrian colleagues.[10] Another potentially more difficult set of conflicts surrounded Sickel's religious affiliations. Like Brentano, Sickel was critical of Austrian Catholicism and the entrenched Catholic faculty at the university. The Austrian Concordat with Rome, chartered in 1855, the year that Sickel arrived in Vienna, strengthened censorship and bolstered the position of the clergy within Austrian society and the university system. By upbringing a Saxon Protestant, Sickel could not help but chafe at the prevalent Catholic influence in his adopted home. Among his favorite betes noirs were the "ultramontanists" of the university faculty.[11] "The ultramontanes are right to complain," wrote Sickel in 1867 regarding his promotion to full professor and the weakening of clerical control over Austrian education, "Beust [prime minister in 1867] upset with one blow the exclusively Catholic quality of the Vienna University and placed everyone on an equal footing."[12] One supporter of Sickel described his appointment as a victory for Protestant science. A less favorably disposed colleague charged that Sickel's lectures on medieval history tended to degenerate into diatribes against Catholicism.[13] Nevertheless, Sickel generally subordinated both national and religious sentiments to professional concerns, a restraint that allowed him to remain productive in an Institute founded on an Austrian nationalist mandate and headed by a Benedictine monk.

Conflicts also emerged, however, around questions of historical methodology and institutional priorities. From its inception in 1854, the Institute for Austrian Historical Research had its detractors. Jäger's Institute seemed superfluous to a philosophical faculty that already taught the subject of history; Sickel's increasing stress on empirical method seemed faddish, unscholarly, and even ahistorical. The Institute and its methods stood for novelty and for Thun's reforms of the 1850s, which threatened the stable posts and inveterate practices of many long-standing professors. Sickel's methodology, therefore, stood on one side of a battle over historiography in Austria that had political and religious undertones as well as scholarly implications. Even the two heads of the Institute parted ways when it came to defining the major focus of the Institute's agenda. Despite Jäger's resistance, the curriculum under Sickel's direction gradually turned away from the promotion of transnational Austrian history and toward the cultivation of training in scientific methods of documentary criticism. By the 1870s, the patriotic agenda of the Institute's founders had all but vanished from its revised mandate.[14]

Sickel's reorganized Institute became the affiliational locus for both students of advanced diplomatics and, after 1874, art historians who studied under Moritz Thausing—students such as Franz Wickhoff, Max Dvořák, and Alois Riegl, the so-called Vienna School of Art History. The condition for this association was a convergence between Austrian historical and art historical research methods stemming from the personal and methodological struggles that transpired at the Institute between 1856 and 1869. By the 1870s, with Sickel's appointment as director, a methodological modernism, stressing scientifically informed empiricism, occupied the center of the Institute's concerns.

Throughout the 1860s and 1870s, Sickel publicized his diplomatic method for historical research and largely succeeded in establishing it as the official course of study at the Institute. He was, of course, not alone in advocating strict empirical methodologies for evaluating documentary evidence. Indeed, nineteenth-century historians were not the first to propose a systematic analysis of documents as the foundation for historical work. Although the spirit of modern documentary criticism dates back at least as far as Lorenzo Valla's attacks on the Donation of Constantine, the doyen of modern diplomatics was Jean Mabillon (1632–1707). A Benedictine monk of the Maurist order, Mabillon published his seminal work *On Diplomatics* (1681) in order to "devise and hand down rules for distinguishing genuine manuscripts from those that are false and interpolated."[15] His formal method of documentary analysis, which concentrated on diplomatic dispatches and treatises, was promulgated in Habsburg territories during the seventeenth and eighteenth centuries by fellow Benedictines Bernhard (1683–1735) and Hieronymus Pez (1685–1762).[16] As nineteenth-century researchers increasingly sought the legitimation of a rigorous scientific method for their disciplines, faculties of history turned to this early modern diplomatic scholarship in order to adapt its research methods and establish schools for training students in documentary source criticism. Recovering neglected traditions of empirical analysis, institutions such as the Special School for Paleography and Diplomatics (reorganized in 1847) at the Ecole des Chartes and the Institute for Austrian Historical Research (founded in 1854) trained their charges in the formal auxiliary disciplines (*Hilfswissenschaften*), such as paleography and chronology, deemed necessary for scientific documentary analysis. In the 1870s and 1880s, taking advantage of newly opened archives in Austria and elsewhere, Sickel's Institute revived and modernized Mabillon's tradition and established itself as a center for training in the *Hilfswissenschaften*. Reacting against the perceived speculations of historicism and claiming for its work the mantle of science, the Institut für österreichische Geschichtsforschung prepared students for careers in Austria's newly opened "libraries, archives, and museums" as well as university faculties.[17]

Sickel's clearest exposition of the history and methodology of diplomatics appeared in his nearly four-hundred-page introduction to the *Acta Regum et Imperatorum Karolinorum: Digesta at Enarrata*, an edited compilation of Carolingian documents. Harking back to the pioneering efforts of Mabillon, Papebroch, and others, Sickel's diplomatics upheld an exacting method for the historical evaluation of official documents.[18]

> [O]fficial documents [*Urkunden*] provide evidence of a particular sort, namely . . . evidence about things of a legal nature, generally written and drawn up in an appropriate form. A document's value must be determined from its unique characteristics, a fact that requires an awareness of all the characteristic qualities of official documents. Therefore the theoretical part of this science comprises instruction in all the unique qualities of this type of documentary evidence.[19]

Before addressing questions of content and interpretation, the *Diplomatiker* had to distinguish empirically among the material features of a documentary artifact. Applying practices drawn from the auxiliary disciplines of chronology, paleography, epigraphy, and sphragistics, Sickel identified the many distinct components of a document and evaluated each using specialized techniques. He divided a document's component features into inner and outer markings [*innere und äussere Merkmale*], or formulae:

> When analyzing a document, the historian distinguishes between the simple content and the form, and thereby speaks of the internal, i.e., content-based criteria of a document's reliability and the external or form-based criteria. The *Diplomatiker,* when he speaks of internal and external criteria, means something rather different, because the inspection of documents reveals a distinction between internal and external markings [*Merkmale*] that does not coincide with the distinction between form and content. . . . There are qualities which are exclusive to original documents and others which both originals and copies share. This essential distinction corresponds to the division within the theory of diplomatics between the study of external and internal markings.[20]

Although internal and external markings varied according to historical period and type of document, Sickel provided a general catalogue of formulae commonly found in medieval documents.[21] Internal markings, designating the formulae of the text itself—the fixed conventions of phrasing and content available in both originals and copies—included the official invocation (*Anrufung* or *invocatio*), the name and title, the date line (including day, year, and indiction) and other markers of time, the various organizational subdivisions of the text (*prologus, formula publicationis, promulgatio, narratio, dispositio, corroboratio, appreciatio*), and the signatures of king, notaries, and chancellors. The external markings described those original material features of a document that could not be reproduced in copies: paper or other writing materials (*Schreibmaterial*); handwriting; abbreviations; written errors and corrections; punctuation; attached seals; and sometimes date line and signatures as well. The evaluation of internal and external formulae required specialized skills, from paleography, sphragistics, and papyrology to linguistics, chronology, and numismatics, all of which helped to evaluate the relationship between a document materially present and a past event that the document registered. Sickel also distinguished between "Special-Diplomatik," which analyzed the separate components of documents using techniques of appropriate disciplines, and "Allgemeine Diplomatik," which synthesized the insights of Special Diplomatics to form an overall evaluation of the document.[22] Thus Sickel's diplomatics offered a systematic, multidisciplinary historical analysis of documentary form and materiality.

The fact that documentary formulae varied from period to period made them helpful markers of historical context and chronology. Diplomatics revealed patterns and precedents "that are handed down from generation to generation."[23] This variance, however, also prevented a historian from being able to rely solely on a fixed register of categories to analyze his materials; each document had to be compared against others. The comparative work of diplomatics depended upon a formal congruity within and at times across epochs; consistent patterns allowed the historian to establish context and succession on the basis of formal similarities and differences. Each era and type of document had formulaic characteristics that could be recognized, catalogued, and used as markers of authenticity and chronology. Thus, it is not quite correct to say that Sickel privileged form over chronological/historical content; it is more proper to state that he treated form *as* historical content.

But what kind of content did diplomatics make available to the historian? According to Sickel, "diplomatics offers us a measure for evaluating the multiple gradations between the true and the false, the clouded truth, the greater or lesser probabilities and the relative worth of each official document. . . . In actuality it provides for nothing less than the application of historical criticism to a particular kind of evidence, this both as a support for and a supplement to the reliable and thorough knowledge of historical reality."[24] A diplomatic inquiry began by bracketing the questions of historical "content" and meaning that oriented conventional research (e.g., What does the information in this document reveal about the era in which it was written?) in order to evaluate authenticity by concentrating on material form. However, diplomatics could do more than simply indicate whether a document was genuine or fake; were it restricted to this, it would offer only the very limited historiographical service of vetting a document and preparing it for a fuller analysis of content and significance. In addition to determining the historical worth of a document, Sickel's diplomatic method claimed to reincorporate chronological information into historical study through an empirical and scientific analysis. Moreover, by comparing a document with materials known to come from the same era, diplomatics could indicate whether that document was authentic or forged; place it chronologically in relation to other documents and historical events; trace the directions of political and intellectual influence, as certain formulae were adopted from one region and carried to another; indicate whether a document was written by one minister or many; and even, at times, ascertain the author or authors of particular documents, revealing the lines of power and influence. These were distinctly historical matters, which, according to Sickel, could not be answered satisfactorily using sources in traditional ways; they required instead a scientific examination of a document's formal and material features. Thus Sickel's method claimed to transcend the form/content dichotomy by revealing the historical content laden within a document's formal and material components. Diplomatics, Sickel asserted, could explain "the historical development of content, form, and formula."[25]

In his *Beitraege zur Diplomatik,* a collection of eight essays analyzing Carolingian documents, Sickel demonstrated the wide historical applicability of his method.[26] In the work, he applied diplomatics toward a conventionally historical end: establishing the chronologies of kings, administrators, laws, and events and thus helping to clarify the historical context of early medieval times. The first *Beitrag,* an analysis of the official documents of Ludwig des Deutschen, set out to establish "the order of chancellors to the eastern Frankish kings."[27] Compiling an accurate chronicle of monarchical and administrative succession required a historian to apply the lessons "of modern criticism and the various results of the historical and auxiliary studies."[28] Accordingly, Sickel opened his analysis with methodological considerations.

> I conduct my discussion of the documents in the following manner: I will group together documents drawn up by the same scribe, characterize them according to their markings and then discuss them with respect to their historical or legal content, form, dating, authenticity or inauthenticity, etc.; these critical considerations deviate as necessary from the chronological order of succession and seek to examine documents that belong together on the basis of other connections.[29]

In this passage, a clear interrelation of historical context and material document emerges in the definition of analytic criteria. Although chronological succession was set aside as a second-order question of content—to be demonstrated, not presumed—Sickel accepted a formal parameter of context defined in paleographic terms: one scribe, one style; the document contained its own formal marker of authorship. Historical context was bracketed in favor of a formal context that provided the scientific basis for inquiry. Form and style offered a materially inscribed context that revealed historical content and succession; indeed, the historical significance of a document could only be determined by comparing it with similar documents to establish the formal and stylistic parameters of its era. Context—the shared set of characteristics that allowed documents to be grouped together—was, first and foremost, a formal relationship materially inscribed in the documents, not a set of qualities, ultimately transcendent, offered up by the historical record to describe a bygone era.

In the end, diplomatics could not escape a certain amount of methodological circularity. Despite the apparent bracketing of historical questions, Sickel insisted that the criteria and formulae applied to documentary criticism were not permanently abstracted from the physical documents or from the eras in which they were written. Indeed, the determination of a document's authenticity demanded a comparative method based in circularity: only from the observation of documents could the formal criteria of evaluation be abstracted, yet a document's reliability could only be gauged with reference to clear criteria.[30] Sickel's diplomatics offered something between a tautologous hermeneutics of material evidence (requiring an awareness of history in order to define the terms of analysis) and a "scientific" critique of documents (determining a manuscript's worth according to fixed categories of inquiry.) It stood uneasily between a general theory of documentary analysis and a critical method relevant to Carolingian documents alone.

In order to conduct thorough diplomatic studies, Sickel emphasized the use of original documents, which became more available in the nineteenth century as Austrian officials opened government archives.[31] "Even the best of copies can offer the *Diplomatiker* certainty only about the internal markings . . . ; good descriptions of individual external markings offer at most a substitute for inspecting the original. Therefore whoever wants to write a thorough and exhaustive documentary study must have the opportunity to look over a great number of original documents."[32] Sickel recruited students at the Institute for massive efforts of archival document collection, analysis, and redaction. Interestingly, in this endeavor, he actively promoted the use of photography to duplicate documents because it seemed to offer exact facsimiles that overcame many of the limitations associated with copies. In 1857, he initiated the photo-duplication of manuscripts for the *Monumenta Graphica,* the multivolume collection of facsimile documents from German, Italian, and French archives and one of the many documentary volumes he helped to edit.[33] The new technology, which was also used at the Ecole des Chartes, provided Sickel with a means for collecting enough material to lead successful paleography courses, although other modes of analysis still required access to original documents. Despite its apparent benefits, Sickel's photography of historical documents was controversial. In an era that was well aware of how to fake images, Sickel's use of the medium raised questions about the authenticity and availability of historical evidence, as well as the link between historical study and technological modernism more generally.[34] Jäger expressed initial concerns that originals would be damaged in the chemical process of copying, that Austria's material legacy would be threatened.[35] Others warned that "the copies could not, or only with difficulty, be differentiated from the originals."[36] Ultimately, it took the intervention of Thun and the Emperor in 1858 to resolve the matter in Sickel's favor.[37] Riegl's ambivalence toward the new medium, discussed later, may have reflected some of these early controversies.

Prefiguring Riegl's early interest in calendars, Sickel wrote about the history of time measurement in his 1862 essay "Die Lunarbuchstaben in den Kalendarien des Mittelalters."[38] With its stress on time as visual, material representation, Sickel's essay claimed to be among the first to apply the tools of chronology, including a meticulous inspection of timetables, calendars, and astronomical charts, to the scientific study of lunar symbols in early medieval calendars. His empirical approach stressed the identification of discrepancies among various lunar and lunisolar calendars—Metonic, Dionysian, Egyptian, Jewish—which he then attempted to chart sequentially; formal relationships provided empirical markers of historical succession. In a theme later adopted by Riegl, Sickel claimed that lunar time reckoning, often used to designate days on official medieval documents, evolved through a formal development and inheritance, rather than natural mimesis. Citing comments by medieval writers such as Bede and Dionysius Exiguus for support, Sickel traced the reconciliation of lunar calendars, prevalent in the ancient world, with the solar calendars increasingly common in the Middle Ages. Lunar reckoning, he wrote, "was not based on immediate observation but on a cyclical computation that was borrowed from the Alexandrians and used through the entire Middle Ages."[39]

Sickel's account alluded to conflicts over calendar organization similar to those discussed more than twenty years later by his student Riegl: the difficulties of reconciling pagan festivals tied to lunar cycles with a Christian worldview, agricultural needs with political and religious vested interests. Sickel rejected the view that the medieval world had adopted a modified Julian calendar, one that marked years according to the nineteen-year Metonic lunar cycle devised in Athens during the fifth century B.C.E. Instead, he insisted that the moon letters found on early medieval documents represented a distinct and novel mode of time measurement and calendar organization. The parallels with Riegl's later argument are clear: apparently familiar forms, which still bear traces of their ancient etiology, take on novel significations in the context of a different epoch. Both teacher and student rejected as ahistorical the view that classical forms persisted unchanged into the medieval world; yet both also insisted that calendar art should be understood as part of a continuous formal tradition. And like Riegl, Sickel believed that late Roman calendars marked a set of decisive innovations within the calendar tradition.

Sickel's essay, however, was ultimately more modest than Riegl's later work. Sickel offered a historical and chronological classification of early medieval calendrical forms, a project that sought mainly to identify distinctions among forms and periods, not to trace clear lines of historical influence and connection. Whereas Sickel focused on late Rome and the early Middle Ages, Riegl's essay suggested a continuous history of calendar development that spanned ancient, medieval, and Renaissance exemplars. Riegl and his art historical colleagues, many of whom trained and taught at the Institute for Austrian Historical Research, expanded upon Sickel's formal and empirical methods and applied them to more ambitious histories and richer theories of temporal development.

4

Max Büdinger's Universal History

In an 1885 review of Alphons Müllner's *Die Krypta in St. Florian,* Riegl attacked speculative historiographies that based grand historical and national claims on limited empirical data. "[P]olyhistory alone," he wrote, "no longer suffices to answer questions that only the scientifically trained specialist can approach without running the danger of wasting time and trouble."[1] Riegl used the term "polyhistory" to designate historical approaches that glanced superficially over many regions and periods rather than specializing in one area. In the context of Riegl's review, the term could be said to characterize Jäger's early Institute practices and models of historicism emanating from German universities, both of which lacked the scientific standards to satisfy a strict empiricist. Margaret Olin points to another likely target of Riegl's attack: the speculative *Universalgeschichte* practiced by his professor Max Büdinger, who directed the historical seminar at the University of Vienna.[2] Although Riegl's criticism may have reflected competition between the traditional historical faculty and Sickel's upstart Institute, it also marked a methodological divide that ran through the discipline of history in late nineteenth-century Vienna. A graduate of Sickel's Institute by 1885, when his book review was published, Riegl threw his allegiance behind a scientific and empirical method that he contrasted to the supposedly unfounded speculations of Büdinger. However, a comparison of Riegl's and Büdinger's work suggests that Riegl did not wholly reject *Universalgeschichte*. Although he eschewed the methods of his former professor, Riegl embraced the universal scope of Büdinger's scholarly enterprise and its goal of seeking connections among widely disparate eras.

It is important to stress that Max Büdinger (1828–1902) viewed himself as the purveyor of an innovative and rigorously scientific historiography based on Rankean *Quellenkritik*.[3] A devoted student of Leopold von Ranke as well as August Böckh and Heinrich von Sybel in Berlin,[4] Büdinger inherited both a commitment to documentary source criticism and a devotion to universal history, a tradition with roots as far back as St. Augustine.[5] Its advocates rejected over-specialization as historically narrow and proposed instead that history should be understood as a universal whole, a unitary expression of human striving that incorporated all world cultures. In the seventeenth century, the philosopher and historian Leibniz (1646–1716) characterized his own brand of universal history in organic terms:

> To judge history distinctly, one may compare it to the body of an animal, where the bones support everything, the nerves form the connection, the spirit moves the machine, the humors consist of nourishing juices, and finally the flesh gives completion to the whole mass. The parts of history correspond thus: chronology to the bones, genealogy to nerves, hidden motives to invisible spirits, useful examples to juices, and the detail of circumstances to the whole mass of flesh.[6]

The organic metaphor described the interconnection of continuous parts within the living whole of historical creation. No event escaped this historical unity, and every study of particulars, if properly understood, revealed universal implications. A natural scientist and mathematician as well as a philosopher and historian, Leibniz insisted that an awareness of the whole must rest on evidence and fact. "Since history without truth is a body without life, it is necessary that one try to assert nothing without a basis in fact, and that gradually one purge history of fables that have crept into it."[7] Like Sickel, Leibniz looked to the science of chronology, with its exact correlation of various forms of time measurement, to provide the foundation for universal, empirical history. "I consider . . . chronology or the knowledge of time as the basis or skeleton of the whole body, which forms the foundation and support of all the rest."[8] Thus Leibniz demonstrated that empiricism and universalism could find some measure of reconciliation in historical research.

The greatest nineteenth-century proponent of universal history, stripped of its medieval religious and Leibnizian organic frameworks, was Leopold von Ranke. "[T]he discipline of history at its highest," he wrote, "is itself called upon, and is able, to lift itself in its own fashion from the investigation and observation of particulars to a universal view of events, to a knowledge of the objectively existing relatedness."[9] In the 1860s, Ranke formalized this conviction under the heading of "universal history," which "comprehends the past life of mankind, not in its particular relations and trends, but in its fullness and totality. The discipline of universal history differs from specialized research in that universal history, while investigating the particular never loses sight of the complete whole on which it is working."[10] Ranke was very careful to distinguish the quality of historical interconnectedness from the Hegelian notion of a universal spirit. "The task of history is the observation of this life which cannot be characterized through One thought or One word; the spirit which manifests itself in the world is not to be so confined."[11] Whereas Hegel's spirit fulfilled itself in the moment when all of History could be apprehended as One, Rankean universal history traced continuity and synthesis but awaited no singular historical consummation. Ranke asserted that all nations enter "the stage of world history" through contact with other nations; cultures develop through mutual influence. Universal history rested on the demonstrable facts of cultural contact, not on speculative notions of a universal spirit working in and through events.

Büdinger subscribed to a more Hegelian-inflected version of universal history than did his professor. A trained philologist like Ranke and Böckh, he practiced a kind of intellectual history based on the analysis of concepts and ideas. Büdinger viewed ideas as the glue that bound together the disparate episodes of universal history. His work traced the evolution of ideas as they submerged, transformed, and resurfaced in the languages and belief systems of various cultures. As one biographer observed, "he struggled to present the continuities of historical development within the framework of his conviction about the power of ideas and the significance of cultural transference."[12] Büdinger's analyses focused on civilizations as culture bearers that inherited ideas from previous peoples and transmitted them to descendants in a continuous process of adaptation and inheritance.[13] He stressed connections among civilizations through the use of a comparative method that traced linguistic, cultural, and religious homologies across time on a global scale. Convinced that the universality and developmental continuity of ideas necessitated a broad research agenda, Büdinger worked on a bewildering array of cultures and topics simultaneously. In one year, for example, he conducted research on cuneiform, Oriental chronology, King Croesus, and Lafayette's sojourn in Austria; he published a work on English constitutional history alongside a study of ancient Greek demagogues.[14] Heinrich von Srbik described him as a figure who, influenced by Hegelian idealism, refused the disciplinary call to specialize.[15] This historiographical attitude may account for his gradual marginalization in Vienna, especially during the 1870s and 1880s when the Institute for Austrian Historical Research encouraged rigorous historical and methodological specialization. Although he championed Rankean *Quellenkritik,* Büdinger did not share the Institute's emphasis on the formal and material analysis of documents; his approach remained determinedly philological. "He persisted in stretching the boundaries of the domain of philological and ancient history," Srbik noted, "always with a touch of rationalism, that ultimately made him appear as more of a venerable holdover from earlier historiographical practices than as the purveyor of new developments."[16] In the 1890s, however, Büdinger found his star rising again as debates about historical method and interest in Hegel grew.

Controversy was not unusual for Büdinger. Raised in Kassel, he studied at Marburg, Bonn, and Berlin before moving to Vienna at the invitation of relatives in 1851. He frequented social and scholarly circles that included Theodor von Sickel and the art historian Rudolf von Eitelberger. In the hope of securing an academic post, Büdinger promptly started research for his first substantial volume, a history of early medieval Austria that was completed in 1858. His scholarship sparked political controversy in the late 1850s when he declared the *Königenhofer Handschrift,* a medieval Czech manuscript testifying to the existence of an autonomous Bohemian kingdom and literary language, to be a forgery.[17] His accusation incurred the wrath not only of Vaclav Hanka, the nationalist scholar who claimed to have discovered the manuscript, but also of influential public figures such as Johann

Alexander von Helfert and Frantisek Palacky, who had referenced it.[18] After his first professorship moved him to Zürich for eleven years, Büdinger returned to Vienna and taught at the university from 1872 to 1899, where he remained an advocate of German historicist trends in Austria.

In the 1880s, Büdinger published two essays that applied cultural and philological analysis to the study of ancient chronology. Both "Zeit und Raum bei dem indogermanischen Volke" (1881) and its thematic sequel, "Zeit und Schicksal bei Römern und Westariern" (1887), were subtitled "universal-historical studies" [*universalhistorische Studie*]. The essays argued that abstract conceptions of time and space existed among ancient Indo-European tribes from the earliest periods of migration, a thesis that contradicted prevalent beliefs that abstraction was a late development in intellectual history, one associated with monotheistic religions. With speculative audacity, Büdinger proposed to trace nineteenth-century idealism back to ancient Indo-European peoples who linked fate and divinities in an original temporal worldview.[19] Perhaps Kant's teachings, he surmised, had roots in the basic concepts of the Indo-European culture and spirit [*Geist*].

> The question appears to me especially important for universal history because the concepts of space and time in a certain sense provide the starting point for metaphysical examinations in modern philosophy. Insofar as they thoroughly preoccupied spirits of such import as Locke and Leibniz, Hume and Kant, it would appear to me that much information regarding the relationships among things could be gained if we can determine the extent to which the Indogermanic character found in these concepts, as in their language itself, was an expression of their conditions of life.[20]

Relying on comparative philology and religion, Büdinger proposed the existence of a pervasive Indo-European belief system linking cultures as distant as Scandinavia, Greece, and India. Cross-cultural similarities in the etymologies of words for time and the characteristics of gods who personified it provided evidence of this widely held, distinctly idealistic conception.

In "Zeit und Raum bei dem indogermanischen Volke," Büdinger asserted a historical relationship between the concepts of time and destiny [*Schicksal*]. Even the earliest Indo-European civilizations linked these two notions conceptually. Ancient Indian Vedic religions, for example, used multiple terms to describe the notion of destiny. The concept of karma described a soul's tally of good and bad deeds, which facilitated the transmigration of souls. The term "Vidhi," a related concept, denoted the "apportioning, ordering, fixing" associated with "the manifestation of destiny."[21] This term suggested to Büdinger the similarity of the concepts of destiny and measurable time, and marked out destiny as a historical phenomenon: "Our German word 'Zeit,' old Norse 'tid,' English 'tides' (die Gezeiten), relates to the Indo-Germanic 'dâ,' that is, 'theilen' [divide, partition]; if this is correct, then partitioning [*Zutheilung*] was the original Indo-Germanic concept of time and corresponds to the Indian representation of fate as Vidhi that we are here considering."[22] A third sense of destiny used in the *Rig Vedas* fell under the label of "Daiva, the Godlike," and suggested an impersonal power, exclusive to the gods.[23] In this sense, destiny transcended human experience and had only abstract reality. Finally, the *Vedas* signified destiny in a fourth way—"Kâla"—that most precisely translated as time, *die Zeit*. This word, not found in the earliest texts, seemed to designate a specific time, an endpoint, a moment.[24] Ancient Indian thought systems, Büdinger contended, viewed time and destiny as abstract phenomena; time was the measured unfolding of destiny, the order or matrix within which fate manifested itself. Its realm encompassed both the earthly and the divine.

Distinguishing between abstract notions and their divine personifications, Büdinger traced the existence of similar conceptions of time through other Indo-European peoples, including the Greeks and Romans. "Time itself," he concluded, "indeed as it continues to endure in modern philosophical theories, is the product or manifestation of an order that governs over everything and corresponds somewhat to our concept of fate."[25] According to Budinger, evidence demonstrated "that Indians, Germans, Greeks, even Slavs and perhaps Italians shared the basic conception that time and fate were almost identical and should be considered with the other godheads a divine power."[26] He designated this relationship between time and fate as "an over-arching universal-historical law, distinguishing and truly characterizing Indo-Germanic peoples in the religious sphere from Semites and Egyptians."[27] Gradually, religious systems elevated time and fate from subordinate positions in the divine pantheon, handmaidens to the gods, to roles of equal importance as the major deities. Gods and linguistic terms, however, ultimately served as mere symbols—personifications and signifiers for a fundamentally non-sensual, philosophically abstract concept. This abstraction, Büdinger believed, allowed Indo-European peoples greater freedom of religious thought, enabling them, for example, to adopt and cast aside religious forms liberally and interpret each as a representation of one and the same underlying phenomenon.[28] Abstract time thereby gradually escaped its confinement in representative forms, so that by the late Roman and early medieval era chroniclers could present time as a matrix within which events transpired, not a god itself.[29] "[T]ime itself, indeed as it continues to endure in modern philosophical theories" he concluded, "is the product or manifestation of an order that governs over everything and corresponds somewhat to our concept of fate."[30]

Büdinger elaborated on this process of abstraction in "Zeit und Schicksal bei Römern und Westariern" (1887). Rejecting critics who claimed that time and space were solely philosophical concepts, he reasserted the ancient origins of abstract conceptions of time among Indo-European peoples; Kant's categories of time and space, he insisted, had historical and ethnological roots. Moreover, while he conceded that similarities between Indo-European and Semitic thought systems had escaped his awareness in 1881, Büdinger reaffirmed the conviction that Indo-Europeans connected time, space, and the gods in a historically unique conceptualization, one that constituted a "universal-historical law that distinguishes the Indo-Germanic way of being."[31] In his second essay on the history of temporal perception, Büdinger investigated two later Indo-European peoples: the Persians (*Westariern*) and Romans. Persian Zoroastrianism, he wrote, transformed Indo-European conceptions of space and time by depersonifying them and treating them as metaphysical principles of religious thought.[32] According to Zoroastrian theology, the god Ahuramazda created time as one of the first principles of the world in order to drag his divine antithesis, Ahriman, from the safety of eternity into the realm of birth and death where he could be destroyed.[33] Time was an abstract container or matrix, distinct from its divine creator, not a god personified as it had been among other Indo-European peoples. This crucial conceptual shift, according to Büdinger, led to the association of space with divinity, time with the earth and mortality. Eternity came to be conceived as a permanent "place" characterized by complete simultaneity.

While the Persians separated temporality from divinity, the Romans desacralized time altogether, severed it from fate, and subordinated it to human control. "Drawing on the hard-won results of scholars," Büdinger wrote, "we can henceforth designate the Roman theory as the overcoming or mastery of time as fate, as the form or effect of destiny."[34] Theodor Mommsen's account of a praetor maximus who marked the date by fastening a nail to the wall of the Capitoline Temple of Jupiter symbolized for Büdinger the subordination of time to man's will and secular reckoning.[35] To exemplify this process, Büdinger cited efforts to establish a calendar that organized both secular events and sacred festivals. Whereas the connection between time and divinity governed the ordering of days in Greek times (and persisted in Roman decorative forms), by the late Roman epoch a new, secular notion of time emerged in struggles to reorient the calendar toward human needs. Covering the terrain of Sickel's earlier and Riegl's later essays, Büdinger noted the gradual liberation of time and space from divine and visual representations, a liberation that culminated in the subordination of abstract time and fate to human control and calculation. By the Christian era, time had become man's to organize.

It is ironic that Büdinger's comparative method, by dint of its almost indiscriminate universal reach and absolute claims, tended to detemporalize time and decontextualize events even as it sought to establish historical origins and continuities. Büdinger treated history as a tableau of events and cultural configurations available for simultaneous comparison. His universal history had an ecumenical embrace that rendered temporality in terms of spatial distance, chronology as an explorer's map. Riegl was exposed to Büdinger's assumptions and ideas in his earliest history classes at the University of Vienna. His connection of temporality and visual forms, in fact, may have drawn on Büdinger's work on time, fate, and the calendar.[36] Riegl's method, however, imposed more stringent analytic and empirical criteria for the establishment of historical connections than did Büdinger's universal-historical studies. Moreover, Riegl struggled to reconcile the analytic synchronicity of universal comparison with temporal and historical diachronicity.

5

Robert Zimmermann's Philosophical Aesthetics

Riegl attended two courses with the philosopher Robert Zimmermann, one on psychology, the other a history of philosophy. While the course titles do not indicate an emphasis on art or aesthetics, several commentators have detected Zimmermann's influence in Riegl's art history.[1] Riegl, remarked William H. Johnston, "exploited his teacher's formalism" and "elevated Zimmermann's Herbartian distinction between tactile and optic art into the polar opposites of haptic and optic."[2] Lambert Wiesing thematizes the connection between Riegl and Zimmermann in tracing the emergence of formalist aesthetics in the nineteenth and twentieth centuries. Riegl, he asserts, shared his teacher's Herbartian aesthetics, which treated form as a matrix of objective relations.[3]

Born in Prague, Robert Zimmermann (1824–1898) studied mathematics and astronomy in Vienna before habilitating in philosophy. Despite a youthful German nationalism, he secured teaching stints in Bohemia on the strength of his early essays on Leibniz and Herbart.[4] In 1861, having already published one volume of his monumental *Aesthetik*, Zimmermann was appointed professor of philosophy at the University of Vienna, a post he held for more than thirty years. In an extensive list of publications on many topics, his work on aesthetics, completed in 1865, remains his greatest philosophical legacy. And as a staunch advocate of academic freedom, Zimmermann influenced Austrian philosophy in yet another way: he was instrumental in the effort to bring Brentano to Vienna.

Zimmermann was arguably Austria's foremost proponent of the Leibnizian philosophies of Johann Friedrich Herbart and Bernard Bolzano.[5] Although Herbart (1776–1841) spent his career in Göttingen and Königsberg, he exerted tremendous influence on nineteenth-century Austrian academia. A philosopher and pedagogue, Herbart espoused an ontology based on "realia," fundamental units of philosophical reality that combined to form complex systems and ideas. Herbart's was a Leibnizian world of interrelating monads; his conception of mental activity, discussed earlier, was based on the mind's ability to order experience rationally and coherently. Herbart's psychology concerned itself with the alternately diachronic and synchronic organization of mental presentations, and his pedagogy sought to cultivate learning through associations that impressed themselves on the mind of a student—much as a composer might seek to combine different notes into coherent harmony.[6] A prolific scholar of pedagogy, Herbart proposed a curriculum that subdivided philosophy into logic, metaphysics, psychology, and practical sciences. Logic dealt with the proper association of ideas synchronically, metaphysics investigated the origin of ideas, and psychology studied their elaboration. Synechiology, the study of continua like space and time, was a fundamental component of metaphysics.

Unlike Herbart, who never lived in Habsburg lands, Bernard Bolzano taught in Prague and tutored Zimmermann when he was young.[7] A mathematician, philosopher, and priest—and like Herbart a disciple of Leibnizian monadology—Bolzano (1781–1848) constructed a system of logic based around "truths as such" [*Wahrheiten an sich*], statements that expressed apodictic truths about their objects. Rejecting Kant's emphasis on a priori mental categories, Bolzano argued that monado-logical truths existed independently of the mind, of expression, and even of God.[8] Propositions in themselves, presentations in themselves, and truths in themselves formed the objective and logical architecture of creation, an ideal reality open for human contemplation. This architecture could be observed in the various phenomena of the world, and its logical workings revealed to an empirical observer the design of divinity. Bolzano's most explicit work on time, space, and continua appeared in the last year of his life. *Paradoxes of the*

Infinite was a mathematical treatise that defined infinity as an uncountable multitude, an indivisible continuum made up of sequences of discrete units. Time, he asserted, was the set of all instants unified as continuity, space the set of all points. Together, these instants and points comprised the fullness of creation. "God's creation is infinitely graded," he wrote, "and each single grade is at every moment occupied by some creature or creatures."[9] Infinite, graded, unbounded, and continuous, Bolzano's reality was transcendent and yet available for mathematical and empirical verification.

Zimmermann readily acknowledged his debts to these earlier thinkers.[10] In *Aesthetics*, he praised Herbart's "distinction between pure form and beauty, which expresses subjective states of excitement," a distinction that secured his "everlasting place in the history of aesthetics."[11] A comprehensive formalist theory of art elaborating Herbartian principles, *Aesthetics* secured Zimmermann's own reputation as a philosopher. The work appeared in two volumes: *Geschichte der Aesthetik als Philosophischer Wissenschaft* (1858) and *Allgemeine Aesthetik als Formwissenschaft* (1865). Its aim was to construct a formalist science of pleasure. "Aesthetics seeks the pleasurable," Zimmermann announced. "[T]he aesthetic worldview perceives it [the pleasurable] realized in the purposeful [*zweckbeseelten*] totality of the world—or historical organism. The world pleases it, and it [aesthetics] investigates and determines what it is about the world that pleases and has to please. A catalogue of the sum of absolute and necessary pleasurable relationships is the end goal of aesthetics."[12]

Zimmermann repudiated Hegelian aesthetics, which in his view confused art history (studying the social reception of art) with aesthetic theory (explaining why a work is beautiful and cataloguing pleasurable relations). Instead, he advanced a model of aesthetics as the formal philosophical science of the principles of beauty based on logical and empirical verification, a task that Herbart had adumbrated without fully elaborating. Zimmermann was careful to distinguish philosophy and aesthetics from other branches of scholarship such as history, mathematics, or the natural sciences. Whereas these disciplines investigated the empirical properties of objects, philosophy and aesthetics studied the concepts behind them. Thus, although it enlisted the support of empiricism, philosophy did not restrict itself exclusively to insights that could be verified by the senses. "Philosophy," Zimmermann declared, "is the science that emerges in the working-through of concepts,"[13] a task that entailed logical development beyond the realm of available sensory data. It is moreover important to distinguish Zimmermann's formalist, relational notion of aesthetic concepts from the more substantive notions of aesthetic beauty in German idealism. Aesthetic concepts such as beauty, he insisted, were not ideal forms or embodiments of a world spirit. This error was found in Hegel's "absolute panlogism," which confounded metaphysics and aesthetics.[14] Instead concepts emerged from the formal interaction between objective presentations and the subjective mind, and could be studied only through mental presentations. Concepts did not exist autonomously in some kind of Platonic ideal realm or noumenal form.

The notion of *Vorstellung* (presentation) was critical to Zimmermann's thought. Modeled on Herbart's concept of the same name, Zimmermann's *Vorstellung* combined the notion of idea or mental image with that of representation or presentation. As such, *Vorstellungen,* like Brentano's in-existent objects, stood at the intersection of subject and object. They were neither the purely subjective products of the human mind nor the pure data of the external world received by the senses; rather, they designated the object's presentation in perception—the mind's impression or apprehension of an object "placed before" it. The mind grasped its objects as *Vorstellungen,* not as things in themselves; presentations, according to Zimmermann, were the objects of philosophy. "We have no other way of arriving at philosophical knowledge except through *Vorstellungen.* . . . The objects of philosophizing can therefore only be things presented, i.e., *Vorstellungen.*"[15] Nevertheless, a description of the objects of perception was not the goal of aesthetics; it sought instead to determine the concepts underlying sensory impressions. A *Vorstellung,* Zimmermann argued, combined two aspects: concept and development. As concept, a *Vorstellung* had objective form and material; it could be analyzed as something independent of subjective perception. This task was the domain of philosophy. "The objects given to philosophy [*das Gegebene der Philosophie*] are indeed *Vorstellungen,* but not understood as merely this, but understood as concepts, i.e., drawn out from [*herausgehoben*] the psychological appearance."[16] Aesthetics was concerned with this objective aspect of *Vorstellungen.* Presentations, however, had another aspect: as a mental production, *Vorstellungen* had origin and development, viz., temporality. This temporal dimension reflected the perceiving subject and was the domain of psychology. Aesthetic philosophy, according to Zimmermann, investigated the synchronic, objective realm of concepts drawn inductively from the diachronic and perceptual domain of *Vorstellungen,* whereas psychology studied change, subjectivity, temporality. Zimmermann posited an atemporal objectivity intrinsic to temporal subjective perception.[17]

Zimmermann structured his aesthetic system around a fundamental separation of form and content. Form determined beauty, and aesthetics therefore privileged the study of form. With this distinction, Zimmermann was reacting in part against romantic and idealist aesthetics, which proposed that content realized itself in form and form became a function of content. Zimmermann proposed instead that aesthetic works combined material [*Stoff*] and form. Form, while interdependent on material, maintained its aesthetic autonomy and conceptual priority. Zimmermann recognized that certain materials required a corresponding form, but this fit was simply a question of appropriate correlation among distinct phenomena. There was no sublation of content and form. In Zimmermann's system, form imbued a work with its aesthetic qualities, and thus the science of aesthetics was necessarily formalist.

We should be careful not to overdraw the distinction between form and content in Zimmermann's work. To treat form as simply an empty geometry, he wrote, was to misconstrue Herbartian aesthetics.[18] Instead, form itself contained as content the spirit [*Geist*] of beauty. As Lambert Wiesing remarks: "[a] purely formal consideration of images does not drive out the spirit but instead discovers the spirit of an aesthetic object only in an unexpected shape. This is identified with form."[19] Content was not jettisoned altogether as an aesthetic category; rather, it was appropriated as a formal quality. Thus, Zimmermann rejected Hegelian idealism on a rhetorical level even as he proposed his own sublation along formal lines. But a crucial difference remained: as opposed to an idealist notion of beauty, Zimmermann's notion of formal beauty could be verified scientifically and empirically in presentations.

Despite its Platonic overtones, Zimmermann's concept of form was heavily indebted to Leibnizian and Aristotelian concepts of immanence. This imprint becomes especially evident in the notion of form as immanent relationship. As Wiesing writes: "Formal aesthetics directs itself exclusively to the immanent relations that the picture's surface components form with each other; not the composition as a whole, the

Gestalt principle, or the arrangement of objects on the plane, none of these interest the formalist aesthetician, but rather the relationship between the component parts of the picture surface."[20] Forms were neither Platonic ideals imposed upon works nor preexisting molds that gave shape to the raw materials of the work; they were immanent concepts, embedded in the very materiality of the canvas, monadic types that inherently defined the architectonics of a work. Aesthetic form was the objective set of relationships among constituent units that structured an artwork—what Wiesing calls the syntax of a work. Form was not so much a conceptual object as it was an object-relation.[21]

The temporal implications of Zimmermann's aesthetics became most clear in his consideration of art forms such as music. Like his mentor Herbart, Zimmermann stayed current on musical matters in the Austrian capital. When Edouard Hanslick published his formalist aesthetics of music, *Vom Musikalisch-Schönen,* in 1854, Zimmermann penned an early and favorable review.[22] In *Aesthetik,* Zimmermann declared that the musical arts demonstrated most clearly the relationship between the individual elements of an aesthetic composition and its overall form: "In the effect of a single tone one hears an individual, in the relationship of tones with each other the purely formal element of musical art [*Tonkunst*]. . . . In the single tone one finds the subjective, in the relationship among tones the objective impact of music."[23] The distinction between objective and subjective aspects of art characterized Zimmermann's aesthetic theory *tout court.* The study of harmony—of the relationship among tones—epitomized the object-relations on which Zimmermann based his aesthetic science. "If we follow the example of harmonic theory in music," he wrote, "the aim of mathematically designating the pleasing and displeasing relations in the other arts does not lie far off."[24] Though both beauty and taste were combined in the experience of a musical performance, a truly scientific aesthetics distinguished between the two. Beauty was determined by mathematical and harmonic relations among notes, not the emotional impact of a performance. Indeed, the distinction between objective beauty and subjective taste, so pronounced in music, shaped judgments on other artistic media as well: "The reduction of beauty to a purely formal conception defined according to objective relationships gives aesthetics a whole new field of inquiry and a new method. No longer dependent upon psychological criteria, it can set forth defining the purely objective domain of pleasing and displeasing positive qualities whose discovery and enumeration will demand continuous work and cooperative effort."[25] The designation of objective and formal relationships of beauty established the foundation for a genuinely philosophical aesthetics.

In stressing the relationship among tones, Zimmermann abstracted formal object-relations from the temporal passage of performance. He characterized harmony as the formal, synchronic relationships underlying diachronic presentation. As we noted earlier, temporality and development in Zimmermann's view were fundamentally subjective, intertwined with the act of perception and presentation. As such, temporal development remained the concern of psychology; only as synchronic, relational forms did aesthetic concepts emerge into the light of philosophy. Like other branches of aesthetics, musical aesthetics sought to explain the permanent forms behind artistic change and perception. Indeed, Zimmermann believed that aesthetics, which studied stable and permanent forms, complemented the natural sciences, which increasingly stressed change and mutability.

> When we consider as well that the more recent natural sciences increasingly understand the whole of nature in terms of unceasing transformation, then all the more must the prospects grow of an aesthetics that seeks its whole significance in the discovery and classification of *enduring pleasurable* [*bleibendgefallender*] forms. When all the natural sciences have recast themselves as morphologies, how much can an aesthetics promise to offer which declares itself to be a *morphology of beauty*? Geology and crystallography, botany and zoology, all deal with the forms taken on by their changing substances, whose type remains even as the material within it transforms from one thing to another. Which among these forms are absolutely pleasing or displeasing, in other words, what is beautiful and what is ugly: this, one cannot deny, is the unique concern of the purely formal science of beauty.[26]

Thus, aesthetics had implications and applicability beyond the realm of art, although art was the domain that offered the greatest prospective insights into the synchronic forms of beauty. Aesthetics could illuminate permanent, formal relationships that characterized a range of human and natural sciences and stood as the very precondition for scientific investigation and typological distinction.

The abstraction of synchronic form from temporal experience had deeper roots in Zimmermann's conception of time itself as a formal relationship among points. Space and time in his system were conceptually analogous in that both could be measured by a formal metric. "There are indeed temporal as well as spatial distances, and thus a temporal as well as a spatial metric, a chronometry, like a geometry, and thus also a chronometric sense of beauty."[27] The basic unit of Zimmermann's chronometric aesthetic was the timeline, "*der Zeitlinie,*" marked by a starting point and an ending point. Temporal forms could be measured along discrete timelines; temporal continuity became chronometric relationship, a quantifiable and synchronic set of contiguous segments. Zimmermann's aesthetic formalism, therefore, rested upon a spatialized conception of time that rendered diachronic continuity in terms of synchronic contiguity. In many ways Riegl accepted his teacher's distinction between the synchronic and the diachronic as an essential characteristic of temporal perception. However, whereas Zimmermann marginalized temporality as outside the domain of formal philosophy, like psychology and subjectivity, Riegl attempted to maintain temporality within his art historical system. He located temporality in the relationship between the diachronic and the synchronic, not in the exclusion of one by the other.

6

Moritz Thausing and the Science of Art History

Many trends of nineteenth-century empiricist philosophy and history converged in the work of the Vienna School of Art History, which championed a scientific approach that stressed the empirical analysis of artworks. In 1873, the appointment of Moritz Thausing (1835–1884) as professor of art history at the Institute for Austrian Historical Research launched an official association between Vienna School art historians and Sickel's institute that lasted into the twentieth century.[1] An often overlooked figure, Thausing was one of a long line of Viennese art historians who sought to establish his discipline on an empirical basis.[2] He applied Sickel's methods of documentary analysis to the study of art, emphasizing form over content and rejecting aesthetic evaluation as a goal for art history. In these concerns, Thausing prefigured Riegl.

The origins of the Vienna School can be traced back before Thausing's time to a circle of artists, collectors, and scholars who gathered at the Vienna residence of metalsmith and collector Josef Daniel Böhm (1794–1865).[3] Profoundly opposed to idealist aesthetic theories, Böhm urged young art historians and archaeologists to practice an inductive method that sought historical patterns in the strictly empirical evaluation of artworks rather than deductive judgments based on aesthetic criteria. Böhm and his circle believed that art objects represented the crystallization of historical forces that could be illuminated only through careful observation. His extensive collections of etchings, drawings, paintings, and ancient cameos, which formed the initial holdings of the Österreichische Museum, provided the material catalogue used for training in empirical methods. His charges, including the young philologist and art historian Rudolf von Eitelberger, accepted and promulgated an inductive method stressing the materiality and individuality of artworks.

In the wake of Thun's education reforms of the early 1850s, Eitelberger (1818–1885) received an appointment as *professor extraordinarius* of art history and archaeology at the University of Vienna.[4] After 1864, he combined his teaching post with the leadership of the newly established Austrian Museum for Art and Industry, which, modeled on London's Victoria and Albert Museum, fostered links between art and manufacture, design and industry.[5] The close contact between university and museum, scholarly study and curatorship, would remain a hallmark of Vienna School art historical practice throughout the nineteenth century.[6] Eitelberger became a devotee of the materialist theories of the German architect Gottfried Semper, who lived in Vienna between 1871 and 1877. Opposed to idealist or romantic theories of art, Semper contended that artistic styles developed in response to functional needs, and that artistic forms originated from ancient technical and utilitarian practices. In *Der Stil in den technischen und tektonischen Künsten,* Semper traced the origin of traditional decorative geometric patterns to prehistoric weaving and wickerwork.[7] Perhaps through Eitelberger's assistant Jacob Falke, who was promoted to museum director when Eitelberger died in 1885, Riegl was exposed to materialist ideas while working at the museum as a volunteer between 1884 and 1887. Falke admired the work of the English historian Henry Thomas Buckle, whose *Introduction to the History of Civilization in England* advanced a materialist theory of the origins of art. "Buckle's social theory," writes Diana Graham Reynolds, "when combined with Semper's technical materialist theory developed into a deterministic and materialistic theory of style."[8] In its stress on empiricism and opposition to idealism, its focus on the immediate and pre-theoretical evidentiary status of art and artifacts, and its attempt to foster links between scholarly, archival, and curatorial work, Eitelberger's art history dovetailed with the historical practices of Sickel's Institute for Austrian Historical Research. Both scholars hoped to claim for their disciplines a set of credentials equal in rigor to those of the natural sciences by dismissing anything that smacked of subjective evaluation. By 1874, in fact, Sickel's revised statutes for the Institute included art history in its obligatory three-year course of study. Artworks were recognized as important historical source documents whose proper analysis required special training and unique skills. Thus, in 1873, the appointment of Thausing, a student of Sickel and Eitelberger, as the Institute's professor of art history affirmed a methodological convergence between the documentary approaches of history and art history by designating the latter as a subfield of the former. Since 1864, Thausing had served as director of the Albertina Museum's collection of etchings and drawings.[9] At the Institute, he dutifully advanced his teachers' scientific methodology for art history by renouncing aesthetic evaluation in favor of empirical analysis. This combination of teaching and curating provided the impetus and the material for his exacting monograph on Dürer, published in 1875.[10]

Thausing's empiricism had another important source in addition to his training under Sickel and Eitelberger. As a director at the Albertina, Thausing had the chance to meet the Italian senator-*cum*-art historian Giovanni Morelli, who made frequent research trips to visit Vienna's newly opened museums. The meetings proved momentous in the development of Thausing's thought and for Vienna School art history more generally, as Thausing became an ardent disciple of Morelli's art historical method.[11] Morelli (1816–1891) was trained in medicine at a time when most art historians emerged from philosophical and legal faculties, and he applied the empirical methods of natural science to the study of artworks. His concerns were primarily in connoisseurship, and his books were filled with new attributions for paintings hanging in European museums.[12] Morelli sought to identify the formal and stylistic tendencies of an artist by observing the often neglected details of his canvases. Faces, clothing, landscapes—these major features could be studied and imitated by lesser artists; they provided the standard subject matter for art students. A master's unique and idiosyncratic style, however, was revealed in the inconspicuous features of his works, those details least affected by his training and most difficult to copy—the ears, the fingernails, the fabric hems. Morelli described the importance of these bagatelles in behavioral terms:

> As most men who speak or write have verbal habits and use their favorite words or phrases involuntarily and sometimes

> even most inappropriately, so almost every painter has his own peculiarities which escape from him without his being aware of them. . . . Anyone, therefore, who wants to study a painter closely must know how to discover these material trifles and attend to them with care: a student of calligraphy would call them flourishes.[13]

While an artist might vary his treatments of major features on a canvas, the minor details showed an almost unconscious consistency across his oeuvre. Close scrutiny of these artistic tics allowed the historian to identify an artist's signature style in the minor features of a painting and thereby recognize the hand of the master. Morelli's method therefore privileged a hyper-empiricism in the service of historical attribution; much as a detective might search the corners of a crime scene for the slightest clues of the perpetrator, Morelli scrutinized the overlooked details of a canvas in order to determine its historical origin.[14]

Unsurprisingly, Morelli's method generated controversy among art historians, several of whom dismissed him as a charlatan. "In its one-sidedness this method can lead to harmful mistakes and misunderstandings," scoffed Wilhelm von Bode. "It's not uncommon that in a single picture various ears are depicted in very different ways, or the form and position of the fingers are shaped in multiple ways."[15] Bode conceded that Morelli's formal method could be a useful tool in the discipline, but he insisted on the need to consider other material aspects of a work as well, such as coloring and inscriptions. Morelli himself was not given to diplomacy in advancing his views; he held a low opinion of the state of art history in the late nineteenth century and did not refrain from attacking even his own devotees.[16] Nevertheless, Morelli enjoyed a considerable following among late nineteenth- and twentieth-century art historians, and Thausing was one of his chief advocates.[17]

Thausing, however, was no mere polemicist for Morelli's ideas. His background and training enabled him both to appreciate the Italian senator's methodological insight and to recognize its limitations. Perhaps it was partly the affinities between Morelli's empirical analysis and Sickel's diplomatics that drew Thausing to the Morellian method. Both of his mentors, after all, stressed the documentary value of their objects, when examined through the close scrutiny of material details. However, Thausing hoped to expand Morelli's narrow connoisseurial focus into the methodological basis for a far more ambitious scholarly project: an empirical art history that studied the universal development of style and form in a purely scientific fashion.[18] Thausing used a strict empirical method not simply to identify the hand of an artist, as Morelli did, but to underpin scientific art historical scholarship.

Thausing expressed his historiographical commitments most explicitly in "Die Stellung der Kunstgeschichte als Wissenschaft," an inaugural lecture delivered in 1873 at the Institute for Austrian Historical Research.[19] The lecture served as a kind of manifesto for art history, a call to sever the discipline from aesthetics and align it with the more rigorously empirical fields of the human sciences. Thausing's primary aim was to define new methods and themes for art history by positioning it within an academic field defined by three established disciplines: archaeology, world history, and aesthetics. Thausing argued that archaeology had the most to offer art history. From the time of Winckelmann's powerful evocations of the classical aesthetic ideal, the development of art history in the German academy was bound together with that of archaeology.[20] Aroused by the classical philological studies of the sixteenth, seventeenth, and eighteenth centuries, German interest in the ancient world blossomed in the wake of Humboldt's education reforms.[21] Archaeologists exploited a philhellenic vogue among educated Germans in order to secure funds for excavations in the Ottoman Empire and the newly independent Greece. Expedition leaders hoped to discover historical and mythological sites and lost artistic treasures. The work of these early archaeologists expressed veneration for the Classical world and provided models of artistic achievement to enrich German museums and inspire young artists. Indeed, the worth of an unearthed artifact was often measured according to Olympian aesthetic standards that art historians were called upon to uphold.

By the mid-nineteenth century, however, the seminal efforts of Alexander Conze succeeded in redirecting the enthusiasms of early German archaeology and redefining its relationship to art history.[22] Sponsored by the Austrian government, Conze led a series of highly publicized excavations of Pergamum in Asia Minor. He parlayed the notoriety gained from these expeditions into powerful museum and bureaucratic appointments that allowed him to shape academic policy. From this eminence, Conze was able to establish archaeology on a scientific and professional basis by promoting specialized research in place of the humanistic and aesthetic aims of earlier dilettantish enthusiasts. This mandate required archaeologists to have technical and scientific expertise. Instead of plundering excavations for art treasures, they should aspire to a historical reconstruction of the sites, utilizing all the artifacts found in the field to construct a historical image of the past. Conze insisted that the distinction between art and artifact was irrelevant to the purpose of historical reconstruction. Only a meticulous cataloguing and examination of all artifacts, fragments, and objects, however negligible, could establish the "physiognomy" of a site.[23] As Suzanne Marchand writes, it was not sufficient "to simply grab the monumental sculptures and run; science required that the city as a whole, including its waterworks and its street plan, be studied in detail."[24] Conze, however, did not merely seek to isolate the characteristics of single archaeological sites. Like Ranke and Büdinger, he aimed to illuminate the interconnectedness of world culture and remained convinced that empirical evidence would affirm a universal vision of history. In his promotion of the scientific credentials of archaeology, his dismissal of aesthetic categories, and his demand that all art and artifacts were of equal historical value as "texts," Conze advocated for many issues that Riegl later raised in his art history. Indeed, Riegl's paradigm for art history could be called a physiognomy in Conze's sense; he treated art objects as sites of historical meaning whose surface forms could be read, or "excavated," by the trained eye.[25]

In Conze's research agenda, the art historian became a philologist or hermeneuticist of the visual artifact, reading historical meaning from physical objects rather than judging the aesthetic beauty of those objects. It was a job description that Thausing found congenial. With archaeology, Thausing wrote, "[art history] shared the two-fold nature of its sources [visual and textual], a method, and an ultimate goal. . . . The two [disciplines] comprise different facets of one and the same science and are only kept separate because a single discipline would have difficulty fully managing the demands of both fields."[26] Art history supplemented archaeology by illuminating the artistic and cultural monuments of ancient civilizations. Using specialized methodologies for analyzing visual artifacts, art historians were, in a sense, archaeologists of the visual; they excavated visual meaning from artifactual sites. Moreover, art historians could apply their unique scientific skills to modern eras of history that archaeologists never considered. Thus, art history could both expand and deepen the insights of archaeological inquiry.

Art history could offer the same benefits to the historical profession as well. Thausing celebrated his Institute colleagues' rigorous empirical methods but simultaneously challenged them to expand their horizon of inquiry. He espoused the kind of *Culturgeschichte* or *Volksgeschichte* offered in contemporary philological and universal-historical accounts, the study of *geistige Leben* in its various manifestations of politics, religion, art, and manners. Although he might have rejected as pseudo-scientific the methods of Büdinger's universal history, he certainly embraced its broad historical vision and its openness to cross-cultural connections: "Despite all the resistance from the historical politicians, history is increasingly developing in the direction of a comprehensive study and investigation of inherited cultural monuments—especially in an era whose greatest statesmen protest from their point of view against the division between the concepts of government and people."[27] Spurning the reduction of history to political and military narratives (perhaps a jab at Prussian School political histories), Thausing believed that art history helped to establish *Culturgeschichte* on a scientific basis. Thus, while he praised the Institute's incorporation of scientific art history in its curriculum, Thausing cautioned his fellow historians not to treat his discipline as a mere aid to conventional historical research. Though it was considered an auxiliary discipline, art history did not simply illustrate the past. Its method of visual analysis opened hitherto inaccessible areas of culture and society for historical inquiry. The project of discarding rigid hierarchies of aesthetics or politics in favor of contextually sensitive and comprehensive historical research seemed particularly appropriate to Thausing in the liberalizing atmosphere of Vienna in the 1870s.

Thausing saved his sharpest rebuke to condemn aestheticizing tendencies in art history. He distinguished forcefully between his discipline and the unfounded speculations of aesthetics.

> Art history for its part is not entitled to reach into the philosophical realm and co-opt for its own purposes or presentations aesthetic formulae or expressions from another system. It has nothing to do with deduction or speculation at all; what it brings to light are not aesthetic judgments, but historical facts that can then serve as material for inductive research. Just as political history does not aim at moral judgment, so the yardstick of art history is not aesthetic; its verdicts are relative, not absolute, tied to the ascent or descent which the development of art in a particular epoch follows.

> The question, for example, of whether a painting is beautiful is simply not justified in art history; and a question, for example, of whether Raphael or Michelangelo, Rembrandt or Rubens was more perfect is an art-historical absurdity. I can imagine the best art history in which the word "beautiful" simply does not appear.[28]

The historical value of an individual artwork, Thausing insisted, emerged only through the empirical scrutiny of the work itself, paired with documentary research into its context and conditions of origin: "Art historical judgments are based on establishing through research and observation the conditions under which an artwork originated. The question 'in what relationship does an artist's ability stand to his will, and in what relationship do these stand to the materials at hand?' can only be answered by a comparison with his contemporaries, his predecessors, and his successors, not by the application of some overarching aesthetic yardstick."[29] Rigid aesthetic hierarchies only confounded a scientific understanding of the conditions of artistic production and the history of artistic style, forms, and values. Aesthetic judgments, Thausing argued, were historically relative, for artworks could only be evaluated in their cultural contexts by comparing an artist's images with those of contemporaries. Whereas Zimmermann tried to define aesthetics as an objective formal science by excluding psychological and temporal considerations, Thausing tied the study of art to formal, cultural, and historical context, and thereby rejected the field of aesthetics as abstract and anachronistic. Although both scholars sought to legitimize their disciplines scientifically, they fell on opposing sides of a divide separating history from aesthetics.

Having defined art history against its related disciplines, Thausing set out to explain what made the discipline unique in its own right. Its positive contribution to historical inquiry lay in its ability to analyze visual sources. Although the art historian, like the archaeologist or historian, made use of written documents, his main objects of study and sources of information were visual; these artworks and artifacts Thausing called "monuments" [*Monumente*], a term that went beyond conventional definitions of art to encompass all artifacts. "Like a document in words, monuments speak to us in visible forms, and to learn how to read and understand this language properly is the task of art history."[30] As monuments, art objects were not judged for their beauty or ugliness but for their historical value, which was registered in the visual language of form. An art historian's trade involved the scientific mastery of this language: "A people's art is also a language; its monuments are like towering mileposts that lead the researcher's gaze back along the path that a nation's genius has followed for centuries, millennia. It conducts us back into eras that written documents do not cover, and which—I think unjustly—are called prehistoric. And the language of this unwritten testimony is ideational [*ideeler*], unbiased, freer of purely subjective impressions and external contingencies than others in word and script."[31] Fluent in the language of visual form and trained in the skill of detailed observation, art historians did more than simply confirm insights gleaned from written documents. They conducted pioneering historical research on eras that had left few written records, and opened up new areas of inquiry into familiar cultures. "[Our artistic monuments] always give us certain information about the ways in which a bygone age thought and felt."[32] Indeed, Thausing believed that art historians had more direct contact with the past than their historical counterparts. Art reflected the world of its producers with greater immediacy than written documents, which were always filtered through layers of thought and opinion. An artwork was a visual crystallization of the values of a past epoch, and an art historian's unique scientific skills could illuminate its position in the historical development of a culture.

These visual skills, however, required meticulous cultivation. "An artwork," Thausing wrote, "will always give you a correct answer when you understand how to question it"—but proper questioning demanded professional, specialized ability.[33] Thausing emphasized the uniqueness of visual analysis by attacking the frequent conflation of art history with the practice of art. Science and craftsmanship were fundamentally different ways of understanding, and Thausing made a sharp distinction between artistic practice and art historical analysis. "The one way is that of imitation, using a group of learned and practiced skills; the other is that of research through pure observation, testing, and comparison."[34] Artists trained their hands; art historians developed their eye and drew their conclusions from observation. To underscore the difficulty and subtlety of the art historical enterprise, Thausing noted the lengthy process of visual development in the human species. "Not only the hand, but the eye of man was originally unskilled, and it took millennia to travel the slow practical path of developing today's sensitive receptivity to art."[35] The very recent development of chromatic theory testified to this slow evolution. That art history was a relatively new discipline, therefore, was not a sign of its naiveté or superfluity, but of an advanced state of human sensitivity and discernment. Tied to the evolution of the human eye, art history was the capstone of modernity's heightened visual relationship with the world. Thausing reiterated this point in the introduction to his 1875 volume on Dürer. Painting, he insisted, was a modern art whose development depended upon the gradual cultivation of human ocular sensitivity; plastic art was more characteristic of the ancient world with its tactile sensibilities.[36] This brief history of perception would become an object of fuller inquiry in Riegl's work.

During Riegl's first semesters as a student, he attended lecture courses on medieval art and architecture taught by Thausing.[37] Their impact was apparent in Riegl's methodology, terminologies, and scholarly concerns. Both men promoted the scientific credentials of art history; both renounced aesthetic judgment, stressed the history of style, and emphasized the uniqueness of visual sources. But the differences between the two art historians were as striking as their similarities. Whereas Riegl insisted on the historical autonomy of stylistic development, Thausing explained artistic style according to historical context and technical ability, thereby tying creativity to the material capacities and cultural values of an age. Thausing charted the historical development of the relation between technical limitations and artistic will or intent. These analyses remained fundamentally contextualist. His Dürer monograph, for example, with its preference for meticulous contextual detail, proposed a close link between biography and the analysis of works. The meaning of an artwork, Thausing suggested, could only be determined by situating it within a broader, extra-artistic context. Thus, although he disputed art history's auxiliary status, Thausing ultimately presented art history as a branch of cultural history. It would be left to the next generation of art historians—to Riegl and his colleagues—to explore fully the themes and possibilities of an art history based solely on formal visual analysis. In contrast to Thausing, Riegl treated art as an autonomous activity. For him, context and historical development were phenomena immanent within, not external to, the visual forms and styles of a work. Whereas Thausing's goal was a history of culture and values told through art, Riegl attempted to write histories of perception, of the visual relationship between man and his world over time.

7

Franz Wickhoff, Alois Riegl, and the Structure of Art History

Colleagues throughout their careers, Franz Wickhoff and Alois Riegl shared overlapping art historical concerns that grew out of a common intellectual background. Raised in Upper Austria and Vienna, Wickhoff (1853–1909) studied under Sickel and Conze, imbibing their views on empirical documentary criticism, artifactual analysis, and methodological specialization. An admirer of both Morelli and Büdinger, Wickhoff espoused an empirical method and a universalist goal for art history in the hopes of establishing the laws of artistic evolution. As a student of Eitelberger and Thausing, he approached the study of art with an ingrained rejection of both classical aesthetic hierarchies and conventional distinctions between art and artifacts. Convinced that the art historian should conduct thorough scientific analyses, Wickhoff, like Riegl, investigated those aspects and epochs of art history that had been traditionally overlooked or discounted; these included craft industries and rural production, as well as periods (such as late imperial Rome) dismissed as degenerate. Like Riegl, he launched an assault on the preeminence of ancient Greek and Renaissance artistic standards. Art history should chart the changing values represented in artworks over time, not the abilities of a culture to approximate an allegedly timeless ideal of excellence.

Many scholars see in Wickhoff's work the emergence of preoccupations that characterized the Vienna School of Art History.[1] His intellectual commitments were presented most clearly in the seminal work *Römische Kunst: Die Wiener Genesis* (1895) (trans. *Roman Art*), which reflected the impact of Riegl's *Problems of Style* (1893) and anticipated the themes of *Late Roman Art Industry* (1901).[2] *Roman Art* grew out of the investigation of an early Greek illustrated codex of *Genesis* held by the Imperial Library in Vienna. Wilhelm von Hartel, professor of classics and later minister of culture, had undertaken to edit the manuscript while Wickhoff provided the commentary.[3] In its discussion of modes of visuality and its revision of the concept of naturalism, Wickhoff's analysis offered a radical departure from conventional perspectives on late Roman art and proposed novel approaches to the practice of art history in general.

Echoing Riegl's argument in "Die mittelalterliche Kalenderillustration," Wickhoff proposed a historiography based on the uneven developmental relationship between form and content. In some eras, formal motifs accurately expressed their intended thematic content; in other periods, novel religious concepts outstripped the representational capacities of inherited artistic forms. Transitional periods displayed this uneven development most acutely. The late Roman/early Christian era, long neglected as decadent, attracted Wickhoff's interest precisely because it exemplified these transitional qualities, and his discussion of the *Genesis* codex aimed at rescuing late Roman art for historical analysis. Wickhoff insisted that the disjuncture between form and content witnessed in the art of late Rome was fundamentally innovative in its development of new forms to solve contemporary representational problems. His progressive model of history, which did not privilege one artistic period over another, offered insights into late Roman art that far surpassed those of conventional art historical models, with their alternating periods of rise and decline.

The broad insights of *Roman Art* sprang from a seemingly modest question: How could early Christian art represent worldly, temporal events within an inherited Greek visual syntax that favored synchronic, mythological depiction? How, in more basic terms, could inherited forms represent the needs and concerns of a culture other than the one for which they were created? "Filling out a framed poetic space with new representations drawn from a different set of symbols and images—a poetic space whose original visual associations and representations had been lost—this was the problem that the first Christian artists had to resolve."[4] As we have seen, the relationship between Christian themes and pagan forms was a topic that Riegl, Sickel, and Büdinger had already addressed. Like Riegl, Wickhoff noted that visual artists lagged behind contemporary poets, who devised original linguistic forms to reflect contemporary themes. What distinguished Wickhoff's treatment from that of his colleagues was a stress on the narrative aspects of religious symbology. Wickhoff limited himself to a consideration of figural scenes and excluded architecture and decorative ornament, which did not fit his interest in narrative depiction. Although he intimated that certain decorative forms could metaphorically suggest narrative continuities, it was Riegl's innovation to trace the narrative capacities of the purely ornamental and decorative arts, and, in so doing, to highlight the underpinnings of narrative in formal temporal continuity.[5]

Wickhoff identified three distinct modes of narrative representation in the history of ancient pictorial art. The oldest mode of depiction, complementary visual narration [*komplementtierende Erzählungsweise*], emphasized continuity through contiguity; it depicted the prelude, progression, and results of a central event—the event in its unfolding—on a single canvas within a single frame, and it did so without repeating any figures. The artist incorporated the consecutive episodes of a story into a singular visual presentation, thereby collapsing the temporal progression of the narrative into a simultaneous visual representation. The second, isolating mode of depiction [*distinguierende Erzählungsweise*], which grew out of the complementary mode, divided a narrative into exemplary scenes and treated each one individually on separate canvases. Crucial narrative moments were depicted in isolation. A story could be framed in consecutive individual images, each containing the same figures; these scenes could be mounted side by side, spatially contiguous, but they remained distinct and separate. The third and most recent mode of narrative depiction, continuous narration [*kontinuierende Erzählungsweise*], was Wickhoff's particular focus in his analysis of Roman art. The Vienna codex exemplified this representational strategy. A continuous depiction presented multiple images of the same individual figures, repeated in consecutive episodes on one canvas. This repetition incorporated narrative continuity and the passage of time into a single scene. Artists of the late Roman period developed continuous narration in order to capture visually the temporal nature of events overlooked by the other two modes. Although it appeared awkward to the modern viewer, wrote Wickhoff, continuous narration actually displayed a heightened awareness of time.

One of Wickhoff's main concerns in *Roman Art* was to trace the emergence of a historical worldview in the visual forms of late Roman art. To do so, he associated each mode of visual depiction with a particular narrative genre and a specific era of preeminence. "As the complementary style corresponded to the epic, and the isolating style to drama, so the continuous style served for rendering . . . historical prose."[6] Complementary narration preceded both isolating and continuous depiction as the earliest mode of visual narrative. It was drawn, according to Wickhoff, from Asian art, with its interpenetrating levels of reality.[7] The isolating mode represented the pure Greek spirit of permanence and stability. Emerging from complementary narration as a means of distinguishing episode from episode, the isolating style lost favor among artists during late Roman times as they sought to render a temporally continuous vision of the world; it reemerged again as an artistic vogue only in the modern world.[8] The isolating mode, therefore, served as a kind of visual fulcrum; artists reduced complementary narrative images to single, instantaneous episodes that would later be recombined to form continuous narrative:

> We see that the narrow isolating method of narration is bordered on either side by broader forms of narration, that each chooses to draw from it distinct means of expression. . . . It is easy to see how the great variety of action brought together within a single frame in the complementary narrative style was split into separate scenes as art developed, out of which only the exemplary were selected for further depiction; but it would be difficult to determine the reasons why these dramatic single scenes were condensed back together into one representation, in which the hero, led hither and thither, presents the whole tragedy to us in one and the same moment.[9]

Wickhoff surmised that religious innovations ultimately necessitated the elaboration of a new continuous mode of narrative; throughout art history, narrative strategies had reinforced and responded to cultural exigencies. Continuous narration was therefore not simply a coarsened borrowing from Hellenic times. Novel and progressive, it grew out of the late Roman need to depict Christian themes in visual form, especially the symbolic interaction between the temporal world of man and the eternal world of God.[10] Early Christian art, like all artistic production, remained embedded in a broader cultural context, which alone could fully clarify its development. Thus, Wickhoff's typology of visual narrative modes represented an effort to historicize the relationship between temporality and visuality, historical context and artistic perception.

In addition to classifying visual narrative modes according to successive historical periods, Wickhoff identified two distinct styles of visual representation: a natural style and an illusionistic style. The natural style sought "firmly to delineate the form, which the observer then reads as something foreign."[11] Using clear lines and borders to separate object from object, the natural style emphasized the distinction between scene and viewer. Naturalist depictions stood outside the viewer as complete and external images. Illusionistic images, by contrast, forced the viewer "to make the last connection of the impression of form himself; and insofar as he is implicated in the act of creating form, the forceful conviction arises in him that the observed image is real, precisely because he was allowed to participate spiritually in completing the deception."[12] The illusionistic style incorporated the viewer into the creative act, into the visual ob-jection (L. *objectus* "casting before") of an object; the viewer became party to the illusion:

> The painter who made this observation and worked in light of it . . . would no longer compile his images as a collection of individually modeled objective units, or from abstract, generalized outlines [*Abrundungen*], but rather he would place hues and colors next to one another corresponding to the actual image and connect these with the objects not by softening the brush stroke on the painting but, as in the act of vision, through the supplemental experience of the observer.[13]

Wickhoff credited the late Roman period with this insight. Early Christian art did not display poor mimicry of Greek ideals; its illusionistic style was deliberate and progressive, motivated by religious and cultural concerns. Wickhoff argued, in fact, that illusionistic art was more natural than naturalistic art. Illusionist art recognized the true nature of visual perception, which does not simply receive objective forms but participates in their construction. Clear borders were a visual abstraction. All art, he insisted, was in a basic sense illusion, a copy of reality that the "naive observer" was urged to accept.[14] Late Roman illusionistic art admitted to its own artistry by engaging the viewer, quite naturally, in the deception of form.

According to Wickhoff, nineteenth-century impressionists were the latest to adopt Roman illusionism as a representative style. But he saw important differences between the ancient and the modern versions of the style. Whereas ancient illusionism strove to represent the organic and essential qualities of the depicted figure or story, modern illusionism selected from the many elements of reality only those necessary to give the impression of an appearance at a particular moment. In other words, late Roman art combined illusionism with continuous narration in order to depict the organic unfolding of an event; temporal continuity was visually represented. Modern artists combined illusionism with an isolating mode of depiction in order to represent single moments in time. However, the very absence of visual representations of continuity in modern art, far from excluding temporality, highlighted the momentary quality of the scene and evoked the fleeting nature of the act of viewing.[15]

Wickhoff's perspectives on modernist art did not remain bound within the covers of a scholarly text. In 1900, he broke ranks with his academic fellows in order to defend a set of paintings designed by Gustav Klimt for the ceiling of the University of Vienna's new ceremonial hallway.[16] By the time of his commission for the university project in 1894, Klimt had become deeply involved in the new Secessionist art movement that he helped to pioneer. He broke with the classical artistic tastes favored by Viennese art patrons and came to advocate a more psychological worldview, influenced by Nietzsche and Schopenhauer, in which passion and will overwhelmed rationality. Instead of a reverent portrayal of the authority of reason, Klimt's painting *Philosophy* depicted a roiling and tangled column of bodies, agonized, half-conscious, buffeted by desires. A shadowy sphinx loomed barely visible in the darkness at the center of the painting, and a medusa-like figure, *Das Wissen*, the most distinctly drawn form, occupied the base of the canvas. Eyes cocked upward, feathers surrounding her head like rays, *Wissen* appeared more necromantic than rational; it was not clear whether she participated in the oneiric world above her, conjured it up, or merely watched from outside it.

Klimt's university paintings provoked indignation among faculty members. Whereas some critics attacked the ideas represented in the works, arguing that they did not befit the dignity of their academic subjects, others, notably the philosopher Friedrich Jodl, rejected the paintings on aesthetic grounds: Klimt's murals were bad art because they were ugly.[17] The latter accusation provoked Wickhoff's response. In a lecture entitled "What is ugly?" he marshaled historical and anthropological evidence to demonstrate that beauty and ugliness were socially constructed concepts, and therefore not subject to timeless aesthetic criteria.[18] In primordial ages, Wickhoff asserted, things that fostered the survival of the human race were considered beautiful, and those that threatened it ugly. Beauty and ugliness were the aesthetic correlates of life and death, growing from a worldview based around struggle, combat, and urgent needs—the very world that Klimt depicted. As expressions of this survival imperative, artistic forms rested on socio-biological and hence natural bases; nature and art were anthropologically linked. As human control over nature evolved, so too did concepts of beauty. Each new transformation was accompanied by a rejection of previous aesthetic forms as outdated and ugly. As civilization progressed, ugliness came to denote not simply that which was life-threatening but also that which was surpassed, gone, dead. The present drew away from the past, and aesthetic preferences expressed the ever-new social and natural circumstances of men in historical context. While this tendency was anthropologically understandable, it could lead to improper artistic evaluations if contemporary standards were applied to the past.

This presentism was no less apparent in Wickhoff's time than it had been in the past. The modern era, he claimed, distinguished itself by a heightened sense of historical awareness.[19] The innovation of the modern, in other words, was to return to the past; paradoxically, nineteenth-century presentism took the form of historicism. Although this attitude fueled tremendous interest in recovering past artworks and advancing historical knowledge, the modern historical sensibility risked degenerating into antiquarianism.[20] Stylistic borrowing, Wickhoff lamented, denied the artistic needs of today by celebrating aesthetic forms inappropriate to current social and cultural circumstances; it perverted the evolution of art by demanding that all artworks adhere to outmoded ideals of beauty improperly understood as timeless. With the late eighteenth-century elevation of a classical aesthetic, both scholars and public measured beauty against the hypertrophied ideals of a bygone era and condemned the pioneering efforts of modern artists as incomprehensible or ugly. Wickhoff defended the Secessionists by lending historical support to their well-known motto: *To the age its art, to art its freedom.* Thus, Wickhoff's progressive model of art history allowed him both to recover neglected works of the past and to defend modern art against the past's heavy hand. That is, an exacting historical sensibility enabled him, paradoxically, to defend modern artists from the overweening influence of history, against the anachronistic imposition of artistic values and standards from the past.

Nevertheless, Wickhoff did believe that each historical era was connected to all others. Much as Büdinger considered ideas to be the glue of universal history, Wickhoff looked to style as the basis for universal interconnections in art history. Borrowing an image from Riegl's *Problems of Style,* he invited his readers to compare metaphorically the movements of stylistic history to the undulations of the acanthus vine that decorated ancient Greek vases:

> [One can] compare the development of poetry and the visual arts to one of those beautiful Greek acanthus tendrils that winds around and sends off a shoot, which, twining about itself, hides in the midst of a wonderful blossom, then sinks to the ground only to rise back up again and begin anew the magnificent wavelike undulations; all the while, from above, unruly offshoots sprout downward, roguishly disrupting any regular pattern of development. Great artists of singular originality always disrupt every regular ascent because it suffocates the imperceptible wellsprings of creativity among future generations, forcing them into constant imitation, ultimately leading to the expressive homogeneity of all artistic products, making art sink down to flatness until, from this level, gradually, gently, fresh sprouts shoot up, once again allowing new innovations to grow.[21]

Art history oscillated between periods of continuity and disjuncture, innovation and imitation, transition and renaissance—each phase equally crucial to the development of art. An analysis of style provided the empirical basis for art historians to understand the continuities and disruptions that characterized the progressive and universal development of art.

Wickhoff's 1898 essay "On the Historical Unity in the Universal Evolution of Art" elaborated his vision of a universal art history.[22] The essay's ostensible topic was the convergence of Japanese and European artistic trends in the nineteenth century, but the broader historiographical point was, in the spirit of Büdinger, to affirm a universal art historical development encompassing traditions around the globe. Noting the impact of Japanese landscape painting on contemporary European art, Wickhoff posited a deep historical interconnection between the two artistic traditions. He argued that cultural contact between East and West had ancient precedence, and that in the modern world both traditions still drew on a common artistic source. As visual evidence of this ancient convergence, Wickhoff cited the ornamental meander bands on Greek and Chinese vases, the decorative motif which Riegl had so painstakingly analyzed in *Problems of Style* five years earlier. Although the meander band was shaped and applied differently in Chinese and Greek decorative art, vases found in Central Europe bore ornamental motifs resembling the broken meander bands and eye patterns of their Chinese counterparts. Wickhoff connected these motifs with the stylistic evolution traced by Riegl: the emergence of the Greek Dipylon style and acanthus ornamentation from an earlier Near Eastern motif. "The meander band is a unique product of historical and ethnic circumstances. . . . It is out of the question that an art form emerging from such singular conditions could have developed elsewhere in exactly the same fashion."[23] Greek art, Wickhoff asserted, must have traveled slowly eastward as trade expanded with the rise of city-states. Athenians in particular actively exported clay pottery that had been unearthed in excavations as far east as Bactria. Chinese decorative motifs, like those of the late Roman Christians, must have been borrowed from Greek models; their cultural distinctiveness emerged in the ways that they were adapted, used, and transformed to meet the particular needs of East Asian societies. That Japanese art should resonate with modern illusionist painting, therefore, indicated a convergence of styles among separate traditions that drew from a common origin.

> It is truly a circle that has come full round, and all art of the modern civilized peoples [*Culturvölker*] descends directly from the art of the Greeks, which spread in all directions.

> And this also explains one of the most remarkable features of the history of art: the ever-recurring periods of renaissance. Because all art has one origin, every one of its branches retains original elements, so that everywhere a loose thread can be detached and the sought-after remains of ancient periods can be connected with new artistic practices.[24]

Artistic traditions evolved by continuously referring back to, drawing on, and adapting aspects of a universal and multifaceted heritage. Just as transformations in modern European art drew on visual and narrative styles inherited from the ancient world, so Japanese art experienced a renaissance during the nineteenth century by adapting and cultivating aspects of its Greek inheritance. The progressive historical oscillation between periods of transition and periods of renaissance was fueled by the regular recovery and adaptation of ancient artistic forms.

Despite his efforts, therefore, Wickhoff never entirely broke from a dominant classical aesthetic. He rejected the hegemony of Greek artistic norms but then rehabilitated Greek art as a universal historical source. He attacked the use of Greek naturalism as a measure of aesthetic beauty but then replaced it with an equally universal illusionism that inverted the classical hierarchy in favor of Rome. Wickhoff did not interrogate the presumptions of universal history. He approached his artifacts—Japanese pottery, Roman manuscript illustrations—trusting that they reflected a universal artistic heritage; his goal was chiefly to determine how (not whether) they fit into this universal history by comparing styles across time and space. Ultimately, then, in his exuberance to assault the classical aesthetic, Wickhoff undermined the contextual relativism of his own argument. In ignoring the historicity of the relationship between art and aesthetics, he exempted the art historian from the historical implications of his own insights. For Wickhoff, the historian alone could make aesthetic prescriptions that escaped the limitations of context. A subtler model of universal history, one that resisted typological fixity and recognized the art historian's own historicity, would appear in Riegl's work.

In *Late Roman Art Industry,* Riegl praised Wickhoff's *Roman Art* for first acknowledging "the true essence of that artistic period."[25] Wickhoff demonstrated that late Roman figurative art could no longer be judged according to classical aesthetic models; he recognized progress and continuity where other scholars had seen only decay.[26] Wickhoff understood that the visual effect of late Roman sculpture was not the result of poor craftsmanship, but instead expressed a deliberate and novel "optical" view of objects in space, a mode of perception that defined objects through the use of light and shadow rather than strong lines and borders.[27] Like Wickhoff, Riegl believed that optical illusionism developed gradually out of problems raised by Hellenistic art forms and received its fullest expression in the late Roman era.

Riegl also shared Wickhoff's opinion that modern art, like its late Roman counterpart, stressed opticality. Wickhoff's universal history defended modern art against those who judged it according to classical aesthetic norms, even as it demonstrated that modern art adapted visual and narrative styles from ancient sources. Riegl, too, accepted the universality of the general development of art as a precondition for the autonomy of each artistic epoch. He affirmed the dependence of modern art on the art of past epochs when he wrote: "We cannot foresee an era that is filled with the conviction to find aesthetic redemption through the visual arts being able to do so without the monuments of past artistic eras: one need merely subtract the works of antiquity and the paintings of the fifteenth to seventeenth centuries from our artistic treasures in order to assess how much poorer would be our ability to satisfy the modern need for art."[28] Riegl tended, however, to invert Wickhoff's defense of modern art, safeguarding the aesthetic distinctiveness of past eras from anachronistic judgments based on contemporary values.[29] He believed that the present aesthetically tyrannized the past more often than the reverse, as Wickhoff had argued in his defense of Klimt. Nevertheless, both Riegl's and Wickhoff's attacks on anachronistic standards drew from a common historical conviction that each artistic era contributed in its unique way to the universal development of art. Riegl adapted many of Wickhoff's insights to the complex and subtle nuances of his own art historical vision. Although he was less rigid in his typologies than his older colleague, Riegl shared the conviction that the artistic autonomy of an era was closely tied to its position in a universal history of art, that each era drew on common historical sources to establish its formal and stylistic distinctiveness. The very historicity of art stood as the condition for its autonomy: each era was at once indebted to formal influences from the past and unique within the historical evolution of art.

But Riegl was also aware of his colleague's analytical shortcomings. Shrewd as he was, even Wickhoff was guilty of making anachronistic judgments about the art of past eras. For example, although Wickhoff recognized differences between ancient and modern pictorial techniques, in his enthusiasm to rehabilitate late Roman styles he presented modern art as a kind of latter-day appropriation of Roman illusionism.[30] This argument reinforced a classical aesthetic, albeit one more flexible than the Hellenic ideal that Wickhoff spent his career attacking. According to Riegl, Wickhoff's view ignored radical differences in the ways that ancient and modern artists depicted objects in artistic space. Late Roman artists used chiaroscuro to outline individual objects; they strove for an even, rhythmic unity, giving each object on a canvas equal treatment rather than representing objects *perspectivally* in three-dimensional space. This technique gave early Christian art its characteristic flatness and cluttered appearance; no single vantage point could organize the figures on the canvas into a coherent hierarchy because each object was distinct from others. Late Roman figural art demanded multiple vantage points. Modern artists, by contrast, used optical light and shadow to highlight the relationship among objects *in space*; space, not figures, received priority. Overlooking this important difference, Wickhoff prematurely ascribed to Roman art a free spatiality more appropriate to the time of Velazquez. Even Wickhoff's description of art history in terms of cyclical adaptations of ancient styles, according to Riegl, misled the modern viewer into seeing his own aesthetic expectations mirrored in the artwork of late Rome. It subverted Wickhoff's own relativist intentions by implicitly accepting a model of historical progress and decay and prevented him from fully recognizing the advances made by late Roman artists. "Where the Genesis and Flavian-Trajanic art meet," Riegl wrote, "there [Wickhoff] finds proof in the Genesis of progress beyond classical art; wherever Genesis and the art of the early Empire diverges, however, he no longer sees it as progress, but as decay."[31] Tied to a rigid typology and "partly informed by a materialistic view of art," Wickhoff failed to remain true to his own historical ideal of treating each era in its own terms. He was guilty of using modern subjective standards to judge past artworks and thereby perpetuating ahistorical notions of artistic beauty and animation. As a result, Riegl's praise for the originality of the unknown manuscript artists of the *Genesis* codex was, ironically, even greater than Wickhoff's. When compared with "Flavian-Trajanic art from the standpoint of a universal-historical perspective on the general development of art,"[32] the manuscript revealed nothing but progress.

Without rejecting it altogether, Riegl discounted Wickhoff's circular historical model in favor of a historiography that linked evolutionary innovation with the constant adaptation of historical forms. In his contribution to the *Büdinger Festschrift,* a short essay entitled "Kunstgeschichte und Universalgeschichte," Riegl applied this historiographical model to an analysis of recent developments in his own field of art history.[33] He opened the essay by announcing his conviction that art history should aspire to the status of a science. Noting that his discipline's late development meant that its goals and methods were not clearly defined, he acknowledged that art history would encounter skepticism from scholars in the natural sciences. Nevertheless, the value of art historical claims, he insisted, depended upon securing scientific credentials for the discipline. Riegl's opening anecdote about his doctor's skepticism toward art history's scientific pretensions expressed more than simply the frustrations of a scholar from an underrecognized field.[34] It suggested, by analogy with the medical field, a model for the new science of art history: the artwork served as the body under observation; the art-historian/doctor determined its place in history from evident symptoms. As Riegl's essay revealed, however, art history could not rely on such a straightforward medical approach to its subject matter because its data were filtered through an ever-changing historical perspective.[35]

Though barely a century-and-a-half old in 1898, the discipline of art history had already passed through several stages of development. The founders of the discipline—Riegl mentioned Seroux d'Agincourt (1730–1814) and Karl Friedrich von Rumohr (1785–1843)—"treated the field of the fine arts as a great unity": "They were not specialists, neither in documentary source criticism nor in useful expertise; but they held every formal example of the visual arts as equally important and worthy of observation, and therefore they actually surveyed the whole colorful world from pyramids to the Nazarenes and apprehended it under the aspect of a singular, unified development."[36] Dedicated to a systematic analysis of artworks, these early art historians labored without the auxiliary disciplines and historiographical advances of the mid-nineteenth century. In their synthetic zeal, they ignored details and failed to differentiate among periods; perceptual transformations went unnoticed, stylistic shifts overlooked. Art history became a kind of museum of objects and characteristics available for simultaneous comparison, oddly synchronic in its universal scope. "Every last 'art buff' knows an enormous number of art monuments," Riegl wrote, "but it is just this sheer amount that will not allow anything more than an undetailed, merely superficial cognizance."[37] Lacking time, available materials, and methodological rigor, these early pioneers were forced to accept both written and visual documents uncritically. Though their impulse to survey the whole history of art was a seminal gesture, advancing the discipline required specialization and the development of scientific and critical methods of visual analysis.

The second generation of art historians, whose number included Thausing and Bode, replaced their predecessors' universalist outlook with an emphasis on exact detail, methodological specialization, and disciplinary professionalization. For mid-century art historians, the greatest triumph "was when [they] succeeded in determining the artist [*Meister*] of a painting or establishing a monument's date of origin, and the pleasure was genuinely heightened when some error in the old biographies could be pointed out."[38] The generation of Riegl's instructors emphasized historical precision, connoisseurship, and physical detail; their preferred genre was the biographical monograph, a form exemplified by Thausing's *Dürer.* Seeking a scientific basis for their discipline, mid-century art historians espoused philological and empirical methods that stressed rigorous documentary and visual analysis as a way to decipher the historical language of artworks. The consequent professionalization of the discipline, as art historians secured posts in universities, accounted for the frequent caricatures of bookish art historians and the growing antagonism among art historians, practicing artists, and amateur interpreters.[39]

Even this approach, however, had its limitations. Riegl's critique of his teachers' generation took two forms, one methodological and the other historiographical. First, mid-century art historians, who stressed the scholarly and theoretical aspects of their calling, tended to lack the practical experience with artworks gained in museums or as a practicing artist. This limitation weakened their analyses of art and their attempts to base art history on empirical induction. (Riegl's critique may have been directed against idealist trends in German art history more than his own Austrian milieu, where close connections between museum and university dated from Böhm's time.) Second, the boundaries of art history accepted by mid-century scholars were too narrow to satisfy the interests of Riegl's generation. Mere connoisseurship could hardly justify the discipline's existence, and it certainly did not exhaust its possibilities. According to Riegl, mid-century art historians treated each artifact as an individual entity to be examined in isolation and then linked to immediate causes and effects. In so doing, they sought to establish a "chronological chain of art objects," link by link, each object in order, connected to but distinguished from its successor. This goal no longer satisfied modern art historians.

> The most modern of the art historians will no longer rest contented with this mere chronological ordering of monuments within the developmental course. They maintain that the establishment of the next cause and effect does not suffice to clarify a monument in its essence and its conditions of origin. They refer to the fact that artworks are not merely divided from one another by individual tendencies, but also bound together by shared qualities. Because the representatives of the philological-historical school attached preponderant significance to the individual mark of distinction and thereby gave it one-sided attention, modern art historians believe that they should direct their attention to the unifying, generalizable qualities.[40]

Modern art historians, unlike their immediate predecessors, felt free to compare works from periods as widely disparate as imperial Rome and seventeenth-century Europe; they noted the differences and recognized the historical progression of art, but were unafraid to highlight the formal similarities and stylistic recurrences as well: "It is justified to bring together artistic periods so distant in time and space, such as those of the second and seventeenth centuries after Christ; indeed, this universal-historical method of observation can be seen as the proper crown of art historical research."[41] Works such as Wickhoff's *Roman Art* combined the methodological rigor and historical sensitivity of the second-generation art historians with the synthetic vision of the first. Specialization and universal history went hand in hand, the former validating the insights of universal history by providing detailed and scientific evidence, the latter justifying specialized research by illuminating its broader significance.

But what justified and legitimized cross-temporal and cross-cultural comparison methodologically? How could historical methodologies honed by the scrutiny of empirical detail support a universal historical enterprise? Riegl addressed this question not on strict methodological grounds but by offering a set of idiosyncratic anthropological assumptions. Universal anthropological laws, he claimed, underlay all human artistic production, a fact that legitimized, indeed necessitated, cross-cultural and cross-temporal analyses of art: "Because it is indeed man that brought both of these images [second and seventeenth centuries C.E.] to life, it becomes gradually more pressing and apparent that the Romans just like the Dutch and the Spanish, in both cases, obeyed one and the same higher law."[42] This law—or what Riegl elsewhere described as the universal and autonomous creative impulse—found expression as "the immediate cause of both [Roman and early modern] images." Anthropology validated a universalist outlook. Art expressed a human creative impulse whose manifestations varied with time and place; art historians sought to uncover the anthropologically based, universal-historical laws revealed in the varied artistic output of each historical epoch.

Riegl's universal-historical outlook was neither cyclical nor purely progressive and teleological, although it combined aspects of each of these historical models. Stylistic evolution, he contended, alternated between periods of innovation and adaptation, renaissance and transition, without either fully mimicking or breaking with the past. With regard to his own discipline, Riegl doubted that a perfect balance would ever be struck between the hyperopia of universal history and the myopia of specialized research. Again, anthropology conspired against it. "The human species," he averred, "moves in relentless, back-and-forth oscillations between extremes. . . . As the trough follows the crest of a wave, so, with the necessity of nature, the one-sided universal-historical mode of observation seen today follows yesterday's emphasis on historical specialization."[43] Just as the history of art revealed the continuous and infinitely varied expressions of a common anthropology, so its historiography oscillated ceaselessly between a stress on the universal qualities of artworks and a focus on the individual details of artist and era—between the two poles of human intellectual inclination: the synthetic and the analytic. Even the most recent generation of artists and art historians displayed this pattern in microcosm. Both art history and painting in the late nineteenth century, noted Riegl, had shifted from an emphasis on naturalism to an emphasis on stylization, from apparent mimesis to clear artifice, from objective verisimilitude to representational abstraction. Each new creative impulse overcompensated for the extremes of its predecessor.

Riegl offered his own analysis as a kind of art historical balance designed to undercut extremism of various sorts. He refused to posit another strict model for art historical evolution, or to characterize universal history in the exclusive terms of endless circularity, progressive evolution, or synchronic similitude. He proposed instead that art history oscillated among all these models, each correcting and counterbalancing the tendencies of its rivals in a never-ending, "Sisyphean" task. "Between the crest and trough of a wave," he wrote, "there lies a dead point at which the extremes touch one another."[44] To understand this elusive equilibrium, we must investigate the model of temporality that informed Riegl's art historical vision.

2
Temporality and History in Riegl's Work

In an 1887 review of Joseph Neuwirth's *Studien zur Geschichte der Miniaturmalerei in Oesterreich,* Riegl outlined two criteria he considered essential to a successful work of art history. An art historical text should include relevant illustrations to "refresh the spirit of the reader" and enable him to evaluate the author's claims; and, although an art history must contain descriptions of visual forms, its language had to be lucid enough to avoid "burying the intellect under a heap of superfluous details."[1] These criteria suggest several themes that that became crucial to Riegl's later work. First, his comments called attention to the fact that an art historical text engaged with an audience of readers, whose judgment it invited and whose approval it sought. Judgment must not simply be made on the basis of an argument advanced in words; it required the reader to evaluate visual artworks. Riegl insisted that a work of art history must consistently test itself against the visual evidence. The artwork was the primary text; it was analyzed and interpreted but not replaced by the historian's descriptive account. The incorporation of visual works alongside the text, therefore, affirmed the priority of visual evidence in the conclusions of an art historian. Moreover, illustrations provided the visual evidence that allowed a reader to judge the historian's descriptions and conclusions. They testified to an art historian's scholarly rigor, his willingness to submit his insights to informed criticism and appraisal. The historian who withheld his visual evidence shunned criticism and thereby weakened his claims.

Illustrations also had a stylistic function: they enlivened a text that might otherwise become turgid and visually unmodulated. Riegl's stress on the stylistic value of illustration suggested an early concern with the relationship between visuality and attention even in the act of reading, a theme that later preoccupied him in his analyses of Dutch group portraiture. To maintain a reader's attention, art historians must not overwhelm their texts with detailed descriptions that were inessential to the analysis at hand. This caution may surprise those familiar with Riegl's work; whereas his conceptual and theoretical impact is still hotly disputed, most commentators agree that Riegl's attentiveness to visual detail and sensitivity of description secured his legacy. In this early book review, however, though Riegl did not discount the role of description in art historical analysis, he did underscore its limitations. He insisted that art historians worked within a medium—language—that was insufficient for encompassing the visual material of their evidence. Visual art had its own formal "language," the language of the image, direct and immediate, whose integrity was partially lost by translation into words.[2] The art historian went beyond written archival material to draw his evidence directly from an exact and sympathetic observation of artworks themselves.[3] Through this enterprise of elucidating an artwork's historicity, temporality, and context in the image rather than the word, the art historian made his unique contributions to the *Geisteswissenschaften*.

Because Riegl's formalist notion of art history was not restricted to the so-called high arts, but embraced the decorative arts more generally (those material artifacts produced for noninstrumental reasons), the insights into perception gleaned from the analysis of a period's artworks applied to a broad social constituency, not simply to those who produced or appreciated fine art. While the fine arts tended to exhibit the perceptual traits of an era most clearly and therefore frequently attracted Riegl's attention, they did not occupy an inherently privileged position among his objects of analysis. We have already seen that Riegl turned his early attention to decorative illustrations on calendars; other quintessentially useful artifacts such as jewelry, potsherds, buckles, and sacred relics also merited his careful descriptive efforts. In fact, not until his later publications did Riegl turn to more traditional art historical subjects, such as Dutch or Italian Baroque painting. Riegl shared Thausing's conviction that art history was not simply an auxiliary historical discipline, as his colleagues at the Institut für österreichische Geschichtsforschung assumed. To investigate art, he believed, was to explore mankind's evolving perceptual relationship with the external world.

As a founder of modern art historical scholarship, Riegl is credited with forging an internalist approach to art history, a theory that rejected the view that art's development was tied to external historical circumstances. Art, he insisted, had its own autonomous formal trajectory and history, driven solely by a creative impulse with deep anthropological roots, not by material and technical circumstances, physiology, or iconographic intent. This did not mean that art existed in complete isolation from the external world, irrelevant to and exclusive of social and political matters. Henri Zerner, in a brief but helpful synopsis of the art historian's thought, remarked that Riegl's internalism was "essentially a methodological tactic," not a claim about social reality: "[Internalism] ensures the proper interrogation of the specific works, the respect for art as a special domain of understanding, and, in the end, the contribution of art history to the social sciences as a particular branch of a more general Geisteswissenschaft."[4] In what follows, I explore Zerner's contention that Riegl's formalist notion of *Kunstwollen* and his concept of the internal development of art was a claim about the methodology and etiology of art history; I attempt to show that proto-phenomenological assumptions about the nature of art lay behind Riegl's internalist history of artistic forms. Far from eschewing any connection between art and other human endeavors, Riegl believed that art reflected and shaped man's temporal and perceptual relationship with the world.

As demonstrated in previous chapters, Riegl's work elaborated many issues raised by his teachers and colleagues. In part 2 of this book, I treat his art historical ideas as an original exploration of themes common within his academic field. By no means do I intend to canvass all the theoretical issues raised in his work; several recent intellectual biographies have surveyed his career with admirable success and breadth.[5] Instead, I focus my discussion on Riegl's conceptualization of time and history, a theme he elaborated throughout his writings and one that preoccupied his professors and colleagues. Time was not simply one topic among the many that held Riegl's attention. Looking retrospectively across his career, one sees that the primary underlying preoccupation of his seemingly varied output was not the examination of this or that artwork or period, but the use of empirical analysis to investigate the relationship between art and history, visual representation and temporality. In his oeuvre, temporal continuity shaped the formal characteristics of individual works and underpinned a historical framework that linked artworks universally. This section examines the relationship between an internal temporality of form and the continuum of art history.

Though cut short by a premature death, Riegl's career was varied and prolific enough to spark disputes among scholars as to its continuity. Throughout the 1880s Riegl contributed numerous articles to such in-house journals as *Mitteilungen des Instituts für österreichische Geschichtsforschung* and *Mitteilungen des österreichischen Museums für Kunst und Industrie;* but it was his books such as *Problems of Style, Late*

Roman Art Industry, and *The Group Portraiture of Holland,* published between 1893 and 1905 that gained him scholarly notice and established his legacy. In 1928, Hans Sedlmayr, attempting to distill "[d]ie Quintessenz der Lehren Riegls," maintained that "almost all of Riegl's ideas are in place very early on, basically from the time when he began work."[6] Dietrich von Loh, in 1986, concurred: "[w]ith Riegl, his scientific thought and finished works from the *Altorientalische Teppiche* (1891) until his final essays fit together in a single whole."[7]

Other scholars have found this claim of continuity "hard to swallow" (to use Wolfgang Kemp's phrase), preferring to view Riegl's development in terms of disjuncture. They see sharp breaks in his development that reflect a fundamental rethinking of basic art historical premises. Kemp, for example, posits a shift in Riegl's work around the turn of the century, signaled in *The Group Portraiture of Holland* by a rejection of the pure formalism that supposedly characterized his earlier work and a new openness to contextual and semantic criteria of interpretation. Kemp situates this shift within a cultural sea change in Austria, a transition described by Schorske in terms of the demise of liberalism, positivism, and, in Riegl's case, formalism.[8] Margaret Olin perceives a crucial transition in the mid-1890s, between Riegl's two lectures on the "Historische Grammatik der bildenden Kunst," the first drafted in 1897–1898, the second in 1899.[9] Whereas the first manuscript postulated a theory of art as a "quasi-scientific mode of description"[10] originating in the human pursuit of knowledge and need for order, the second offered a theory of art as will, rooted in human desires for harmony. This shift from an emphasis on knowledge to a stress on will, Olin claims, informed the method of analysis Riegl practiced in *Late Roman Art Industry* (1901). Still other commentators sidestep the debate between continuity and disjuncture and focus instead on synthesizing Riegl's thought within a broader nineteenth- and twentieth-century trends.[11] This synoptic approach, of course, presupposes a unified core that can be drawn from his work.

Intellectual biographers, such as Margaret Olin and Margaret Iverson, have attempted to show both continuity and discontinuity in Riegl's evolution. In their accounts, *Problems of Style, Late Roman Art Industry,* and *The Group Portraiture of Holland* mark phases in Riegl's thought, defined according to specific historical topics and related thematic issues. I too hope to strike this balance in my discussion of Riegl's work. His thought developed through various phases, each providing a distinct perspective on his underlying scholarly preoccupation with the history and temporality of artistic representation. What appears to be a fundamental assumption of Riegl's thought—that the analysis of art rested properly on a historical basis—was actually, I contend, the point he sought most stringently to interrogate. The empirical analysis of specific artworks and periods provided Riegl with a method for addressing a broader historiographical concern. His strategies changed over time, from an affinity early in his career for constructing grand historical narratives that encompassed many cultures ("Die mittelalterliche Kalenderillustration," *Problems of Style*) to a narrower focus on specific transitional periods after the mid-1890s (*Late Roman Art Industry, The Group Portraiture of Holland*).[12] And as he shifted his attention from decorative motifs to late Roman art and Dutch group portraiture, he allowed each topic to dictate a set of questions, themes, and methods specific to its own elucidation. However, by subdividing Riegl's work too strictly into discrete periods, one risks ignoring the thread that unified his art historical enterprise. While the questions raised in *The Group Portraiture of Holland* differed noticeably from earlier topics, recurrent themes permeated his writing and demonstrated the persistence of a set of underlying intellectual interests. "The Modern Cult of Monuments," written late in his career, recalled the grand historical scope of his earlier works in its effort to outline the temporal dimensions of the modern appreciation of historical monuments. In part 2 of this book, which is part intellectual biography and part thematic exposition, I try to highlight the ways in which Riegl's later writings reflected the thematic concerns of his earlier work even as they employed markedly different methodological strategies. Foremost among these interests were historicity and temporality.

8

History and the Perception of Monuments

In 1902, Riegl was appointed editor of the journal of the Central Commission for the Research and Preservation of Artistic and Historical Monuments (*Mitteilungen der k. k. Zentral-Kommission für Erforschung und Erhaltung der Kunst- und historischen Denkmale*). Established in the mid-nineteenth century partly through the efforts of Rudolf von Eitelberger, the commission modeled its program on a similar organization headed by Eugène Viollet-le-Duc in France.[1] In 1903, the year he joined the commission itself, Riegl drafted his essay "The Modern Cult of Monuments" as a theoretical analysis of the social and aesthetic implications entailed in the commission's work of monument preservation.[2] Rarely did he address the topics of time and history as explicitly as in this essay. Published in folio form, "The Modern Cult of Monuments" entered into the debate over whether historical buildings should be restored to their "original" state or simply preserved to slow their decay. In 1882 and 1883, Thausing had vigorously condemned the fashion for monument restoration in a feuilleton written for the *Neue Freie Presse*, and he intervened to prevent the restoration of the Giant Portal of St. Stephen's Cathedral.[3] Like his teacher, Riegl also favored a cautious approach toward renovation.[4] "The Modern Cult of Monuments" presented, among other things, a case for preserving monuments as historical documents that register the passage of time.

But Riegl's essay also had far broader historical implications. Instead of taking a polemical stand in the heated debates over architectural restoration, the essay offered an elaborate theory of the various historical suppositions that determined the relationship between monuments and observers. In this regard, "The Modern Cult of Monuments" outlined the broad scope of Riegl's modernist historical vision:

> We call historical everything that once was and today is no more; in modern conceptions we add to this the further idea that what once was can never be again, and everything that once existed constitutes an irreplaceable and unremovable link in a chain of development, in other words, that each successive step is determined by the first and could not have happened as it did had any of the earlier links not preceded it. The central point of every modern conception of history is the idea of development. In these modern terms, every human activity and every human fate of which we have evidence or testimony can without exception claim historical value: every historical event is in principle irreplaceable.[5]

The historical worldview, shared by Riegl and his contemporaries, subsumed human events and products within a developmental framework. This perspective informed all modern schools of thought to one degree or another. Idealists, materialists, and positivists alike accepted some form of evolutionary history in their systems; they understood the past in terms of a continuous, causal process linking cultural phenomena to their predecessors and successors. This worldview was not universal; instead, it was a historically specific conceptual framework that organized the modern perception of the social and cultural world and provided structure and meaning by conferring on each event or artifact a significance based on its position in the historical chain.

In identifying his own modern perspective as a conceptual paradigm, Riegl set out to historicize contemporary notions of history. Thus, although he affirmed the premises and insights of his contemporary historical scholarship, he recognized that even its emphasis on universality, equality, and evolutionary development grew out of a specific nineteenth-century intellectual milieu. History itself, as a mode of organizing knowledge, was culturally and historically conditioned. Just as Riegl assailed the absolutism of classical aesthetics by arguing that all artistic judgments were historically determined, he followed a similar logic by criticizing the tendency to evaluate historical artworks according to modern standards. Even his own scholarly commitments, Riegl believed, reflected a distinctly modern historical sensibility that shaped his approach to the study of art. Aware of the historicity of his own scholarly enterprise, Riegl sought to devise an art historical approach that remained true to its own relativist and subjectivist implications yet at the same time allowed phenomena to be studied objectively and scientifically so that they might "speak" in their own terms and reflect their own time. In "The Modern Cult of Monuments," Riegl set out to examine the temporal and cultural constitution of historical perception. Because there was no absolute vantage point from which to render aesthetic judgment, the art historian had to reflect on the temporal dynamics inherent in the act of judging itself; he had to investigate the historical relationship between artistic form and cultural perception.[6]

Historical awareness itself had a history, developing from late antiquity through Renaissance Italy (when "the past won a present-day value [*Gegenwartswert*] for modern life and production") and into the nineteenth century. "It took several centuries," Riegl wrote, "before [historical awareness] gradually acquired the modern shape we see today, especially among the Germanic peoples." The modern historical worldview, a sensibility broad enough to embrace the hyperempiricism of Sickel and the universal history of Büdinger, nurtured "an interest in everything, including the smallest facts and events of even the most remote peoples set apart from our own nation by insurmountable differences in character; and an interest in the history of mankind overall, in which every individual allows us to glimpse a piece of ourselves."[7] How could an art historian, conditioned by his own historicity, grasp the temporality of artworks or make sense of forms of time that were not his own? How could a nineteenth-century Austrian scholar understand the temporal universe of ancient Rome on its own terms?

The historicization of historical awareness enabled Riegl to identify two distinct notions of time: time as a historical concept and time as a phenomenon embedded in artifacts. The former changed from one era to the next, whereas the latter at once escaped perception and underpinned it. By examining the dynamics of historical perception—the ways in which one era perceived the cultural products of another—Riegl hoped to clarify not only the notion of temporal continuity that informed the modern historical worldview, but also the ways a modern worldview affected the reception of historical artworks. He hoped to suggest ways that a contemporary art historian, conditioned by his own historicity, could make sense of forms of time that were not his own by perceiving the material signs of alternate temporalities in artworks, the "objective" traces of time "written" across the surface of a work. Only in perception could the traces of a proto-phenomenological, artifactual time emerge. By analyzing the relationship among modern historical perception, the artifacts it attempted to organize, and the alternate constructions of temporality they envisioned, Riegl identified a new project for art history: like chronologists without the benefit of a fixed calendar, art historians strove to understand the interaction among various conceptions of time.

Riegl organized "The Modern Cult of Monuments" as a typological study of the various modes of historical and artistic valuation. As the commission title suggested, his first task was to distinguish between artistic and historical monuments. Every human event or artifact had value as a historical monument, he contended, although sheer quantity required historians to focus their energies on those objects that exemplified cultural attributes or transitions most clearly.[8] Riegl rejected the hard distinction between historically significant and inconsequential artifacts. A historical outlook considered all objects unique and significant in the progress of history; its reach was potentially limitless. Artistic value was also broadly construed, and it overlapped significantly with historical value.

> Every artistic monument is at once and without exception an historical monument in that it represents a specific step in the development of the visual arts, for which, strictly speaking, no real equivalent can ever be found. Conversely, every historical monument is also an artistic monument; even a literary example as insignificant as a short, inconsequential note on torn-off scrap paper contains (in addition to historical information about the manufacture of paper, the script, writing materials, etc.) a series of artistic elements: the external form of the paper, the form of the letters, and the ways in which they were put together.[9]

It is important to recognize the radical revision of aesthetics proposed here. We have already seen that Riegl rejected the distinction between high and low, classical and decadent art, on historical grounds. His challenge to aestheticians went even further, however, for he also ignored the conventional distinction between art and non-art. In Riegl's view, art did not designate a distinct class of aesthetic objects, but rather the formal and decorative aspects of all human production; it described the products of a non-instrumental creative drive that shaped the relationship between human perception and the objective world. All objects had artistic value, in that all objects possessed formal attributes that did not directly serve a practical function; and all artifacts had historical qualities as well. A mere scrap of paper, Riegl remarked in language reminiscent of Sickel's diplomatics, could become an indispensable artifact from both a historical and an artistic point of view. It formed a potentially irreplaceable link in "der Entwicklungskette der Kunstgeschichte"; indeed, it might be one of the few artifacts available from a particular era. What determined the artistic value of an object, then, was its ability to exemplify the perceptual tendencies of a given period, to express its position in the developmental chain of history. "The division between 'artistic and historical monuments' is unfounded," Riegl wrote, "because the former is at once contained and absorbed within the latter."[10] For Riegl, artistic value was a historical category.

It must be stressed, however, that historical value and art value, though interrelated, were not synonymous. In this regard, Riegl was not simply a crypto-historicist, basing all aesthetic value on historical significance. Whereas historical value characterized the clues to the past offered by an artifact, art value concerned its "spezifisch künstlerischen" qualities of concept, form, and color insofar as they possessed intrinsic worth beyond their historical significance.[11] It was entirely possible to appreciate form and color without regard for the historical information they conveyed. For the art historian, however, an exclusively artistic perspective was insufficient, for it ignored the developmental tendencies inherent within the formal qualities of artworks, the historically determinant character of those works, and the culture of perception they revealed. Art both escaped from and embedded itself within history.

In "The Modern Cult of Monuments," Riegl characterized the historicity of artifacts in two ways. First, objects were historical insofar as they provided information about life in the past, evidence that could be classified chronologically. The indexical qualities of an artwork—the traces of its time and place of origin—legitimized its historical status in the eyes of the modern viewer; an artifact had historical value if it elucidated the past. But Riegl identified a second, more fundamental form of historicity that he dubbed "age value" [*Alterswert*]. An artifact could possess age value even if it offered no clues about a specific historical era:

> The ruins of a castle, for instance, whose decayed walls display little of their original form, technique, floor plan, etc. to gratify an art or art historical interest, and to which moreover no chronicled memories attach, offer no simple historical value that can explain their clear and evident interest to the modern observer. When regarding an old church belfry, we also have to distinguish between the more or less localized historical memories of various forms that are awakened in us when we observe it, and the general, non-localized presentation of time, which the belfry has "joined in" [*mitgemacht*] and which it reveals in its clearly evident traces of age [*Alterspuren*].[12]

Artifacts—written, visual, or architectural—represented the passage of time in traces of age accumulated over the course of their existence. This representation was not a function of either the artifact or viewer alone, but something they both "joined in" or "made with" [mitgemacht] each other, literally a re-presentation of time emerging within the visual dialogue between an artifact and a viewer. Admirers of age value cherished monuments not for their ability to illuminate this or that historical period, but because they revealed "the past alone and as such."[13] Why should age value captivate modern viewers? What was revealed in the re-presentation of time in artifacts? According to Riegl, age value "brought forth in its observer the sense [*Stimmungswirken*], which among modern men, generates an awareness of the regularized cycle of becoming and passing, of the emergence of the particular from the whole and its gradual but necessary dissolution back into the whole."[14] The dilapidated ruins of a castle, for example, reminded observers of fate, passage, and the cyclical impermanence of life. To the historical and anthropological roots of this modern appreciation of age, Riegl added a religious one as well: "age value is based in a truly Christian principle: that of humble acceptance of fate and the will of the

Almighty, which feeble man must not audaciously presume to grasp."[15] Whereas the nineteenth century privileged historical value, Riegl believed that the twentieth century would come to accept fully the necessary implications of the "historischen Entwicklungsgedanken." It would become an era of age value, recognizing the relativity of even its own valuations, and appreciating works of the past more for their traces of age and timeliness than for their original intent:[16]

> It is much more the pure, regular cycle of becoming and passing according to natural laws whose unclouded perception modern men from the beginning of the twentieth century enjoy. Every human artifact is hereby conceived as a natural organism, in whose development no one should interfere. . . . Modern man glimpses in a monument a piece of his own life, and he finds all interference in its development as disturbing as interference with his own organic growth.[17]

Evoking an anthropological sense of time or passage, age value recalled the temporal experience of each viewer by presenting it back to him in traces of age and decay, by offering a present pastness. Thus artifacts could be described as historical in two ways: they marked time chronologically, recalling a work's original state; and they re-presented time "rhythmically,"[18] recording the passage of moments as "traces of age" [*Spuren des Alters*].[19] The historicity of an artifact was based not only on its chronological content but also on the fact that time traced its movements across the very face of the object. Art historical monuments gratified the modern observer by both illuminating the distant past and linking artwork and viewer in a common temporal experience.[20]

When it concerned the preservation of monuments, historical value and age value sometimes contradicted each other. Whereas a historian might call for renovating a monument to its original state, an admirer of age value insists on leaving it to a natural process of decay. This dispute was further complicated by the antagonism between age value and its social and artistic antithesis: newness value. Harking back to Wickhoff's defense of Klimt and foretokening the twentieth-century cult of novelty, Riegl noted that most people in the modern world celebrated newness for its own sake, prioritizing youth over age, innovation over tradition. "Only the new and the whole appear beautiful in the eyes of the majority," he wrote. "[T]he old, fragmented, and discolored are ugly."[21] Both the cult of newness value and the cult of age value reflected a nineteenth-century obsession with time and history. "On the one hand we see an appreciation of the old for its own sake which rejects on principle all renovation; on the other hand, the appreciation of the new in itself, which seeks to remove all traces of age as obtrusive and displeasing."[22] The coexistence of historical value, age value, and newness value set up the complex temporal matrix of Riegl's modern perceptual culture.

Using language evocative of generational social conflict, Riegl's essay characterized artworks according to historical, perceptual, and temporal attributes, not aesthetic criteria of beauty or ugliness. History registered temporal passage visually for admirers of age value and established a measurable relationship between past and present for historians; advocates of newness value dismissed history as worthless. Monuments occasioned a struggle over meaning among cultural groups committed to distinct visual constructions of time. Whereas proponents of age value admired the traces of time's passage on objects, advocates of newness value called for the elimination of preterit marks. Historical value treated time as chronology and art as indexical. It is important to note that in these competing perspectives, the Rankean historicist invocation to extinguish the self during research disappeared altogether. Riegl's historian did not abolish the present in order to illuminate the past. Instead, he preserved the historical value of an artifact by placing it in a meaningful visual relationship with the present—a present that conferred significance on the objects of the past. "Whereas age value appreciates the past for its own sake, historical value has the tendency to single out a moment in the historical development of the past and set it clearly before our eyes as if it belonged to the present."[23] Treating art as indexical and time as chronological, Riegl's historian recognized the present as a critical point of reference and perspective.

Artistic and historical monuments embodied yet a fourth form of temporality inscribed in them by the monument builders themselves. Because memorials were created to preserve memory, the act of constructing a monument was in Riegl's view a claim to stop time, to fix or monumentalize the moment of an event. Like historians, monument builders believed that certain moments in chronological time (the origin, the date) were irreplaceable and should be immortalized. However, like the advocates of newness value who celebrated the eternity of the now, monument builders asserted the permanence of a memorialized moment by attempting to remove it from the temporal passage that both age value and historical value registered in different ways. Riegl summarized the relationship among these temporal valuations in the following terms: "Whereas age value is based exclusively on passage, historical value, though its existence would lack justification without the passage of time to the present, nevertheless wishes to suspend the whole passage of time from today onward; intentional commemorative value simply makes a claim to immortality, to an eternal present, an unceasing state of becoming [*Werdezustand*]."[24] Reminiscent of Nietzsche's paradox of the eternal return, this curious model of commemorative value describes a continuous temporal development coinciding with a succession of static eternal moments.[25] This seemingly paradoxical relationship between an "eternal present" and an "unceasing state of becoming" in artworks was a temporal puzzle that Riegl sought to capture in his concept of the *Kunstwollen,* discussed in the next chapter.

9
Temporality in Visible Form

Under the influence of Theodor von Sickel's Institute training, Alois Riegl conceived of artistic form in material terms, a notion that enabled him to base formalist conclusions on empirical research methods. Sickel's *Merkmale*—material clues to the chronological record—expressed in Riegl's eyes the formal attributes of a universal-historical development. He adapted the diplomatic method, designed to secure facts and dates, by broadening its artistic and historical scope beyond the goals of chronology. Unlike Sickel or Morelli, Riegl did not strive mainly to date objects, pinpoint their origins, and coordinate them along a fixed timeline. Without renouncing chronology altogether, he sought to elevate art history from a chronicle of artworks to an analysis of the developmental logic expressed in artifactual form. This logic, or grammar,[1] was fundamentally temporal, chrono-logical; it worked itself out formally through time.

In "The Modern Cult of Monuments," the temporal nature of visual perception shaped the relationship between a modern historical worldview and the art of the past. Riegl noted that contemporary art patrons often preferred historical artworks that only partly shared their own artistic sensibilities over modern art emerging from their own culture. Given the modern tendency toward aesthetic relativism, Riegl wondered on what basis these preferences could be held. How could modern viewers judge art of the past, or even contemporary art, without a fixed standard? Riegl's answer to this question stressed the tension in the relation between artworks and viewers. "Certain old artworks correspond, if not completely, at least in part, to the modern *Kunstwollen*. It is precisely this apparent correspondence of certain aspects when set against conflicting aspects in the same historical work that exert such a powerful effect on us modern viewers. A modern art work, which necessarily lacks this contrast, can never offer such an effect."[2] Modern viewers perceived historical artworks as force fields made up of some elements that were compatible with their sensibilities and others that were not. The aggregation of familiar and foreign elements in a single work created lively viewing. Historical paintings with modernist resonances revealed contrasting artistic sensibilities and thereby offered immanent criteria for comparison, criticism, and evaluation. Neither purely modern art nor utterly foreign historical works could provide this visual stimulus; the former obliterated critical distance whereas the latter offered no opening for evaluation.

This evaluative discrepancy between past and present aesthetic judgments, embodied formally in a tension between the congruous and incongruous elements of an artwork, became Riegl's main focus or "object" of analysis. It emerged in the relationship between viewer and object, between a contemporary observer and the objectified vision of a past made present as material form. This tension was not exclusively in the eyes of the beholder. Although the designation of congruous and incongruous elements in the art of the past was partially a subjective and cultural construct, historical artworks presented themselves to the modern viewer as an *objective* tension—a tension among formal elements in a work, elements that resisted complete subsumption into the subject. Even modern art, Riegl wrote in *The Group Portraiture of Holland,* preserved a "tense separation [*Auseinandersetzung*] between a subject, on the one hand, and things (i.e. extension, space), on the other, never a complete merging of the object in the subject, which would ultimately signal the end of the visual arts."[3] Relating past to present through a visual medium, this tension had a profoundly temporal character; it allowed the discerning art historian to trace temporal change (between past and present, progressive and regressive elements) in formal, visual juxtapositions. As I will argue, it stood as the basis of Riegl's formalist notion of time.

In "The Modern Cult of Monuments," Riegl distinguished between intentional monuments (those works constructed as memorials by their creators) and unintentional monuments (those artifacts that gained historical value with age). The former had a commemorative value inscribed at the time of their completion, whereas the latter had historical value and age value attached by subsequent observers.[4] The distinction is crucial because each type of monument embodied a specific form of temporality. Intentional monuments possessed historical worth because they withstood decay; they memorialized an incident for all time and thus in some sense escaped from time's grasp. Unintentional monuments, by contrast, gained historical value as a result of their ability to register the past, to show visible traces of age. Whereas intentional monuments staked a claim to eternity, the value of unintentional monuments resided in their "mortality" and appreciated over time. Most monuments, of course, had both intentional and unintentional qualities. An artwork's original meaning competed with its history of reception up to the present in determining its significance; the viewer and the work engaged in a kind of negotiation over meaning. Thus, an artwork's meaning was both objective (it had an identifiable era of origin, an original significance, and an irreducible materiality) and subjective (it changed with each successive present and needed the viewer to complete its meaning). The "tension" or "distance" between past and present itself became an object of art historical analysis, as did the relationship between successive presentist readings. The art historian Henri Zerner calls these relationships art historical "data" and describes Riegl's strategy as an attempt "to 'formalize' meaning"[5] within the visible space and depth of a work. By reading historical significance into the formal aspect of artworks, Riegl attempted to trace historical continuity perceptually in visible data.

An account of Riegl's formalist conception of time and history would be incomplete without an examination of his famously enigmatic notion of the *Kunstwollen*. By the time of *Late Roman Art Industry*, the term had come to designate an autonomous "art-will" that acted as the historical motor or impetus for artistic development.[6] An art historian's primary task was "to read the *Kunstwollen* . . . in works of art [*in den Kunstwerken . . . das Kunstwollen herauszulesen*]."[7] Not surprisingly, commentators dispute the meaning of this injunction.[8] The concept of *Kunstwollen* is elusive both because it seems highly abstract and because its meaning varies from context to context in Riegl's work. Most scholars agree that the *Kunstwollen* represented Riegl's conceptual effort to secure the independence of art among human pursuits. *Kunstwollen* designated the autonomous creative impulse expressed in all artworks. The development of new art forms, Riegl claimed, should not be attributed primarily to extra-artistic influences such as new materials, improved techniques, or changing social circumstances. Against the technical and functionalist theories of neo-Semperians, Riegl argued that the impulse to create art was anthropologically prior to technique; the *Kunstwollen* appropriated material and technical innovations to serve its purpose, not the reverse.[9] "This *Kunstwollen,*" he wrote, "freely calls on and chooses the appropriate artistic genre to fit its needs."[10] Moreover, commentators generally agree that Riegl identified style and form, rather than content, as the unique expressive medium of the *Kunstwollen.* Riegl's student Max Dvořák, for example, equated "Stilgeschichte" with "Geschichte des *Kunstwollens.*" "[B]uilding upon a clear and singular idea of development that identified the history of style with the history of art, [Riegl] believed that he had found the historical law of this development."[11] Beyond this general agreement about Riegl's hope to secure the anthropological autonomy of art through the study of stylistic history, however, there has been little concord as to the meaning and application of the term *Kunstwollen.* Scholars have given it variously cultural, psychological, symbolic, and formalist readings.

Wilhelm Worringer's *Abstraction and Empathy* is the best known, if not the most respected, cultural interpretation of *Kunstwollen.*[12] Citing Riegl's inspiration, Worringer argued that art history oscillated between periods of denaturalized abstraction and naturalistic empathy; each period produced its own cultural and anthropological type: Renaissance man, Baroque man, and so on. Worringer's *Kunstwollen* designated reified cultural and perceptual types that were expressed in artworks. The term described the sensibilities of cultural and racial groups as filtered through the psychology of an artist, who objectified the "latent inner demand which exists per se, entirely independent of the object and of the mode of creation, and behaves as will to form."[13] Although not all cultural readings of the *Kunstwollen* had such essentializing implications, they all tended to interpret individual artistic psychology as the filter for broader cultural or spiritual perception. Hans Sedlmayr, for example, disagreed with Worringer's claim that *Kunstwollen* could be reduced to the expression of an individual type, racial type, or *Zeitgeist,* but he insisted that it functioned as a "supra-individual will . . . like the 'Spirit,' something real, indeed a real force."[14] It is not surprising, then, that after World War II such theories came under stringent attack. In his renowned *Art and Illusion,* Ernst Gombrich condemned the "single-mindedness" of Riegl scholarship, attributing the fault to Riegl himself, whose will-to-form (the *Kunstwollen*) "becomes a ghost in the machine, driving the wheels of artistic development according to 'inexorable laws.' . . . It is not difficult to see in this picture of world history a revival of those romantic mythologies which found their climax in Hegel's philosophy of history."[15]

The cultural reading of Riegl's *Kunstwollen* did not lack challengers. In an essay entitled "Der Begriff des Kunstwollens," Erwin Panofsky proposed an alternate symbolic interpretation of the term.[16] The concept of *Kunstwollen,* he argued, did not reify either individual or social psychology; this interpretation falsely conflated the meaning of a work with an artist's intent. *Kunstwollen* did not describe an abstract synthesis of qualities—an essence—that somehow stood above and beyond the work; indeed, multiple *Kunstwollen* could exist within any artwork. Moreover, the *Kunstwollen* should not simply be read as a manifestation of the artwork's original cultural content; to reduce the meaning of artworks to their etiology was to commit a genetic fallacy that ignored the relationship between a work and its audience. Each of these misinterpretations worked to the same end in Panofsky's mind: each treated art solely in terms of content—historical, philosophical—that is, as the expression of largely extra-artistic circumstances and concepts. By contrast, Panofsky distinguished artworks from political or social "events"; the latter exhausted their meaning in historical explanation, whereas art demanded clarification in extra-historical terms. He attempted to sever the notion of *Kunstwollen* from historically reductive accounts that treated stylistic form only as a straightforward reflection of original cultural content. Instead, the concept of *Kunstwollen* designated an immanent *Sinnesgeschichte,* encompassing the internal symbolic expressivity of art in all its disjunctive signification. This symbolic potency bridged both the content and form of artistic images. To the extent that symbolic meaning was historical, its significance rested as much with the viewer as with the original artist.

Several recent theorists have downplayed cultural, psychological, and symbolic readings of the *Kunstwollen* and emphasized instead its expressly formalist implications. Interpreting *Kunstwollen* as a will-to-form, devoid of necessary content, Lambert Wiesing uses the term to characterize the formal, relational coordinates of a work. In a reading with Schopenhauerian and Aristotelian overtones, Wiesing interprets *Kunstwollen* as a kind of entelechy of creative will realizing itself in visual, material form.[17] Henri Zerner's interpretation, by contrast, emphasizes Riegl's training in empirical methodologies and his dedication to the rigors of positivistic science. To establish art history as *Wissenschaft,* Zerner writes, Riegl needed to outline an empirical method and establish positive, observable data for art historians to study. The concept of *Kunstwollen* was his attempt to designate as a scientific phenomenon the relationship between artistic form and historical development. Zerner disputes various commentators who have interpreted *Kunstwollen* as meaning one thing or another (nation, psychology, intention, will); he insists instead that *Kunstwollen* denoted "the whole complex of cultural connotations suggested by the individual work of art," a complex perceived as sensible form rather than expressive content.[18] According to Zerner, Riegl used the notion of *Kunstwollen* to define an immanent formal datum that could be registered empirically and described, not a conceptual meaning that demanded hermeneutic clarification. "It is the very *Kunstwollen,*" Zerner asserts, "this most elusive entity, that makes [Riegl's] approach scientific."[19] That the notion of *Kunstwollen* stretched the boundaries of "empirical datum" serves for Zerner to underscore the determination of Riegl's positivistic allegiances. It also shows, we might add, that Riegl held a very broad understanding of positivism, that he did not accept an empiricism narrowly restricted to straightforward sensory verification. A passage from Riegl's essay "Naturwerk und Kunstwerk" highlights the flexibility of his empiricism.

> There exists today a widespread philosophical trend, which in principle rejects all metaphysics and is determined to hold itself exclusively to the things given: this is dubbed positivistic (in the widest sense). If one carries the principles of this system of thought over into art history, then one would have to say that the production of art finds expression as a purely aesthetic impulse: from those (artists) who represent things in nature in a particular form and style, enhancing some aspects and suppressing others; for others (the public), who perceive these representations of nature in the very same

> form and style as they are given by contemporary artists. Of those things through which this impulse is determined—be it raw materials, technique or function, or visual memory—we remain no less than ignorant, perhaps will always remain ignorant: only the *Kunstwollen* remains as that single certain given thing.[20]

Riegl's aim was not, like Sickel, to use empirical criticism to establish, once and for all, "a succession of facts or events"; it was instead to trace development as such within art, according to an analytic and scientific framework that rested on empiricism but was not restricted to the immediately observable facts. The concept of *Kunstwollen* presumed a kind of evidence that took into account the subjective vision of the observer as well as the visual "data" of the observed object. It also offered an inherently temporal and historical account of cultural perception.

> The question is: how is development possible within this *Kunstwollen.* Just as the study of monuments themselves teaches us about the well-known phenomenon of temporal succession, it is apparent that development does not attach itself to things in nature as such, which tend to remain the same, but instead to the manner in which humans choose to represent things in nature at a given time. . . . I aim to show the developmental stages of the *Kunstwollen,* as it manifested itself in the conventionally recognized and distinct periods of style.[21]

Riegl's *Kunstwollen* cast the history of artistic style as first and foremost an empirical history of perception. Zerner's interpretation, however, limits Riegl's concept of *Kunstwollen* by reducing it to an unnecessarily empty sense of pure form and thereby ignores the imbrication of artistic and historical value that Riegl outlined in "The Modern Cult of Monuments." For example, Zerner describes the figure-spectator relationship in *The Group Portraiture of Holland* in terms of vectors, thereby draining rich historical content from visual forms by reducing them to pure geometry. Riegl's treatment of psychology and his "data of art history," however, comprised more than the narrow two and three-dimensional formal qualities of art that Zerner cites.[22] As Panofsky reminds us, even the purely formal aspects of art and artifacts had historical and temporal content. The dichotomy of form and content, therefore, is simply too schematic for making sense of Riegl's work. Moreover, Zerner hastens to psychologize the *Kunstwollen* along early Brentanian lines when he maintains that all artistic forms are presentations in the minds of viewers. Riegl would have rejected this claim as a totalizing imposition of modern subjectivism. As material and perceptual forms, artworks were themselves real objects possessing an autonomous external existence. Throughout his writing, Riegl defended external objectivity as a counterbalance to modern psychologistic and subjectivist tendencies.

> Modern subjectivism wants above all that things should no longer be considered things, that is, as outside our immediate objects, but instead be seen as merely subjective color-sensations. But this can only go so far. In contrast to earlier periods, which emphasized the tactile qualities of artworks above all, today one strives to emphasize the chromatic properties of an object to the point of forgetting all its other properties; things (that is, extensions) remain as the necessary substrata of color, and a color without an object . . . is indeed today still not possible.[23]

A painted human figure, for example, had an objective independence of line and form that existed in dialogue with a viewer's perception of it. An artwork retained an irreducible objectivity regardless of the subjective interpretations that would inevitably help to determine its meaning. Objectivity and subjectivity, artist and viewer coexisted in the work. Riegl's notion of *Kunstwollen* encompassed this interpenetrating subject/object duality in art as a historically conditioned, formal relationship. This duality was immanent within the work of art (both form and content had subjective and objective significance) and within the viewer/artwork relationship (both determining the significance of a work). Crucial for our purposes is that the *Kunstwollen* had its own distinct and constitutive mode of temporality, one that linked form and content in works of art and connected art with the external human world.

The *Kunstwollen* was more than a mere artistic principle in Riegl's oeuvre. In *Late Roman Art Industry,* he argued that the "visual *Kunst-*

wollen regulated the relationship of men to the sensual, perceptible appearance of things." The *Kunstwollen* was a component of a broader human *Wollen,* directed toward "the gratifying construction of [man's] relationship with the world." It governed the form-giving and form-perceiving capacities of this *Wollen* and bridged the gap between passive reception and active creation.

> All of man's will [*Wollen*] is directed toward the satisfying fashioning of his relations with the world (in the broadest sense of the word, as both internal and external to man). The visual *Kunstwollen* regulated the relationship of men to the sensible, perceptible appearances of things: it gives expression to the manner in which men at the time want to see things shaped or colored (just as the poetic *Kunstwollen* expresses the manner in which he wants to see things presented). But man is not only a being who receives things with his senses (passively), he is also a desiring being (active); thus he wants to interpret the world so as to openly and obligingly fit his desire (which varies with people, place, and time).[24]

Both *Kunstwollen* and *Wollen* were in turn determined by "what we call the worldview [*Weltanschauung*] (again in the widest sense of the word) of the time."[25] As comprehensive phenomena in Riegl's catalogue, the *Weltanschauung* and *Wollen* of an era shaped its religion and philosophy, science, state, and law. The *Kunstwollen,* in turn, governed the perceptual forms of human desire and shaped man's visual relationship with the world. As manifestations of the *Kunstwollen,* artworks registered this all-encompassing historical and cultural matrix. Thus, despite Riegl's rhetorical and methodological insistence on the autonomy of art, we must understand form not as a purely isolated artistic concept, but instead as a principle of spatial, temporal, and historical orientation connected with all aspects of life.

Riegl's notion of *Kunstwollen* was teleological in a very specific sense. "In contrast to the mechanistic conception of the essence of the artwork," he wrote, "I have adopted in *Problems of Style* a teleological view, in that I see in works of art the result of a definite and purposeful *Kunstwollen* that triumphs in conflict with function, raw materials, and technique."[26] The *Kunstwollen's* teleology was in fact quite distinct from that of historicist models, which developed progressively from one era to the next, perhaps culminating in some supreme end. As an expression of artistic form, the *Kunstwollen* was localized in the space of an artwork, not extended across historical time. Any particular *Kunstwollen* manifested specific artistic characteristics within the sharply delimited temporal and spatial boundaries of an artwork—framed, localized, chronologically fixed. Riegl's teleology, therefore, as Wiesing suggests, described the realization of a formal entelechy, an actualization of expressive formal features, not a historical progression toward some ultimate future goal. Francesco dal Co recognizes this feature of Riegl's thought when he writes that "every 'artistic event' shows . . . an autonomous will that is different from the norms of the times," distinct from the historical context that holds it.[27] In this regard, Riegl followed his Austrian forebear Leibniz by characterizing an artwork as an expressive monad, a visual form encompassing its own process of self-realization.[28] Artistic form contained inherently temporal impulses that progressed toward a self-actualization that was *prior* to progressive historical time. Thus, the temporality of the artwork must be understood as conceptually distinct from historical time. The nature of their connection—what Sergio Bettini cites as the creative will "alluding" to the "direction of artistic culture in the order of history"[29]—might again best be conceived in Leibnizian terms: the artwork-monad, though self-sufficient, reflected its historical world as a kind of mirror. It was at once a temporally constituted work that staked a claim to its own formal self-sufficiency, and an expression of the cultural context from which it emerged. Art monuments possessed a formal temporality, a duration and protensity that recalled the work of production, recognized the time of viewing, and anticipated formal development. They were visual objectifications of temporal relationships, at once materializations of time's traces and physical registers of its multiple, sometimes conflicting forms. Art expressed *Zeit* as well as *Zeitgeist*.

Though Riegl did not embrace a historicist notion of teleology, his universal outlook was punctuated by local teleologies that shaped individual epochs and particular artworks. In *Problems of Style*, for example, vegetal decorative motifs developed with a kind of relentless inner momentum toward their fulfillment in the naturalized tendrils and acanthus leaves of Greek ornament. A single, unified development encompassed apparently distinct motivic forms, and innovation was driven by a kind of inner formal logic. Similarly, Riegl's *Late Roman Art Industry* traced the gradual, step-by-step emergence of space as an object of artistic concern in the late Roman Empire, an evolution revealed in various artifacts in subtle, often unexpected ways. Finally, *The Group Portraiture of Holland* traced the emergence of a "typically Hollandish painting,"[30] which emphasized space and attention, through three stages that displayed progressive and retrograde features depending upon the influence of non-native artistic demands. Art history for Riegl passed through successive stages, each with its own teleology, yet each a phase in a continuous and universal artistic development.

Riegl's simultaneous reliance on universal history and an explicitly localized *Kunstwollen* set up a tension between the dehistoricized (but not detemporalized) artwork and the diachronic movement of history. "Step-by-step development," Riegl announced at the outset of *Problems of Style,* "[is the] basis of the historical method";[31] but this commitment to stepwise analysis did not make historical continuity and localized temporality conceptually synonymous. The *Kunstwollen* designated a micro-teleology of localized artistic traits manifested in the artwork; each work staked a claim to a kind of trans-historical value in that it was predicated on a dehistoricized notion of temporality as entelechy. Each *Kunstwollen,* however, defined a self-contained work or period that connected up with other works to form stages—"steps"—in a universal history of artistic development. These steps could be national or epochal periods—ancient, medieval, and modern; Greek, Roman, Italian, French, or Hollandish—or individual artworks. Riegl's tendency to posit seemingly synchronic historical eras, therefore, coexisted with a fascination for artistic transition and change. In fact, the distinction between transitional eras, such as late Rome or the Baroque, and golden ages, such as the Renaissance or classical Greece, was not absolute for Riegl. He tended to find transitional qualities in even apparently stable artistic periods and seminal innovations in times of supposed decadence. *Problems of Style,* for example, traced the continuous internal transformation of decorative motifs across and within periods, from ancient Egypt through Greece and into the medieval Arab world. Within each era, individual artworks revealed stages in the self-contained historical development of that period as well as steps in a wider historical development. Thus, the internal development of an artistic period mirrored the progression of universal history as a whole. Progressive history and the local teleologies of artworks upon which it was built were conceptually distinct but complementary phenomena in Riegl's thought.

Riegl's notion of progressive history closely resembled Bergson's concept of a vital creative impulse, elaborated most fully in the 1907 volume *Creative Evolution.* Bergson described evolution as an "original impulse" that passed from one generation to the next, "bridg[ing] the interval between the generations."[32] "Life evolve[s] before our eyes as a continuous creation of unforeseeable form"; evolution was not mere appearance or idea, but intrinsic to the matter of life itself.[33] "What is real is the continual change of form," Bergson asserted. "Form is only a snapshot view of transition." The essential continuity of organic forms conflicted with our mental tendency to parcel time in discrete units.

> For I speak of each of my states as if it formed a block and were a separate whole. I say indeed that I change, but the change seems to me to reside in the passage from one state to the next: of each state, taken separately, I am apt to think that it remains the same during all the time that it prevails. Nevertheless, a slight effort of attention would reveal to me that there is no feeling, no idea, no volition which is not undergoing change every moment: if a mental state ceased to vary, its duration would cease to flow. . . . The truth is that we change without ceasing, and that the state itself is nothing but change. This amounts to saying that there is no essential difference between passing from one state to another and persisting in the same state.[34]

Bergson described this temporal passage in terms of "real time," which, he argued, was the stuff that made up psychic life. Each of our states amounted to the creation of "self by self," so that our "existence" could only be properly understood in terms of constant change.[35] Creative evolution was the fundamental quality of life. It is easy to hear in his words an echo of Riegl's own emphasis on the temporality of form and the continuity of history. Bergson in fact compared life to an artwork in that both represented a kind of continuous transformation and creation. Yet while the organic world was subject to the duration and rhythms of continuous transformation, inorganic objects fell outside the scope of Bergson's time and history.[36] Riegl, as we have seen, diverged from Bergson in his belief that art objects also possessed a formal temporality.

In Riegl's analysis, artworks embodied temporal juxtapositions. Monuments expressed a localized temporality of self-realization, embodied time in the formal traces of age, and comprised integral links in a universal historical chain. These marks of art's temporal constitution registered on the physiognomy—the visible surface—of an artwork, so that viewing and interpreting art were temporally and historically charged activities. This complex interaction between time and art can perhaps be clarified by recourse to an analogy with photography, a medium toward which Riegl was cautiously favorable.[37] According to Roland Barthes, the photograph is a perfect *analogon* of reality. Its peculiar hold over us does not result from symbolic or iconic qualities. Instead, the power of photographs derives from the fact that they contain objective traces of the past. "The realists," Barthes writes, "do not take the photograph for a 'copy of reality,' but for an emanation of past reality: a magic, not an art."[38] The photograph is "somehow co-natural with its referent";[39] it depicts the having-been-there of an object as a being-there-now with the viewing subject by showing the past as an objective "thereness," a presence that is at once temporalized and detemporalized. In simultaneously bridging the temporal distance between past and present and depicting that distance as irretrievable loss, photographs provide absolute evidence of the past and at the same time portray death as their fundamental *eidos.*[40] Though Riegl would probably dismiss the thaumaturgical and thanatological aspects of Barthes's analysis, his conception of art as a depiction of temporal passage can be understood in terms similar to Barthes's conception of the photograph. The artwork's objectivity resided in its visual re-presentation of temporality and history as form.

10

Seeing Time in *The Group Portraiture of Holland*

Riegl's last major work, *The Group Portraiture of Holland* (1902), was written contemporaneously with "The Modern Cult of Monuments" and displayed a similar interest in historiography and temporality.[1] Toward the end of the volume, in a historiographical excursus, Riegl dismissed the view that "individual evolutionary phases succeeded each other in discrete, strictly divisible stages." Art history taught us instead that artistic evolution "proceeds in gradual but steady transitions."[2] This process was uneven: "An artwork can make tremendous progress in an aspect that the artist concentrates on solving while other aspects appear more backward; and yet because the aspects compensate for each other, on balance the work retains its normal position in the development."[3] This uneven continuity unified various strands in the development of Dutch group portraiture and connected the tradition with a broader, universal art history. At the same time, however, the artistic and historiographical insights Riegl gleaned from group portraiture remained closely tied to the rules and conventions of that period genre.

When discussing *The Group Portraiture of Holland,* scholars tend to highlight four crucial themes. Foremost among these is Riegl's concept of attention [*Aufmerksamkeit*], which indicated a psychological state linking figures in a scene with viewers outside the canvas.[4] Along with will and emotion, attention designated a mode of psychological expression displayed throughout the history of the pictorial arts. Wolfgang Kemp notes that the categories of will, emotion, and attention define more than simple pictorial modes; they illustrate, to use Kemp's phrase, "Riegl's more or less homespun anthropology":[5] three psychological attitudes toward external objects, three ways in which men relate visually to the world. Classical and Renaissance art, which emphasized will and emotion through action, tended to isolate individuals from their surroundings and depict them in struggle with the external world. Dutch art, by contrast, fostered an attentive psychology that calmly bound men to their surroundings.

> The individual opens up to the outside world, not in order to subjugate it [in an act of will], and also not to unite with it in pleasure or retreat from it in displeasure [in an act of emotion], but in pure, selfless interest. Attention is passive, in that it lets external things affect it without seeking to overcome them; at the same time, it is active, in that it searches things out, but without trying to make them subservient to selfish pleasure.[6]

Group portraiture only became comprehensible through an attentive viewing that preserved both subject and object by setting them in an interdependent relationship. Margaret Olin thus recognizes attention as more than simply an impartial aesthetic category for Riegl; his celebration of "pure, selfless interest"—as psychological mode and as anthropology—implied an "ethics of attention" as well as an artistic analysis.[7]

Riegl's concept of attention gives rise to a second oft-remarked theme in *The Group Portraiture of Holland:* the dissolution of the plane between scene and viewer. Riegl analyzed the development in Amsterdam and Haarlem of painterly techniques for incorporating the attentive viewer as a participant in the activity of a scene. Figural gestures and gazes were used to draw the viewer into the painting, enacting in the painted medium the joint subjective and objective conferral of meaning that Riegl discussed in "The Modern Cult of Monuments." The figures in Dirck Jacobsz's portraits, for example, had eyes that gazed steadfastly from the canvas toward the viewer and hands that "spoke" in expressive gestures. These devices unified the painted scene in both space and moment, and expressed a Dutch attentiveness toward their environment that was unique in the history of art.[8] Wolfgang Kemp sees in this emphasis on the spectator a forerunner of *Rezeptionsästhetik* and a shift in Riegl's thinking away from his earlier formalist preoccupations;[9] I argue, by contrast, that throughout his career Riegl encompassed the space and time of viewing in his formalist history of art.

A third theme that commentators highlight in *The Group Portraiture of Holland* is the compositional depiction of free space [*Freiraum*]. *Late Roman Art Industry* had traced the emergence of space as a bounded object in late Roman artworks, which like all ancient art tended toward depiction on the plane. *The Group Portraiture of Holland* picked up this theme by presenting three-dimensional free space as a device used by Dutch painters to unify otherwise isolated figures into psychological collectives. Even wholly separate objects could be clustered together within a palpable space. In Rembrandt's paintings, for example, objects were "so softly bound with the surrounding space"[10] that, as Riegl argues earlier in the volume, "figures (the cubic space of bodies) and free space presented a single homogeneous whole. . . . Solid shapes become merely denser accumulations scattered here and there in free space."[11] Space and objects were quantitatively but not qualitatively distinct. Moreover, free space helped to incorporate the viewer into the scene by establishing a continuum between the space of the scene and the space of the viewer. Along with disinterested attention, which linked figures and viewers on a psychological level, visible free space helped to dissolve the plane between a painting and the world.

Finally, many commentators have lamented the substratum of national stereotypes that seem to underpin Riegl's otherwise subtle analysis. Indeed, *The Group Portraiture of Holland* applied the concept of *Kunstwollen,* seemingly universal in implication, to the task of identifying attributes of a typically Hollandish art. Here as elsewhere, however, Riegl's recourse to cultural archetypes and binary oppositions masked an analytic sense that was anything but dualistic or essentialist. For example, although his lecture on "Salzburg's Stellung in der Kunstgeschichte" (1904) apparently relied on a pat distinction between northern European and Italian aesthetic norms, it mitigated that dichotomy by arguing that geographic boundaries were porous and that artistic forms grew from cultural cross-fertilization.[12] Although modern commentators tend to balk at Riegl's cultural typologizing, especially in its more overt moments when stereotypes supplant analysis,[13] *The Group Portraiture of Holland* is rich enough in other themes to maintain its intellectual currency.[14]

A theme that has not yet been significantly examined is the concept of temporality that informed Riegl's history of group portraiture. The general history of pictorial composition, according to Riegl, revealed several distinct modes of temporal depiction in paintings. The first mode he called "subordination." A strategy specific to history paintings, from which group portraiture emerged,[15] subordination marshaled figures around a common, central action. A favored genre of Italian Renaissance artists, history paintings achieved pictorial unity by depicting a specific event—often a recognizable moment in chronological or mythological time—and orienting figures hierarchically according to their involvement in the central action.[16] A spatial punctum (point of view, vanishing point) organized the visual scene and marked the moment of action (the historical event, the chronological date). Spatial and temporal punctuality determined figural arrangement. As we saw with Wickhoff's notion of complementary depiction, spatial contiguity indicated temporal proximity and figural priority. History paintings emphasized "historical events," those deeds that occurred just once, not repeatedly, in the lives of the men depicted.[17] Italian painters attempted to capture such events and acts of will in a single image of momentary narrative action. The very singularity of the event required the artist to arrange figures around a central point. Like a courtier whose influence depended upon access to the duke, a figure's importance hinged on its proximity to the scene's central action. Chronology found its spatial *analogon* in single-point perspective, for each demanded a punctuality that marshaled its subjects hierarchically.

One of the innovations of Dutch group portraiture, on the other hand, was to develop pictorial techniques for conveying the fraternal spirit of Dutch civic guardsmen.[18] The move away from the hierarchy and subordination of historical painting toward greater equality and figural coordination covered more than a century and comprised several phases. Early group portraitists such as Dirck Jacobsz applied a strategy of depiction that Riegl called coordination, aimed at de-emphasizing action as the unifying element in a painting. These artists reduced the activities in a scene, confounded its temporal coherence, and depicted everyday events that lacked singular historical significance. In Jacobsz's "Civic Guard Group Portrait of 1529," for example, symbolism replaced action as the source of pictorial coherence.[19]

The figures gaze intently out at the viewer, and their hands gesture earnestly in various directions. The gazes and gestures do not indicate a central action or single vanishing point; they point in many directions and cannot be linked to a single event that prompts them. Riegl argued that these actions need to be read symbolically, not narratively. "[S]ymbolism requires the viewer to associate specific attributes and figures with particular abstract qualities (in this instance, that of civic spirit)."[20] As the unifying hierarchy of action disappears, we are left with a symbolic unity of space, attention, and fraternity.

For pictorial symbolism to establish its connection among objects and abstract qualities, it had to appear in a scene that was suspended from historical time. Dutch artists depicted everyday scenes with activities so common that they could not be recognized as historical events and could not be attached to a particular moment. In Jacobsz's "Portrait of a Man," for example, the figure is engaged in the mundane activity of computing with chalk on a table. The temporal coherence of the scene is disturbed by the fact that the man stares off into space at the viewer, an unlikely pose to accompany his calculations. Furthermore, a wine glass, an apple, a fruit peel, and the hilt of the man's sword act as symbols; they are not evidently relevant to the man's activity, and so they disrupt the sense of a unified moment or action.[21] Riegl interpreted the banquet in Teunissen's "Civic Guard Group Portrait of 1533" not as a historical event, but as a "symbolischen Kunstzweck," memorializing the custom of sealing brotherhood with a drink.[22] And of the anonymous "Civic Guard Group Portrait of 1541," Riegl wrote: "One wonders if we really have before our eyes a specific historical moment, as we did with Geertgen and Scorel, or a purely symbolic reference to type, which formed the conceptual basis of the civic group portrait of Dirck Jacobsz. . . . One is soon convinced that this master also strove to depict the psychological coherence among the seventeen portrait figures through the use of objective symbolism."[23] Early Dutch group portraiture made elaborate use of symbolism to disrupt the temporal punctuality of historical paintings and assert a new mode of pictorial coherence and temporality that was not based on the singular moment. Whereas action marshaled figures according to a hierarchy of punctuality, symbolic paintings coordinated them through the use of associative symbols.

While historical paintings sought coherence in the fixed temporal moment and symbolic works relaxed temporal punctuality in favor of symbolic equality, genre painting, the third and most typical category of Dutch group portraiture, achieved pictorial unity by combining elements of both the subordinating and coordinating modes. "[G]enre painting elevated the everyday to the status of the eternal," Riegl wrote, "whereas earlier historical painting believed that the eternal could only be expressed through exceptional events."[24] The incidents chosen for depiction by genre artists were "no longer historically meaningful"; instead, they were often unusual or awkward, inducing the viewer to ponder their "irresistible necessity."[25] Genre artists strove to capture both the singularity of historical paintings and the rich significance of symbolic art. Under the pioneering influence of Pieter Breugel the Elder, genre painting achieved a kind of transcendent timeliness by revealing the symbolic imperatives of the merely temporal (as opposed to the historical) incident. Thus it attempted to overcome the "äußere Bedeutungslosigkeit" of the unhistorical incident depicted. Once again, Dirck Jacobsz exemplified this trend. Of his "Civic Guard Group Portrait of 1563," Riegl wrote: "For the first time we see a unified pictorial treatment used to express the unity among the members of a civic guard group. This is not a 'historical' treatment of action that took place only once, but rather a recurrent event whose meaning rests simply in this frequent and typical repetition: in other words—a genre treatment."[26] The painting combined a common unified action with the presence of numerous awkward details—stray gazes and broken lines—that disrupted the overall coherence.[27] Despite resistance to the hierarchy of historical scenes, genre painters gradually and hesitantly reincorporated common action, pictorial subordination, and even a limited spatial and temporal coherence, all of which symbolic painting had abandoned when it renounced the conceptual subordination of history painting. In genre art, chiaroscuro and free space were used to mute the effects of a renewed hierarchy and create a localized atmosphere that Riegl described as "introspective" and "soulful" [*Gemütsausdruck*].[28] Dutch portraits, remarked Riegl, "portray soul [*Gemüt*] not size."[29]

Each compositional mode of early Dutch portraiture privileged its own characteristic temporality. Historical painting organized a scene punctually and hierarchically; symbolic painting stressed a detemporalized coordination of figures; and genre painting evoked the transcendent moment, at once temporal and eternal, hierarchical and coordinated. In Riegl's account, these modes interwove throughout the sixteenth- and seventeenth-century flowering of Dutch portraiture, achieving their greatest expression in the work of Rembrandt and Hals. Riegl's typology of pictorial modes, therefore, was not a set of exclusive categories but, rather, a group of recombinant traits and temporalities that generated new pictorial forms according to the *Kunstwollen* of the period.[30]

Riegl situated group portraiture within the more long-term development of a universal historical will, or *Wollen,* that shaped the medieval and early modern *Kunstwollen* and extended beyond the Netherlands. He characterized the medieval Christian worldview in terms of an intellectual dualism between mind and body, between an isolating, psychological subjectivity and an external objectivity that constrained human beings. The evolution of the relationship between subject and object was a historical theme that ran throughout Riegl's work and manifested itself in the particular equipoise of each artistic era. In ancient times, material objectivity predominated over subjective interpretation. In the medieval worldview, the subject confronted an all-powerful divine objectivity. By modern times, subjective interpretation played an increasing role in man's relationship with the world of objects. Art history revealed the visual manifestations of this dualism. Pictorially, the struggle between subject and object was expressed in depictions of the human form, especially the eyes. Whereas classical antiquity focused on the face—objective, mirrorless, flat—medieval Christian artists highlighted the eyes as "mirrors of the soul."[31] Citing Wickhoff's *Wiener Genesis,* Riegl noted that typical medieval figures "whose bodies face the viewer nearly or completely, strain their eyes sideways in the direction of the other figures in the scene. This effect is enhanced in some medieval figures in that individual limbs move in impossible directions and even appear dislocated. From a modern perspective, this would be considered clumsiness, but this dismissal overlooks the particular stylistic will [*Wollen*] exhibited in the scene."[32] The position of the eyes and the body came to stand for the relationship between subjective vision and the objective world. Classical composure oriented eyes and bodies in the same direction, whereas medieval psychomachy emphasized "a bifurcation in two directions."[33] Thus, when early modern artists manipulated eyes and gestures to express inner soulfulness, activity, or attention, they were reworking the relationship between subject and object by drawing on traditional visual tropes in figural composition.

The early modern sense of visuality took multiple forms. In a comparison of Italian Renaissance art and early Dutch portraiture, Riegl distinguished between two distinct modes of vision: "der Blick" and "der packende Blick."

> Take the example of an Italian portrait from the fifteenth century, such as that of Cardinal Francesco Gonzaga painted by Mantegna, hanging in the Camera degli Sposi in Mantua, with its riveting gaze [*packenden Blick*], its palpably sensuous eyeballs and lips which directly affect the viewer. The objects have such a powerful sensuous influence that the observer, the subject, completely forgets himself. When we compare this with our Knights of St. John [in Geertgen van Haarlem's "Legend of John the Baptist"], who direct their glances [*Blick*], unassuming but full of inner life, inwards as well as outwards, one does not even perceive the material, three-dimensional eyes as they watch. Only intimate observation by a thoughtful subject, who devotes the time to rediscover himself within the scene, can do justice to its inner sense and meaning.[34]

Evelyn M. Kain and David Britt's 2000 translation of *The Group Portraiture of Holland* rendered "der Blick" and "der packende Blick" as "the glance" and "the gaze."[35] For our purposes, the importance of Riegl's glances and gazes was not what they revealed about the figures on the canvas but the effect they had on the viewer. The gaze could express a figure's soulful and attentive engagement with the external world, or it could have the effect, as it did in Mantegna's "Portrait of Cardinal Francesco Gonzaga," of abolishing a viewer's autonomy by absorbing him into the scene before him. In the latter case, the painting effectively fixed an audience with *its* gaze. By contrast, the glance in Geertgen's painting, although its furtive restlessness suggested distraction, actually belied a deep introspection, a soulful attentiveness that engaged but did not dominate the external world. It is important to recognize that the glance and the gaze were not irreconcilable modes of visuality in Riegl's pictorial catalogue; in Dutch art, the glance transformed an external gaze that subordinated its viewers into an internal gaze that invited them into penetrating association and communion. This transformation, according to Riegl, passed through several historical stages. Initially, figures in Dutch paintings gazed directly out at their subjects. More soulful than their Italian counterparts, these intense gazes served as an overt method for inviting the viewer to calm reflection on the portrait. Because multiple figures stared off in many directions, Riegl asserted that early group portraiture presumed multiple subjects, not a single ideal viewer or vantage point. By the seventeenth century, however, figures gazing out of the canvas gave way to figures who did not directly acknowledge the viewer through eye contact; these later figures glanced at one another, at objects on the canvas, or at transactions taking place in the scene. The glances, sometimes oblique and sidelong, served to unify the figures around a particular action or moment. However, although they incorporated aspects of Italian subordinating composition, seventeenth-century Dutch portraits still managed to convey a deep and thoughtful inner life through the use of free space and the attitude of attention. Unlike early group portraiture, the pictorial unification of later Dutch scenes invoked a single psychological and temporal viewer, intimately engaged with the scene in a state of attentive participation. The singular viewing subject, Riegl insisted, was conjured *psychologically,* without either the overwhelming reliance on action or the commanding gaze of Italian art.

In *Vision and Painting: The Logic of the Gaze,* Norman Bryson points out further distinctions between the gaze and the glance. Like Riegl, Bryson claims that the gaze absorbs and dominates the viewing subject. He describes its effect as an erasure of the traces of time, both the time of painting and the time of the subject matter depicted.

> Like the stylus in the mystic writing pad, the brush traces *obliteratively,* as indelible effacement; and whatever may have been the improvisational logic of the painting's construction, this existence of the image in its own time, of duration, of practice, of the body, is negated by never referring the marks on canvas to their place in the vanished sequence of local inspirations, but only to the twin axes of temporality outside durée: on the one hand, the moment of origin, of the founding perception; and on the other, the moment of closure, of receptive passivity: to a transcendent temporality of the Gaze.[36]

Paintings of the gaze mask the inherently temporal process of their own creation by presenting scenes with an auratic timelessness and eternity. This *aoristic* gaze, as Bryson calls it, recognizes only moments abstracted from temporal flux—the origin, the now—and obliterates duration (*durée,* production, viewing) as an object of depiction. The image becomes "pure idea,"[37] and the subject, viewing in time, is absorbed by the timeless gaze of the scene. The gaze privileges the now-moments of Riegl's newness value and the originary moments of intentional memorials. For Bryson, Titian's "Bacchus and Ariadne" exemplifies this viewpoint "of an all-knowing eternity" exempt from the change and decay that shapes the sublunary world. The Italian artist's "constellation" of visual meaning is an abstraction, a myth, an image that dominates an eye that can never quite take it in and must therefore approach it with awe and humility. The term Bryson chooses to describe this operation of the gaze is "consideration": "In its root form, the word *consideration* refers to exactly this transcendent operation of vision, where the stars (*sidera*) are seen together, the constellations made and named by subduing the random configurations of the night sky to the order of celestial geometry: the constellation is that which just exceeds the boundary of the empirical glance."[38] Constellations establish synchronic relationships in an otherwise empirically undifferentiated field of stars. In the consideration of a gaze that obliterates traces of time, constellations suppress the different temporalities and origins of the stars, whose light seems to emanate from a synchronous source.[39] The glance, by contrast—brief, furtive, indirect, distracted—denotes a less transfixing activity of the eyes. "Painting of the glance," Bryson writes, "addresses vision in the durational temporality of the viewing subject; it does not seek to bracket out the process of viewing, nor in its own techniques does it exclude the traces of the body of labor."[40] Whereas the gaze transfixes temporality and renders images in the monumentalized form of myth-history,[41] the glance preserves traces of the time of production and the time of viewing.[42]

We do not find in Riegl's work any pure examples of the gaze or the glance; instead, both modes of visuality combine in ways that alternately reinforce and mitigate each other. Clearly, the painting of the "packende Blick," or gaze, predominated in Italian art, whereas Dutch portrait painters preferred "der Blick," the glance. The absorbing gaze of Mantegna's "Cardinal Gonzaga" found its proper setting in the transcendent timelessness of Italian historical painting, which absorbed the viewer into a scene extracted from the temporal flux of moments and monumentalized as a timeless scene. As Bryson suggests, the aura attached to the historical image reflects its parthenogenesis in an act of inspiration idealized and classified according to date of completion. Punctuality privileged the moment of inspiration over the work of realization by ignoring the temporality of production; it thus mythologized the artwork as a work of genius. Chronology and myth served the same function here, for they both lifted extraordinary events out of temporal *durée* and monumentalized them in historico-chronological time. The gaze, in Riegl's analysis of Mantegna, effected this abstraction of both subject and scene; the gaze froze temporality and rendered it in the fixed time-points of chronology, the scene of myth.

Dutch portraiture, by contrast, used glances to depict unity and coherence in the durational moment. In early group portraiture, according to Riegl, glances still betrayed the remnants of medieval dualism,[43] for the eyes were positioned awkwardly within the face. By the late sixteenth century, figures began to gaze out of the canvas, setting up "an instantaneous tension"[44] by making eye contact with viewing subjects. This overt gesture, inviting viewer attention, established external pictorial coherence at the expense of internal coherence; the disconnected figures often stared off in various directions, which suggested multiple viewers. This compositional tactic gave way during the seventeenth century to a unity centered on internal glances among figures. Instead of historicizing/mythicizing a scene by depicting it as a timeless point or date, the glance invited the viewer's involvement by acknowledging the duration of viewing, at once distinct from and continuous with the scene. Even when the scene took place in a coherent moment, as was the case in later group portraits, that moment was open to the temporal world of the viewer. In lieu of direct gazes, external coherence was established psychologically by creating a pictorial atmosphere that fused with the time and space of the viewer. By the era of Rembrandt and Hals, the overt gaze was no longer needed to attract the subject's attention.[45] Glances among figures on the canvas animated a painting and established spatial and temporal coherence without relying on gazes between figures and the viewer. Thus, Dutch painting evolved from treating viewers as objects to be addressed by an "apostrophic" gaze, to invoking them as singular subjects attracted to communion by the inner reflectiveness of the scene. Later group portraiture invited attention but did not demand it.

> As a result of this intense process of his conscious experience, the viewing subject becomes implicated in the inner coherence of the scene, and is so deeply engaged in the reality of its happenings, that the scene shifts from an external occurrence to an inner experience. . . . The baroque dualism was no longer emphasized and the object and subject were brought closer together through the psychological mechanism [neutralizing attention] mentioned above.[46]

The combined work of gazes and glances mitigated the dualism between mind and body, human subject and divine object. As a viewer was drawn into the scene, so the scene was drawn into the viewer. The scene implied its own continuation, not simply in narrative action, but in the "space" of viewing. Whereas the punctuality of Italian Renaissance art privileged a timeless point of view, Dutch group portraiture stressed the durational moment of production and of viewing. A scene did not just happen; it was a happening.[47]

This temporal relationship between artwork and viewer had specific formal parameters. Artworks rendered temporality observable according to what Riegl called the fundamental law of rhythm, a concept I examine in detail in chapter 12. It is important to note here that Bryson too applies the term rhythm, normally associated with the musical arts, to the visual field. "To dissolve the Gaze," he writes

> we must willingly enter into the partial blindness of the Glance and dispense with the conception of form as consideration, as Arrest, and try to conceive of form instead in dynamic terms, as matter in process, in the sense of the original, pre-Socratic word for form: *rhuthmos,* rhythm, the impress on matter of the body's internal energy, in the mobility and vibrancy of its somatic rhythms; the body of labor, of material practice.[48]

"Rhythm" impressed temporality on matter as dynamic form, externalized, objective. For Riegl as for Bryson, the term designated form as a temporal inscription. We can conceive of this notion in a phenomenological sense. Like Husserl and Brentano, Riegl recognized that time submitted to examination only indirectly, as it *appeared* in objects or artifacts. "[A] phenomenological analysis of time," declared Husserl in his 1905 lecture on inner time consciousness, "cannot explain the constitution of time without reference to the constitution of the temporal Object."[49] Objects were, in a phenomenological sense, objectifications of time insofar as they were temporally constituted. Phenomenological *avant la lettre,* Riegl's art history sought to trace temporality objectified in artworks. Indeed, visual art was in some sense the quintessential medium of time's presentation. Art objects, to use Husserl's phrase, "not only are unities in time but also include temporal extension in themselves."[50] They are not simply objects that appear *in* time, but objects that appear *as* time.

11

The Anthropological Autonomy of Art

In the introduction to *Problems of Style,* Riegl announced his formalist allegiances by defining art's unique historical significance in terms of perceptual form, not expressive or mimetic content. "A random scribble is not a form of art,"[1] he asserted, not because it wanted meaning but because it lacked articulate form. Riegl based his artistic formalism on a ostensible human impulse to visualize and create forms in matter, an anthropological urge that he called the "immanent artistic drive" [*immanenter künstlerische Trieb*].[2] "The urge to decorate," he wrote, "is one of the most elementary human drives, more elementary even than the need to protect the body."[3] An admiration for the disciplines and methods of anthropology and ethnology permeated Riegl's thought and informed his art historical claims. In 1896, for example, he compared art history unfavorably to ethnology, praising the latter for the inclusiveness of its scientific study; scholars in his own discipline, by contrast, tended to exclude from examination whole categories of relevant artifacts.[4]

Riegl's earliest book, *Altorientalische Teppiche* (1891), only hinted at the role that anthropology would play in his historiography. Unlike his more renowned works, *Altorientalische Teppiche* tied artistic development—in this case, the history of Near Eastern rug patterning—to technical and economic change, invoking a kind of cultural sociology that bore surprising affinities with Semper's technical-materialist thesis, which he later attacked. The so-called geometric style of decorative rug patterning, for example, which Riegl incorporated into his ornamental history in *Problems of Style,* grew out of needs specific to a particular stage of nomadic life and social conditions related to the mode of household production peculiar to Near Eastern peoples. Even the development of naturalism in Oriental rugs was linked to economic considerations, in this case the growing demand for Persian luxury rugs used for decorative, nonutilitarian purposes (as opposed to nomadic rugs used to cover floors and walls). Naturalism and figuration contributed to the development of distinct national styles, gradually fragmenting the tradition of rug design into various indigenous branches.[5]

By the time of *Problems of Style,* Riegl had moved away from technical and materialist accounts of art history. He used anthropology not to propose an externalist account of art history but to demonstrate that a creative drive was embedded in the very origins of human society. "All of art history presents itself as a perpetual struggle with material; not the tool, which is determined by technique, but the artistically creative idea is primary. It strives to expand its formal domain and increase its productive capacities."[6] Art expressed a fundamental human need, equal in priority to other aspects of primordial human culture. In an early lecture on the history of ornament, Riegl remarked that anthropology and formalist theory had at times to make up for a paucity of empirical evidence.[7] Anthropological speculation served just such a purpose in *Problems of Style,* where it replaced material evidence for those periods when artifacts were insufficient to establish formal trends; anthropology was especially useful in clarifying art's origins in the prehistoric past. Riegl argued that the "Schmuckbedürfniss,"[8] a desire to decorate, was an "elementary need [*elementare Bedürfnis*]" so basic to human psychology that it mooted efforts at pinpointing a chronological origin for art. The origins of creativity, embedded deep in human culture, were accounted for by anthropology and psychology not empirical history. The architectural theorist Francesco dal Co describes the *Schmuckbedürfniss* as a "primitive desire for the world [fulfilled] by putting into practice representational strategies capable of dominating the 'world's material' by bending it to fit the forms of desire."[9] The pleasure taken in formal beauty preceded and catalyzed technical innovation. Technique served the creative drive, not the reverse. According to Riegl, decorations found on ancient artifacts or on the walls of the Dordogne caves suggested that a primal *horror vacui,* an anthropological fear of empty space, motivated early man to cover blank areas with decorative forms.[10] Decoration created a visual presence and fullness that exorcised the unfathomable void of death, eternity, and emptiness. All early art, therefore, whether figural or geometric, was first and foremost decorative; its main purpose was apotropaic, to allay a primal fear by filling empty space. These anthropological claims secured the formal autonomy of Riegl's art history by providing a theory of human motivation to underpin the empirical data of artworks.[11]

In *Problems of Style,* Riegl sought to demonstrate the "inner genetic coherence" of ancient art.[12] "All art," he famously asserted, "is inextricably tied to nature. Every artistic form is based on a form of nature."[13] In the opening pages, Riegl designated the fundamental laws of art as "Symmetrie" and "Rhythmus." These basic principles corresponded to rudimentary natural forms: "The same laws of symmetry and rhythm are indeed those that nature uses in the formation of its phenomena (man, animals, plants, crystals), and it does not require a great insight in order to notice the basic planimetric forms and configurations latent within natural things."[14] Both art and nature adhered to common, formal principles, Riegl noted that "the geometric art forms behave with regard to other forms of art just as the laws of mathematics do in relation to living natural laws."[15] The regular patterns of rhythm and symmetry, expressed most basically in geometric art, governed the forms of naturalistic and figural art as well, just as mathematical relationships characterized even the most intricate forms of life and nature.

Though Riegl stressed the "close connection of all art forms with the physical appearances of nature [*körperlichen Naturerscheinungen*],"[16] he did not propose a mimetic theory of art. According to most mimetic theories, art strove with greater or lesser success to emulate objects and patterns from nature. This commitment tended to limit art to realistic and naturalistic modes of depiction, thus ignoring or dismissing the wide variety of nonrealist artistic styles. A formalist approach, by contrast, analyzed artworks in terms of color, line, shape, and figural relationship and thereby allowed for a much broader definition of art. Whereas artworks followed the same formal laws as nature, according to Riegl artists did not apply those laws in order to copy natural scenes. Nature offered discernible formal patterns, not themes, styles, or subject matters that had to be reproduced. Riegl reiterated this point in his first lecture on the *Historical Grammar of the Visual Arts* (1897): "As soon as man felt the urge to fashion a work from dead material for decorative or utilitarian purposes, it became natural for him to use the same laws as nature used in forming inorganic matter, that is, the laws of crystallization."[17] The influence of crystalline structure was more evident in decorative patterning—symmetrical and geometric, linear and planar forms—than in later figurative art. This connection to nature, however, did not make decorative art more primitive than figuration; instead it revealed the creative principle that provided the condition for art's autonomy. "Only in inorganic creation does man appear fully equal [*ebenbürtig*] with nature, creating from a purely inner drive without external models; as soon as these boundaries are overstepped and man begins to recreate the organic creations of nature, then his production is no longer fully independent, but something imitative."[18] The creative drive was most purely expressed in nonnaturalistic, nonimitative art forms.

In *Problems of Style,* Riegl set out to demonstrate that the history of decorative art could be explained solely through inner formal imperatives. The book can be read as a lengthy counter-argument to "materialist" and "mimetic" interpretations of art, which he denounced for explaining art by external factors such as technical innovation, mimetic skill, or cultural influence. Riegl's attack on mimetic theories of art grew out of the belief that imitation was not a "schöpferischen That," and it led him to some surprising exclusions. He did not, for example, consider primordial three-dimensional sculpture a part of art history because, while it may have implied a nascent anthropological urge to create, it offered only products of the human "Nachahmungstrieb," the capacity for imitation. Photography as well held a dubious claim to the status of art because its images were akin to copies. Only with representation and decoration on a flat surface did formal innovation and thus art history begin.

> In [two-dimensional images], they did not copy the representative, three-dimensional objects that were before them, but the silhouette, the outline that in reality did not exist but first had to be devised by men. From this moment onward art first won its endless representational abilities; in relinquishing three-dimensional corporeality and accepting appearance, men took the essential step of freeing the imag-

> ination [*Phantasie*] from the constraints of the strict observation of real natural forms and enabling it to treat and combine these natural forms more freely.[19]

Art did not imitate three-dimensional nature directly; instead, it creatively rearticulated natural patterns in two-dimensional matter and form. Formal innovation, therefore, began with a break from nature that nevertheless retained nature's regulative patterns. Art history also marked its beginning with this break, buried in a prehistoric past that was the domain of anthropology. Art historians traced the transmission and adaptation of creative transfigurations, not technical improvements in the ability to copy.

The theory of the natural and anthropological origins of art had important ramifications for Riegl's historiography. The postulate of a human *Schmuckbedürfniss* justified his assertions of art's autonomy and his own focus on its internal formal development. In *Late Roman Art Industry,* Riegl chided the art historians of his teachers' generation for relying on extrinsic factors to explain the development of art.

> The characteristic feature of historical scholarship in this generation, which today prepares to make room for another new goal, lies in the one-sided preference for auxiliary disciplines. In art history—ancient as well as modern—this manifested itself in the one-sided concern for and overestimation of iconography. No doubt, the evaluation of an artwork finds its certainty essentially weakened when one is unclear about the content of the presentations, within which the meaning of the work can be found. But in the middle of the last century, the holes in this method began to be felt severely. Because the holes could only be filled in through the extensive use of literary sources, which were not directly related to the visual arts, art historians produced immense, extensively researched investigations whereby our art historical literature of the last three decades largely exhausted itself. No one will deny that this provided an indispensable foundation for the future edifice of art history; but one can also not deny that iconography established only stronger foundations and that the erection of the actual building can only be accomplished by art history.[20]

Iconography produced two distortions in art history. First, because it tended to perpetuate classical aesthetic ideals, non-classical monuments were often valued only in terms of their "antiquarian-historical content"; their unique "artistic form" was generally overlooked.[21] Second, iconography did not address the uniquely artistic qualities of a work; like functionalist and technical theories, it served mainly an auxiliary role for art historians.

> The antiquarian significance of such iconographic investigations can not be contested; for art history, however, they have primarily an auxiliary value in that they help to establish the external coordinates of place and time. The iconographic is indeed altogether different from the artistic; the goal which the first serves is extrinsic like the utilitarian functions of craft or architectural works, whereas the actual artistic goal is solely directed toward presenting the thing in outline and color, in the plane or in space in order to arouse the free appreciation of the viewer. An iconographical observation therefore can only gain true art historical value when it is demonstrated to express the same will [*Wollen*] that—absolutely unique—shaped the distinct visual-artistic [*bildkünstlerische*] aspect of the artwork.[22]

Riegl's skepticism toward art historical iconography was reiterated in a passage at the beginning of the posthumously published essay "The Place of the Vapheio Cups in the History of Art," composed during the period when he was writing about late Rome.

> In every work of art in which things of nature are recreated, one must distinguish between the idea that led to the selection of the particular models of nature and the manner and style in which these models were represented by the artist's hand. The artistically decisive factor is unconditionally the latter. Indeed, the question could be raised whether the idea, the given representational purpose, should not, like the purposes of use and decoration, be dismissed as external and be strictly separated from the artistic purpose as such.[23]

In light of these claims, it comes as little surprise that Riegl ultimately severed iconography from the realm of art historical concerns. "In the establishment of a clear division between iconography and art history," he declared, "I see the necessary prerequisite for all progress of art historical research in the near future."[24]

Riegl also attacked "materialism" in art history, a term he used rather loosely to condemn a variety of scholarly assumptions and shortcomings. He decried the "dogma of materialist metaphysics"[25] for ascribing art's origins to the development of technical ability and complained that materialism had failed to designate "where the domain of the spontaneous generation of art ends and the historical law of transmission and acquisition begins."[26] In the work of Semper's epigoni, for example, art historical materialism encouraged lazy scholarship and unsystematic investigation.[27] Riegl dismissed his "natural scientific age" as "restlessly concerned for causal explanations,"[28] "anti-historical,"[29] "lifeless [*todten*],"[30] backward looking, and simplistic.[31] Scholars were frequently too timid to propose historical or cultural interconnections except among neighboring time periods and regions, a faintheartedness that Riegl once again ascribed to the dominance of materialism.[32]

To be sure, Riegl's polemic indulged in reductionist treatments of art historical trends. He conflated iconographic, mimetic, materialist, and functionalist theories of art's origin and history, accusing them all of overlooking the anthropological autonomy of art. However, his attack should be understood for what it was: a clearing operation meant to establish the validity of his own formalist credo by distinguishing it from contemporary scholarly trends. His main assault was against neither materialism nor iconography per se, but against the tendency to explain art history in terms of extrinsic, nonartistic factors.[33] Riegl affirmed that iconography, technique, and materialism played crucial auxiliary roles in shaping our understanding of art by helping to establish the cultural and chronological context of a work. But they could not account for a work's position in the *internal* history of artistic form. Chronology as well was a useful tool for art historians, but not an end in itself.[34] Materialist and iconographic histories reduced artworks to a set of lifeless characteristics by placing them side-by-side as points in chronological time. They defined the category of history in exclusively nonartistic terms that failed to grasp the essential formalism of creative art, which, he insisted, had its own inner historical imperative.

In distinguishing Riegl's formalism from art historical materialism, we must beware of associating him with a tradition of art historical idealism that he equally condemned. After all, Riegl remained committed to an empiricist methodology that based universal history on the documentary evidence provided in artworks. Forms did not have independent existence outside the material and perceptual world in which they were embedded. Although creative and formal imperatives shaped the history of art, these imperatives were inherent in artworks, not free-floating concepts. Form was not an abstract idea; it was a history inscribed in matter, and, as such, immanent within the perceptual relationship between man and the world. *Pace* Kemp, Riegl was no historical idealist.[35]

Riegl called on fellow historians to treat artistic motifs as "form and color on the plane and in space," not as "objective meaning."[36] Rigorous art historical scholarship found its sine qua non in the close empirical study of forms; only through painstaking description of an artwork could historians reveal the inner formal imperatives that produced it. These impulses demonstrated continuities with both earlier and later artworks, and thus situated the work within a formal and continuous history. Artworks were temporally constituted material forms that contained their own inherent temporality, not static objects that could be fixed and classified serially along a lifeless axis of dates. Each work of art manifested a tense formal constellation of elements with progressive impulses; it possessed a formal temporality—an entelechy—that implied its own transformation and linked with other works to constitute a progressive, internally driven history of art.[37] The art historian's task was "to arrange the individually discussed monuments within [a] historical development" that illuminated form, autonomy, and continuity.[38]

12

Rhythm and Temporality in *Problems of Style* and *Late Roman Art Industry*

In the final chapter of part 2, I examine Riegl's concepts of artistic form and historical continuity more closely by analyzing the fundamental regulatory principle of rhythm. In Riegl's work, rhythmic form organized art and nature, man's perception and the historical world. In *Problems of Style,* he used the term "rhythm" with an often loose and offhand frequency, but its very prevalence underscored its importance to his thinking. Rhythm governed both regularities and irregularities in nature, as well as fundamental artistic laws:[1] it defined formally the earliest Geometric Style of decoration;[2] determined the decorative placement of animals in the ancient Egyptian and Assyrian Carpet Style;[3] designated the coherent filling of decorative space in Egyptian art; generated new decorative forms such as the spiral and guilloche in the Near East;[4] excluded certain common but arhythmic forms, such as the tree, from the decorative catalogue of Mesopotamian art;[5] determined tectonic harmony in Greek times; described the undulating movements of the Greek tendril motif that culminated the ancient decorative progression;[6] and organized the coherent filling of surfaces, flat or otherwise, which was the "endpoint and goal of the whole development."[7]

Such a widely applicable principle—rhythm—received frustratingly little definition in *Problems of Style.* Its clearest exposition emerged in a concluding discussion of the Byzantine and early Islamic notion of infinite rapport, an eternal, almost timeless state that Near Eastern artists conveyed in the decorative loops of the arabesque.[8] The perceptual psychology expressed by the arabesque recalled Riegl's anthropological claim that art responded to mankind's *horror vacui,* its fear of empty space. Near Eastern artists succeeded in developing Egyptian and Greek vegetal motifs to the point where they expressed infinity, not as an empty space or void, but in the harmonious rhythm and symmetry of endless tendril loops—the negation of absolute emptiness. Infinite rapport, Riegl argued, stood in the "closest relationship" with "late Roman colorism."[9] Whereas a concept of space as "the negation of matter and therefore nothing" still dominated during late Roman times,[10] Byzantine artists depicted space as a visual object in its own right, with rhythmic form as its organizing principle.[11] Artistically, the demarcation of visual space involved the manipulation of light and color "directed toward rich and subtle rhythmic change between pattern and ground, light and dark."[12] The emergence of space as an object of perception during imperial Roman times and its rhythmic organization against the flat plane gradually led to the Near Eastern perception of an articulated infinity. Rhythm organized an otherwise undifferentiated and seemingly empty space (bounded or infinite) in terms of line, pattern, and fullness.

Most relevant for our purposes is the metaphorical connection between Riegl's rendering of space as rhythmic form—full, perceptible, and demarcated, not empty or contourless—and his conception of time and history. Like artistic form, history had a rhythmic structure that linked art with the world and space with time in a formal continuity that rested upon empirical contiguity.[13] In elaborating this argument, I will first consider the metaphorical connection between rhythmic formalism in art and rhythmic order in history. Then I discuss Riegl's extrapolation of a rhythmic temporal continuity from the sensory experience of contiguity.

The role of rhythm in establishing a relationship between temporal continuity and sensory experience is most clearly expressed in the concluding section of *Late Roman Art Industry.*[14] As in *Problems of Style,* Riegl insisted that formal qualities defined the unique and specifically artistic aspects of an artwork; form reflected the *Kunstwollen* of an epoch, man's perceptual relationship with his world. But in *Late Roman Art Industry,* he defined form in the ancient world more precisely as rhythmic articulation. "Like all of antiquity, the essential artistic medium which late Roman art used to fulfill its stated artistic intentions," declared Riegl, "was rhythm."

> By means of rhythm, that is, the sequential repetition of like appearances, the coherence of the respective parts of a unified whole is made absolutely clear and convincing to the viewer; and where several individual elements were brought together, there it was once again rhythm that was able to give shape to a higher unity. . . . Like all of ancient art, late Roman art strove to represent individual unified forms through rhythmic composition on the plane.[15]

Rhythmic composition allowed late Roman artists to establish pictorial unity while still preserving the individuality of separate artistic components, much as the use of free space and attention allowed seventeenth-century Dutch portraiture to establish unity among figures without obliterating their individual distinctiveness.

In Riegl's analysis, late Roman art served as the transition between a form of rhythmic composition suited to two-dimensional, planar depiction and one that could organize objects in three-dimensional space. Roman artists emancipated spatial intervals as strictly bounded entities organized rhythmically on the canvas. In so doing, the artists showed that rhythm was a flexible principle of artistic form that need not be restricted to a particular era or genre. Light and darkness, space and figure, mass and depth, each became a feature of an emerging late Roman *Kunstwollen* organized according to a rhythmic balance between individual parts and the collective whole. Even as late Roman artists struggled with the three-dimensional implications of the emancipation of space, ancient rhythmic composition adjusted itself to new artistic requirements: "The isolation of form has also exerted its influence on the rhythmic modes of expression in that rhythm no longer had to concern itself only with articulation and change, which always have unifying effects, but also with simplification and the construction of mass [*Kommassierung*]. While classical rhythm was concerned with contrasts (contrapposto, triangular composition), late Roman rhythm became one of uniform series (quadrangular composition)."[16] In its simultaneous articulation and unification of shapes, rhythm became a basic principle of form that characterized more than simply one artistic era; rhythmic depiction changed over time, incorporating new representational capacities in its orderly regulation of visual material. Rhythm provided the basis for artistic form and development, and was subject to art's fundamental condition of historicity.

Even as it came to organize three-dimensional artworks, however, rhythmic composition retained the traces of its original two-dimensionality. As we have seen, Riegl claimed that art history began with the creative transposition of three-dimensional nature onto two-dimensional surfaces. Ancient rhythmic composition regulated the depiction of objects on the plane, not in space; it separated elements beside and above, not behind one another. The emancipation of bounded space in late Roman times signaled a move toward three-dimensionality that culminated in the infinite fullness of Byzantine arabesques. In this process, rhythm came to govern three-dimensional articulation—"interval, ground, and space"—as it had the planar and linear art of classical antiquity.[17] But rhythmic composition still regulated space and depth in terms of line and measure; it translated dimensionality into linearity for the purposes of visual representation. Infinite rapport, with its implication of boundless three-dimensional space, found its typical representation in two-dimensional arabesques. This representation of three-dimensional objects in two-dimensional forms expresses a central characteristic of rhythmic composition. Indeed, many architects and sculptors plan their works on two-dimensional blueprints; photographers and cinematographers cast three-dimensional images onto two-dimensional screens. And at the same time as Riegl was highlighting the essential two-dimensionality of rhythmic form, post-Impressionist artists such as Cezanne and Matisse were rejecting naturalism and emphasizing the flatness of their canvases. In Riegl's art history, it was the inherent two-dimensional linearity of rhythm that made it such an apt metaphor for temporality. Just as rhythm organized artistic form in two-dimensional models, rhythmic temporality organized multidimensional and semi-autonomous art histories in terms of linear continuity.

Uncharacteristically for a scholar who rarely referred to outside sources, Riegl turned to St. Augustine's aesthetic writings to support his characterization of the late Roman *Kunstwollen*.[18] Augustine argued that, instead of privileging one style over another, ancient artistic creation sought harmony by emphasizing the twin goals of "unity (isolated perception of singular forms) and rhythm."[19] The fundamental rhythm of an artwork balanced "intervals" of "beauty" and "ugliness" in a unified whole. "Evil is merely the lack of good, ugliness just an interval of beauty," wrote Augustine. "They are just as necessary as the intervals between words in language, between tones in music. We tend to see evil and ugliness up close, and then they naturally appear to us as evil and ugly. But whoever observes the whole from a distance grants that beauty would be nothing without its complement, ugliness, and that both together present an image of consummate harmony."[20] Ugliness was simply an interval or gradation of beauty, not its negation. Because true beauty, according to Augustine, resided exclusively with God, artists could only capture *formal* traces of the divine in created works. Form expressed divinity to the senses, and individual works had to be understood in the broader context of divine creation as intervals balanced between beauty and ugliness, good and evil. "Consummate harmony" was achieved by properly balancing all visual and historical components in a unified, composite whole. Thus, Augustine's theory of beauty, with its assertion that all objects contain vestiges of beauty, bolstered Riegl's attacks on the aesthetic exclusivity of modern classicists.

In *De Ordine* and *De Musica*, Augustine defined rhythm, or numerical order, as the very basis of reason in the sensible world. "We must therefore acknowledge," he wrote, "that in the pleasure of the senses, what pertains to reason is that in which there is a certain rhythmic measure."[21] Musical and visible forms alike were governed by "the supreme eternal presidency of numerical rhythm."[22] Riegl notes that Augustine cited lunettes, the perforated windows in Roman halls, as architectural examples of rhythmic composition, and colorism in painting as a rhythmic exchange between light and dark patterns on the canvas.[23] For Augustine, rhythm was more than simply the ordering principle of sensory experience, although this was one of its roles. Rhythm was the very "Law of God,"[24] the rational and beautiful essence of all temporal human activity, sensible form, and divine structure. Thus, rhythm did not apply to temporal experience in a merely metaphorical sense. In visual form, rhythm was *experienced* temporally, as a movement of the eyes from point to point, as a series of successive observations; rhythm emerged as the basis of artistic form in the temporal succession of instantaneous perceptions. Augustine noted that man perceived rhythm "in time [as a] silent movement."[25] If properly contemplated, this temporal rhythm of the senses evoked the divine balance of eternal design. "So earthly things are subject to heavenly things," Augustine wrote, "seeming to associate the cycles of their own duration in rhythmic succession with the song of the great whole, universitatis."[26]

Augustine's providential and universalist vision of history, which served as a basic framework for medieval chroniclers,[27] offered Riegl a Christianized version of both artistic formalism and art historical ecumenism by extending the thematic relevance of rhythmic form to encompass man's spatial and temporal relationships with the world around him. The Augustinian theory of rhythmic harmony provided Riegl with a model for an art history comprising the rhythmic progression of eras and artworks within a continuous historical whole. Just as rhythm governed intervals of space in Roman art, so it regulated intervals in the temporalized space of history as well. Indeed, for Riegl, rhythm held priority over even symmetry and proportion as the fundamental regulating principle of form.

> Symmetry and proportion are only special forms of appearance of a higher universal medium of the visual arts: rhythm. The medium through which unity—that is, the individual, self-contained form of natural objects in artworks—achieves its evident expression is also called rhythm (numerus) by Augustine. . . . All other aspects of beauty in works of visual art (to symmetry and proportion . . . we can add a third aspect: order) are simply particular modes of the expression of rhythm.[28]

Rhythm preserved the unity of the self-contained form even as it established a relationship among individual forms; it thus became the very agent of formal coherence and articulation. Riegl's application of rhythm as a visual analytic inscribed the temporality of viewing into the artwork itself. Rhythm linked the formal articulation of the work with the temporal character of its perception, a connection easily masked by the apparent synchrony of the completed work "gazing" steadily out at the viewer. The viewer's perception was actually a composite of instantaneous glances, a temporal series, open to cultural and historical influences. Art depicted the rhythmic intervals of this formal temporality, and the viewer organized these intervals into visual and historical continua.

How did rhythm achieve this continuity among instantaneous perceptions and individual objects? Did continuity describe the objective character of art history and temporality, or was it merely a supposition built upon empirical discontinuities? Was temporal continuity a perceptible phenomenon, or was it, like Augustine's divinity, that which always escaped human perception? Riegl's answers to these questions emerge in an earlier section of the volume on late Roman art, in a passage that outlines his now well-known distinctions among modes of visuality: *haptisch* and *optisch*, *nah-sichtig*, *normalsichtig*, and *fern-sichtig*.[29] More important for our purposes than these modes of visuality themselves is Riegl's discussion of the ancient perceptual constitution of objects, which, he argued, organized the world into bounded individual entities in order to tame an otherwise chaotic external reality. "Fine art of the whole ancient world sought as its ultimate goal to represent external things in their clear, material individuality."[30] Because its point is so crucial to the culmination of this chapter, I will quote at length Riegl's description of the evolving relationship between perception and objects in ancient times.

> First one tried to comprehend the individual unity of things by way of pure sensory perception, excluding as much as possible all notions derived from experience [*Erfahrung*]. As long as the assumption prevailed that external things were actually objects independent from us, all help from subjective consciousness had to be instinctively avoided as a factor disturbing the unity of the particular object. The sense organ that we use most frequently to take notice of external things is the eye. This organ shows us things merely as colored surfaces but never as impenetrable, material individual entities; it is precisely this optical perception which presents the external world to us as a chaotic mix. We possess certain knowledge about the bounded individual unity of single objects only through the sense of touch. Through touch alone we gain awareness of the impenetrable borders which enclose individual material objects. These borders are the tactile surfaces of things. Yet what we touch immediately are not extended surfaces, but only individual points. Only in the perception of single individual points following each other in quick succession, repeated beside each other on one and the same material thing, do we arrive at the conception of an extended surface with its two dimensions of height and

> width. The conception is not gained through an immediate perception of touch but through the combination of several such perceptions, which necessarily presupposes the intervention of the subjective thought process. It follows, therefore, that the notion of tactile impenetrability as an essential condition of material individuality was achieved not merely on the basis of sense perception but also with the supplementary aid of the thought process. In ancient artistic production, there must have existed from the very beginning a latent inner opposition; in spite of the fundamentally intended objective conception of things, from the beginning a subjective admixture could not be avoided. In this latent opposition lay the seed of all later development.[31]

Man's perceptual relationship with the objective world, Riegl believed, was a production of the eye, the touch, and the mind.[32] This relationship passed through historical stages, oscillating between an emphasis on vision and touch, subjective constitution and objective presentation. Haptic, or tactile, periods (emphasizing touch, linearity, and shape) alternated with optic periods (emphasizing vision, color, light and shadow); the modes of visuality in art history shifted between *nah-sichtig* (stressing a close optical view of objects that de-emphasized depth and space in favor of impenetrable material objectivity), *fern-sichtig* (stressing a distant, subjectively constituted optical focus that muted tactile objects by combining them into a whole), and *normal-sichtig* (incorporating both tactile and optical qualities, balanced between *nah* and *fern-sichtig*). Both touch and vision enlisted the cooperation of the mind to transform sense perceptions from isolated experiential units into a sustained awareness of the continuous contours and borders of objects. The fingers could transmit impenetrable points; the eye could convey isolated color stimulants. But only the mind could combine these immediate sense perceptions into an awareness of physical continuity and depth. Pure perceptual experience was pointillist; only subjective thought translated percepts into a unified, dimensional, individual object, the immediate sense of contiguity into the perception of continuity. Riegl's perceptual anthropology challenged the Kantian assertion that a priori mental categories such as space and time organized human experience. In his view, these categories were perceptual, produced through the combined operation of sight, touch, and thought. This operation was so basic to the act of perception that it passed nearly unnoticed.

In Riegl's account, the visual aspects of perception rapidly came to mask tactile and mental contributions, a tendency that led to basic misunderstandings about the nature of empirical perception and the unity and continuity it affirmed.

> The sense of touch is indeed indispensable in order to confirm for us the impenetrability of external things, but not in order to teach us about extension. Regarding this, it is far surpassed by the abilities of the visual sense. Yet the eye transmits only color stimulants, which, like the sense of impenetrability, are expressed in points. And we arrive at the notion of colored surfaces as multiplied points through the same process of thought used for tactile surfaces. But the eye executes the operation of multiplying singular perceptions far quicker than the sense of touch, and therefore it is mainly the eye to which we owe our notion of the height and width of things. As a result, the thinking observer arrives at a new combination of perceptions in consciousness: where the eye recognizes a coherent colored plane in one unified perception, there arises the notion of an enclosed material individuality based partly on the experience of a tactile impenetrable surface. In such a way, very early on it could happen that optical perception alone was considered sufficient to produce certainty about the material unity of external things, without need of the immediate testimony from the sense of touch.[33]

The ancient prioritization of vision, whereby a pointillist optical experience assumed a coherence and authority that led to its dominance over the other senses, was based on the anthropological tendency for sight to presuppose the proofs of touch. The investigations of optical experience by impressionist painters of Riegl's era succeeded in weakening the certainty of vision in its own right, but they did not undermine its dominance over other forms of sensory experience in the modern world.

Because time and space were perceptual categories produced in a temporal relationship between subject and object, they themselves were affected by historical change along formal and cultural lines. Art historical continuity emerged through a perceptual process similar to that which Riegl used to describe the awareness of physical continuity. Individual artworks were apprehended in singular perceptions or moments; these were combined into a chronological succession of contiguous works and then transformed into a perception of historical continuity through the subjective involvement of the art historian-viewer. Historical continuity was both subjectively constituted by the viewer and objectively anchored in a succession of moments; it became an act of perceptual composition, a presentation in form, a work produced. History as a concept was itself an inherently historical form; it both organized relationships among artworks and maintained its own temporal constitution.

This insight into the temporal nature of artistic and historical form provided the basis for Riegl's history of ancient perception in *Late Roman Art Industry.*[34] Throughout antiquity, societies offered different explanations for the perceived connections among phenomena. Whereas earliest antiquity believed that arbitrary and omnipotent religious forces determined the order of things, classical antiquity sought necessary, regular connections among objects and thereby developed mechanistic and atomistic notions such as force, impact, and sequence—in a word, cause. Late antiquity, in turn, emphasized magic as the medium linking objects. This worldview was not, in Riegl's view, a mark of intellectual decline; instead, it affirmed the fundamental gap between subject and object, between perception and experience, that the classical world had overlooked. Late antiquity unwittingly acknowledged the subjective aspect of perception by noting the seemingly illusory constitution of objectivity, continuity, and time. This conviction explained why late Roman illusionism did not strive for the deceptive realism of its classical predecessors. Modern man adopted yet a different attitude toward the objective world. Riegl used the notion of *Stimmung* to characterize in almost mystical terms the sense of space and time that governed the relationship between modern man and the surrounding world. In his essay "Die Stimmung als Inhalt der modernen Kunst," Riegl argued that modern artworks aimed to express to the viewer the vast unity of the world of objects and historical moments linked together by causal connections. The viewer was made to feel at once a sense of subjective distance from the passage of time and a perceptual and "spiritual" oneness with the causal chain of universal history.[35] He felt both above and within space and time. Throughout history, artworks have manifested this historically changing relationship between form and perception, objective world and creative subject.

Artistic form for Riegl was temporally inflected, implying its own continual transformation into ever new and future forms. Moreover, artworks contained the traces of their own production by revealing the time and context of the artist. The viewing act was also fundamentally temporal in its duration. The subject received a succession of single, separate perceptions over time, and these were transformed into a continuous perception of durability. The resulting sense of a unified object both presupposed and produced an awareness of temporal continuity. These unities grew out of the formal imperatives of artworks, the temporal duration of viewing, and the subjective perceptual constitution of objects. Continuity always exceeded what could be empirically verified, yet it was inherent in the very nature of perception, which itself entailed a continuous process of rhythmic negotiation between subject and object, back and forth, constituted by the viewer but anchored in a succession of contiguous objective moments.

Physical and temporal continuity, in Riegl's analysis, were human perceptual productions that art realized in visible form. Artworks became the sites of a ceaseless enactment of contig/nuity, the visible markers of an ever-ongoing perceptual negotiation between subject and object, artist and viewer, man and the world. Riegl's art history acknowledged both creative subjectivity and empirical objectivity as equiprimordial in the perception and development of form. They defined two fundamental poles of a perceptual experience that was organized by the rhythmic balances of time. Riegl thus depicted human temporality as neither a Kantian mental category nor a noumenal reality, neither chronological fixity nor pure undifferentiated flux, but instead as a perceptual *relationship* in constant production. Temporality constituted the productive space between objectivity and subjectivity, the historical interaction between observer and observed. The immanent temporality of the artwork was actively transformed in the act of viewing, as Riegl demonstrated in his consideration of monuments. Although temporality could be fixed in times and dates that made it available for chronology and history, chronological time offered merely a handy set of coordinates for grasping the development of perceptual form and did not adequately reflect the temporality of artworks. For Riegl, art provided far greater insights by offering a privileged locus for witnessing man's temporally and historically constituted perceptual relationship with the world.

In *Techniques of the Observer,* Jonathan Crary posits that a sweeping change in European visual culture occurred during the first half of the nineteenth century. Under the influence of physiological research and new visual technologies, nineteenth-century scholars developed theories of pure opticality that distinguished sight from the other senses, severed the image from the external referent, confounded the distinction between viewer and object, and exposed the inherent temporality of vision. Visual theorists no longer presumed a transcendent subject who organized an otherwise chaotic perceptual world. Instead, they submitted both "observer and observed" to the same "modes of empirical study" and redefined vision "as a capacity for being affected by sensations that have no necessary link to a referent."[36] Crary also notes a rising interest, shared by Goethe, Schopenhauer, and other nineteenth-century scholars, in the temporality of vision. The discovery of retinal afterimages, for example, which link successive visual impressions together into a perceptible continuum, provided empirical evidence for the temporal continuity of vision.[37] Though Riegl tied vision more closely to objective referents than Crary's analysis of nineteenth-century visual culture allows, he clearly reflected the nineteenth-century fascination with temporality and visuality. It is easy to see how Riegl's notion of art as "form and color on the plane" participated in Crary's discourse on opticality.[38]

Interestingly, however, some of Crary's categories of *eighteenth*-century visual culture also seem to characterize Riegl's work. We have seen that in Riegl the apparent separation of the senses (haptic and optic) belied a deeper *embodiment* of vision in a "more unified human sensorium" of sight, touch, and mind.[39] Thus when Crary describes Riegl's haptic and optic perception as a "dualist" and "transcendental" system "severed from the immediacy of the body,"[40] he offers an oversimplified reading of Riegl's language that fails to acknowledge a complex and underlying theory of perception. In fact, a passage that Crary uses to describe the prototypically eighteenth-century paintings of J. B. Chardin could just as well be said to describe Riegl's thought. "His apprehension of the coidentity of idea and matter and their finely set positions within a unified field discloses a thought for which haptic and optic are not autonomous terms but together constitute an indivisible mode of knowledge."[41] Although Riegl proposed a historical oscillation between predominantly haptic and optic periods, his perceptual anthropology emphasized the cooperation and interaction of both sight and touch in the production of our sense of continuity.[42] Riegl maintained Crary's eighteenth-century faith in the human ability to unify a chaotic world perceptually, a faith that Leibniz, whose influence in Austria we have already noted, expressed in the following terms: "And as the same city regarded from different sides appears entirely different, and is, as it were, multiplied respectively, so because of the infinite number of simple substances, there are a similar infinite number of universes which are, nevertheless, only the aspects of a single one as seen from the special point of view of each monad."[43] For Riegl, the human sensorium effected just this kind of unity from discrete, discontinuous percepts to perceptual unity and continuity. He refused to treat empiricism as either purely subjective or purely objective, and he resisted merely physiological theories of vision as insufficient to explain the act of perception or the development of art history. Instead he translated the divine unity of Leibnizian perspectivalism into the human temporal unity of subjective/objective perception. Along with Brentano and Husserl, Riegl acknowledged an intentional referentiality—an objective trace—within perception; like Sickel, he believed that the object was external and material as well.

Although Riegl attempted to explain the anthropological roots and perceptual constitution of temporal continuity, he avoided the question of time's ontological status. Perhaps he considered questions of ontology ancillary to his art historical concerns, something better left to philosopher-colleagues such as Brentano, Meinong, or Husserl. Or perhaps he accepted Brentano's dictum that time could be perceived indirectly in objects but not abstracted from them. In Riegl's art history, temporality constituted artworks in both form and perception and could be known empirically. Localized artistic temporalities combined to form a continuous universal history of art that reflected the development of formal innovation and creative impulse. But as for the correspondence of this internal temporality and continuous history with an objective time external to the work or the viewing, Riegl remained quietly agnostic.

And so, finally, what about the historian? If the form and meaning of artworks are constituted in temporal acts of perception, then the historian has a crucial role to play. The artwork mediated between past and present, its meaning irreducible to either. For Riegl art was, to use

Margaret Olin's term, a "dialogue" between subjective present and objective past about the conferral of meaning through time.[44] By holding both subject and object, present and past, in a dialogic relationship, artworks allow viewers in the present to grasp past constructions of temporality different from their own—grasp them not as utterly foreign, but as both familiar and distinct. Although each viewer plays an active role in this dialogue, the historian, as an analyst and spokesman for bygone cultures, has an especially prominent voice. His subjective sense does not vanish before the objective evidence of the past, but he does attempt to read as judiciously as possible the original forms of perception and temporality exhibited in artworks. He does not stand transfixed before the object "as it really was," but instead attentively engages with it in the attempt to discern its empirical tensions, reanimate its temporal forms, and discover its fundamental historicity. Like a stargazer pointing out constellations in the heavens, the art historian both shapes and witnesses the past.

Conclusion

In *The Culture of Time and Space,* Stephen Kern surveys what he calls the "distinctive new modes of thinking about and experiencing time and space" that emerged between 1880 and World War I.[1] He explores the effects of technological and social changes on late nineteenth-century temporal experience, the ways in which philosophers, writers, artists, and social theorists reflected the novelties of modern life in their work. *Time's Visible Surface* has presented Riegl's art history, which rethought the temporal dimensions of art and perception, within the modern context of these turn-of-the-century transformations. I have addressed two main themes in my analysis: First, I sought to illuminate Riegl's concept of temporality and indicate its relevance for twentieth-century thought. Second, I used Riegl's work as a lens for viewing his contemporary Austrian intellectual milieu and demonstrated the prevalence of a discourse on history and time in fin-de-siècle Vienna. In the conclusion, I will revisit each of these themes. To gain a broader perspective on Riegl's significance, I first consider Walter Benjamin's reception of his ideas on temporality. Then I return briefly to the problem of context in fin-de-siècle Austria for my final remarks.

Walter Benjamin's Reception of Riegl's Temporality

Walter Benjamin was not the only member of postwar Germany's robust Marxist community to engage with Riegl's work. In his 1922 article "Reification and the Consciousness of the Proletariat," Georg Lukàcs praised the Austrian art historian for noting that "the essence of history lies precisely in the changes of these structural forms which are the focal points of man's interaction with the environment at any given moment and which determine the objective nature of both his inner and outer life."[2] Theodor Adorno also saw fit to mention Riegl on numerous occasions, despite a deep skepticism about the concept of *Kunstwollen,* which he felt established a false continuity between artistic and historical subjectivity. Perhaps responding to Benjamin's enthusiasm, Adorno acknowledged that the notion of *Kunstwollen* "free[d] aesthetic experience from timeless abstract norms" even though he feared its relativistic implications.[3]

But it was Benjamin's encounter with Riegl's art history that proved decisive for the development of twentieth-century cultural theory. Over the course of a tumultuous career, Benjamin incorporated, adapted, and transformed Riegl's ideas in his own work.[4] Benjamin found in Riegl a scholar "who penetrates so far into the historical conditions that he is able to trace the curve of their heartbeat as the line of their forms."[5] Explicit references to works by the Austrian art historian appear throughout Benjamin's corpus. Riegl, he declared, anticipated the move away from indiscriminate eclecticism and universal history in art historical analysis by focusing on marginal historical phenomena, on the monumental significance of seemingly insignificant objects and epochs.[6] More important, in seeking the cultural and intellectual meaning-systems revealed by individual art objects, Riegl offered a new method and direction for art history. *Late Roman Art Industry* and *The Group Portraiture of Holland* exemplified Riegl's fundamental awareness that the "meaning-content [of artworks] is bound up with their material content."[7] Benjamin celebrated *Late Roman Art Industry* as an epoch-making work of early twentieth-century *Wissenschaft*, revolutionary in both content and method.[8] Indeed, Riegl was one of two scholars whom Benjamin singled out for special acknowledgment in his Curriculum Vitae of 1928.[9] He credited Riegl's notion of *Kunstwollen* with weakening the reliance on territoriality in art history in favor of an eidetic or physiognomic "definition of those aspects of artworks that make them incomparable and unique."[10] Benjamin employed the notion of *Kunstwollen* in his *Habilitationsschrift, The Origin of German Tragic Drama* (1928), using it to highlight the "expressionist" strivings found in periods often dismissed as decadent.[11] Acknowledging Riegl's inspiration, he reinterpreted overlooked artistic eras such as late Rome and the Baroque as periods when the artistic will strove toward realization in form even at the expense of producing well-wrought individual works.[12] A further reference to *Die Entstehung der Barockkunst in Rom,* Riegl's posthumously published seminar notes, lauded its analysis of the "conflict between sensibility and will," which Baroque artists settled in favor of the latter.[13] And in a more personal citation, Benjamin noted that Riegl's work opened his eyes to the contemplation of decorative artifacts and jewelry, including a late imperial ring he gave to his fiancée, Grete Radt.[14]

Uncited references often reveal greater appreciation than direct citations, for they affirm that a thinker's ideas are a common part of the intellectual landscape. Benjamin referred to Riegl's *Problems of Style* in a review of Karl Blossfeldt's volume of plant photographs, *Urformen der Kunst: Photographische Pflanzenbilder* (1928), by describing the vegetal images as "forms of style" observable in art and architecture.

> One senses a gothic *parti pris* in the bishop's staff which an ostrich fern represents, in the larkspur, and in the blossom of the saxifrage, which also does honor to its name in cathedrals as a rose window which breaks through the wall. The oldest forms of columns pop up in horsetails; totem poles appear in chestnut and maple shoots enlarged ten times; and the shoots of a monk's-hood unfold like the body of a gifted dancer. Leaping toward us from every calyx and every leaf are inner image-imperatives, which have the last word in all phases and stages of things conceived as metamorphoses.[15]

The magnified images reveal patterns unavailable to the naked eye; their forms suggest inner "imperatives" shared by nature and art. Indeed, the paradox of Blossfeldt's magnified plant images lies precisely in their ability to arrest metamorphosis in the felt-like grey of the tinted photograph. One need only observe the dancing boxwood stems (photo 18), the mechanized thistle (photo 44), or the wailing birthwort (photo 58) to witness the movement espied—indeed, produced—by Blossfeldt's clinical camera.[16] This momentary flash of visualization revealed art forms in nature, at once static and motive, that exemplify Riegl's notion of the inner formal development of artworks. Benjamin's discussion of Blossfeldt linked these stylistic motifs with Goethe's concept of *Urpflanzen*—in fact, *Urphänomene* in general—which offered privileged access to the world of original ideas. This insight into originary forms, Benjamin believed, held forth the possibility of redemption from an unfulfilled historical experience by revealing (to use more Aristotelian language) a kind of phenomenal entelechy that had yet to be realized. "There takes place in every original phenomenon a determination of the form in which an idea will constantly confront the historical world, until it is revealed fulfilled, in the totality of its history."[17] The "forms of style" that Benjamin found in Blossfeldt's photographs suggested to him that such original ideas lay hidden in objects, offering the possibility of a redemptive (or entelechic) overcoming of unfulfilled existence.

This survey of references alone shows that Riegl's work occupied a central place in Benjamin's thought. Doing fuller justice to the influence, however, requires a consideration more integral conceptual affinities between Benjamin's and Riegl's work. While its roots in Jewish Messianism (especially Kabbalistic thought) and a Marxist/Lukacsian philosophy of history have long been acknowledged,[18] Benjamin's *Origin of German Tragic Drama* owes a tremendous debt to Riegl's art history that has yet to be fully recognized. The essay shared with *Late Roman Art Industry* the desire to recover overlooked periods of "decline," and echoed Riegl's premise that in "decadent" periods objects disrupted temporal coherence, their decay allegorizing the transience of all cultural production.[19] Along with several specific references to the Austrian art historian in the main body of the work, Benjamin offered an introductory characterization of the Baroque period in German drama that explicitly adapted Riegl's late Roman framework.

> [T]he baroque is not so much an age of genuine artistic achievement as an age possessed of an unremitting artistic will. This is true of all periods of so-called decadence. The supreme reality in art is the isolated, self-contained work. But there are times when the well-wrought work is only within reach of the epigone. These are the periods of "deca-

> dence" in the arts, the periods of artistic "will." Thus it was that Riegl devised this term with specific reference to the art of the final period of Roman Empire. The form as such is within the reach of this will, a well-made individual work is not.[20]

Benjamin's rendition of the *Kunstwollen* (artistic will) in this passage differed from Riegl's interpretation of the concept. First, for Benjamin artistic will described a relationship between will-to-form and technical ability, especially a relationship in which the desire for the production of the new in art outstripped the technical mastery necessary for its achievement. This formula contained the germ of a formalist art history with which Riegl might have concurred: technical innovations in material and practice follow on the need or desire for formal innovation, on the realization of the poverty of existing artistic forms for expressing contemporary cultural circumstances. Creative will, therefore, precedes innovation in technique and material, not the reverse. However, for Benjamin, this characterization was specific to periods labeled "decadent," eras such as late Rome or the German Baroque. Artistic will, or *Kunstwollen,* did not therefore amount to a philosophy of artistic creation or a theory of the temporality and historicity of artworks *tout court* as it had for Riegl; instead, the concept expressed a particular relationship between creative desire and technical mastery that prevailed during certain historical epochs.

At the same time, Benjamin's passage stresses the essential quality of isolation, self-containment, and discontinuity of the artwork within the literary history of the German Baroque. This discontinuity emerged in numerous ways in Benjamin's "Epistemo-Critical Introduction." First, discontinuity characterized the form of the essayistic treatise that Benjamin wrote. A treatise lacked the purpose and continuity of a formal thesis that drove progressively toward its conclusion. "The absence of an uninterrupted purposeful structure is its primary characteristic. Tirelessly the process of thinking makes new beginnings, returning in a roundabout way to its object."[21] This "continual pausing for breath," as Benjamin described it, established an "irregular rhythm" for the treatise, whose primary aim was the representation of truth in fragmentary form.[22] This goal required a descriptive analysis that stressed detail, digression, fragment: "The value of fragments of thought is all the greater the less direct their relationship to the underlying idea, and the brilliance of the representation depends as much on this value as the brilliance of the mosaic does on the quality of the glass paste."[23] The thought fragment in a treatise represented by digression the fragmentary quality of a perceived whole. In visual terms, truth understood as sacred image, as mosaic, comprised a fragmentary whole made up of contiguous but disjunct shards, not a continuous unity of parts. Essayistic treatises attempted to grasp the whole and the detail in their indirect, unsublated, discontinuous relationship. "The relationship between the minute precision of the work and the proportions of the sculptural or intellectual whole demonstrates that truth-content is only to be grasped through immersion in the minutest details of the subject-matter."[24] It is easy to see in Benjamin's analytic method a celebration of the kind of descriptive art historical formalism that Riegl practiced. Riegl constructed context and historical progression through the meticulous analysis of individual works, traits, and features, and thereby built historical characterizations from a contiguous series of detailed descriptions. This emphasis on physical detail, minute and discrete, preserved a materialist core to Riegl's and Benjamin's otherwise seemingly idealist projects.

Benjamin, however, proposed a new project for historical analysis, one that used detailed description to transcend history and seek ideal truths that had timeless reality. He aimed to identify and describe ideas, which existed as a higher order of truth than historical knowledge. History, in Benjamin's treatment, provided an example of conceptual analysis that organized its data by linking them together according to evolutionary patterns. Benjamin drew a crucial distinction between "concepts" and "ideas." Whereas concepts structured material along analytic lines, ideas defined no progression, class, or analytic terminology. Instead, an idea existed entirely outside the realm of intentional or reflexive knowledge as an objective interpretation of phenomena. "The world of philosophical thought," Benjamin averred, "does not evolve out of the continuum of conceptual deductions, but in a description of the world of ideas."[25] Citing his and Riegl's joint philosophical forebear, Benjamin compared ideas to Leibnizian monads, each absorbing its own history, each containing an image of the world.[26] As we saw in the introduction, Benjamin explained his doctrine of ideas through analogy with constellations. "Ideas are to objects as constellations are to stars. . . . [B]y virtue of the elements' being seen as points in such constellations, phenomena are subdivided and at the same time redeemed."[27] In this regard, Benjamin's project went beyond Riegl's effort of historical explication. Riegl sought to rescue overlooked periods of art history from scholarly oblivion and in so doing offered an explanation of art history in terms of temporal continuity and physical contiguity. Benjamin appropriated these aims and methods for a project that sought to transcend historical and conceptual analysis by placing the notion of "context" at a phenomenological level, outside of time, beyond the conceptual convenience of continuity, as a kind of luminous constellation whose objectivity existed equally for the perceiver and the phenomena it organized.

Benjamin elaborated his astronomical analogy by further describing the relationship among ideas in terms of "discontinuous finitude."

> [I]deas subscribe to the law which states: all essences exist in complete and immaculate independence, not only from phenomena, but, especially, from each other. Just as the harmony of the spheres depends on the orbits of the stars which do not come into contact with each other, so the existence of the *mundus intellegibilis* depends on the unbridgeable distance between pure essences. Every idea is a sun and is related to other ideas just as suns are related to each other.[28]

In its purported aim, therefore, Benjamin's project in *The Origin of German Tragic Drama* of isolating a set of ideal contexts—the suns of the *Trauerspiel* or the Baroque—would seem wholly in conflict with Riegl's effort to discern the temporal constitution of artworks in their empirical and historical forms. The two thinkers, however, converge in a crucial way: what Benjamin left unsaid in his analogy between ideas and suns was the sky "in" which the ideal suns shone. As we have seen, in Riegl's analysis, temporal continuity ceased to exist as an empirical phenomenon; instead, it became a perceptual process, a proto-phenomenological context for separate perceptions—a kind of Benjaminian ideal that organized distinct and contiguous moments of sensory experience into a perceptual whole. Benjamin stressed that the world of ideas was discontinuous. Isolated and monadological, the suns illuminated each other but did not come into contact. Riegl's notion of temporality shares with Benjamin's model this structure of discontinuity. Time, in Riegl's analysis, was based ultimately upon a series of successive contiguities drawn together in the perceptual process. Riegl's art history had no *chronological* beginning or ending, and historical time, as the perceptual unification of separate temporalities in artworks, could not be characterized as objectively finite. (This open-endedness, as we have seen, forced Riegl to rely on a speculative anthropology of origins.) It is indeed apt, therefore, to consider Riegl's notion of temporality in terms of Benjamin's formula of discontinuous infinitude: Like Benjamin's sky in which suns shine (not the container, but rather the dimensional space, the through-ground of the suns), time was an infinitude from which individual works shone out. The horizon where sky and land merged was only a boundary of perspective, a movable limit of sight. In this way, Riegl's notions of history and temporality aspired to the status of Benjaminian ideas.

Benjamin's later works, including his two renowned essays "The Work of Art in the Age of Mechanical Reproduction" (1936) and "Theses on the Philosophy of History" (1940; first published 1950), demonstrate the continual appropriation and adaptation of Riegl's thought. In "The Work of Art," Benjamin characterized the modern era as one in which artworks, mechanically reproduced on a mass scale, gradually lost their "aura," a term that has occasioned much debate among scholars. Benjamin used the term to characterize an artwork's uniqueness in time and place, the almost expressionless quality, tied to authenticity and origin, that captivates a viewer and holds his attention. Aura was at once a quality of an artwork in relation to a viewer and the expression of a work's originality and presence. The aura was temporally constituted in that it registered the work's traces of origin and its unique existence through time. In his "Little History of Photography," Benjamin described "aura" as "[a] strange weave of space and time: the unique appearance or semblance of distance, no matter how close it may be. While at rest on a summer's noon, to trace a range of mountains on the horizon, or a branch that throws its shadow on the observer, until the moment or the hour become part of their existence—this is what it means to breathe the aura of those mountains, that branch."[29] The aura did not define a distinct quality of a perceived object existing *within* time, but rather, designated the very timeliness of the object itself. The aura existed *as* space-time—origin, passage, and distance—"woven into" the very fabric of an artwork. "Uniqueness and duration" are "intertwined" in the original work.[30] "Breathing" the aura of an object, one perceived its immanent temporality, a timeliness tied to the moment of viewing as well as the moment of creation, at once produced and in production. The artwork, then, was not simply an object; as the term "work" suggests, it was both product and process, a profoundly temporal relationship between viewer and world. In this regard, Benjamin's discussion of an artwork's aura recalled Riegl's analysis of the *Kunstwollen,* the inner formal and temporal imperatives of an artwork. Henri Zerner equates the aura to Riegl's notion of age value, which distanced the art object from its moment of origin and highlighted its temporal constitution.[31] Yet, despite its wide appeal in Riegl's account, age value maintained a somewhat auratic quality commanding aesthetic respect. In exploring the social implications of the decline of aura and the emergence of new technologies such as photography and film, Benjamin observed the disappearance of this quasi-sacred aspect in the modern market for artistic production and consumption. He acknowledged that his discussion of art's social implications pushed Riegl's ideas to conclusions the art historian could not reach. "However far reaching their insight," he wrote of Riegl and Wickhoff, "these scholars limited themselves to showing the significant, formal hallmark which characterized perception in late Roman times. They did not attempt—and perhaps, saw no way—to show the social transformations expressed by these changes of perception."[32]

Benjamin's appropriation of Riegl's art history for wider social analysis is clearest in the "Work of Art" essay, especially in its exploration of photography and film. The photograph, Benjamin argued, opened up realms of perception unavailable to the naked eye. "Everyone will have noticed how much easier it is to get hold of a painting, more particularly a sculpture, and especially architecture, in a photograph than in reality."[33] Two things account for this accessibility: First, through technical innovations, a photograph could bring out aspects of a work that the eye could not see. And second, technical reproduction could place copies of artworks in the hands of those who could not travel to observe them. Time, space, and human perception ceased to be barriers as photography technologically altered the context of art's reception. Furthermore, photographic reproduction dispelled the aura of authenticity surrounding works of art; originality lost its authority in the circulation of copies.[34] Artworks no longer stood above the viewer as objects commanding reverent appreciation. The decay of the aura had a revolutionary significance in liberating art from its ritualistic trappings and "reactivating" its social potency. "[T]he technique of reproduction detaches the reproduced object from the domain of tradition.

By making many reproductions it substitutes a plurality of copies for a unique existence. And in permitting the reproduction to meet the beholder or listener in his own particular situation, it reactivates the object reproduced."[35] The loss of aura did not strip "art-as-photography," a term Benjamin coined in 1931, of its temporal dimension. Instead, the art object was drawn down into the profane world of temporal circulation; a work registered the traces of its technical production and reproduction as well as those of the many hands and eyes that viewed it. The timeless auratic distance separating a ritualized originary moment from a secular now-moment disappeared, and the art object was reanimated in the acts of viewing and circulation. Art became a revelation of its own production and reproduction, a visible marker of modern temporality. In tracing the aura's technological counterpart, Benjamin dispersed the ritualistic haze of Riegl's age value to reveal the social predicament and radical potential of modern art.

Or, more precisely, film did so. Benjamin argued that the photograph could arrest life at a pregnant moment and discharge its historical tensions in a potentially redemptive way. But in cinema he found a technological medium capable of mechanically "freezing" and reanimating temporal development as such. Out of single images, captured in "the dynamite of the tenth of a second,"[36] the filmmaker could create a scenario of continuous visual movement. The actor's work became "a series of mountable episodes," which were isolated and then reconnected when the projector rolled.[37] What Riegl described as the temporal structure of art history, the relationship between artworks and continuous temporality, could now be technically realized and publicly displayed through cinematography; separate, contiguous images moved in fluid continuity across the screen.[38] Where Riegl showed that time could be rendered in visible form, Benjamin offered cinema as the temporal reanimation of spatial forms. Riegl analyzed the spatialization of time at work in art and history, whereas Benjamin described the dynamization of space in film.[39] Of course, both procedures presumed the inherent temporality of visual perception.

This technological actualization of Riegl's art historical metaphor had monumental implications for the social history of perception. Riegl considered attention as the privileged mode of viewing artworks, capable of recognizing temporal and historical significance in even apparently insignificant artifacts; Benjamin saw in this attitude a residue of the art's traditionally ritualistic, "parasitical" position.[40] Instead, Benjamin posited the revolutionary potential of distraction as a modern mode of viewing that collapsed the distance between art and the social world. "In the decline of middle-class society," he wrote, "contemplation became a school for asocial behavior; it was countered by distraction as a variant of social conduct."[41] The difference between attitudes was embodied in the distinct modes of viewing called forth by paintings and film. "The painting invites the spectator to contemplation; before it the spectator can abandon himself to his associations. Before the movie frame he cannot do so. No sooner has his eye grasped a scene than it has already changed. It cannot be arrested."[42] Modern viewers perceived architecture as well in a distracted manner. Adopting Riegl's categories but rejecting his perceptual psychology, Benjamin noted that architecture was apprehended "by use and by perception—or rather, by touch and sight."

> Such appropriation cannot be understood in terms of the attentive concentration of a tourist before a famous building. On the tactile side there is no counterpart to contemplation on the optical side. Tactile appropriation is accomplished not so much by attention as by habit . . . [Optical reception], too, occurs much less through rapt attention than by noticing the object in incidental fashion.[43]

Benjamin noted that "[a] man who concentrates before a work of art is absorbed by it," whereas "the distracted mass absorbs the work of art."[44] In this regard, both concentration and distraction displayed one-sidedness, the former abolishing the subject, the latter the object. Thus, although the mass availability and receptivity of artworks held redemptive potential, it also threatened to obliterate the objective autonomy of art. Benjamin and Riegl would have agreed that historical analysis should preserve the relationship between subject and object.

Like Riegl, Benjamin extrapolated from the temporality of artworks to the work of the historian. "To articulate the past historically," he insisted, "does not mean to recognize it 'the way it really was' (Ranke)."[45] This historicist attitude abolished the defining moment of subjectivity in the perceptual constitution of history. Benjamin also criticized historicism's fetishization of empirical fact for producing universal histories devoid of historical insight. "Universal history has no theoretical armature. Its method is additive; it musters a mass of data to fill the homogeneous, empty time."[46] Like the photographer's, the historian's goal should exceed mere chronicle. The historian-photographer sought to seize the past "as an image which flashes up at the instant when it can be recognized and is never seen again."[47] Unlike the chronicler who treated the past as mere dead matter, he sought to reanimate an artifactual past that had direct concern for the present. Historian-photographers achieved insight not by "blot[ting] out everything they know about the later course of history,"[48] but by putting the tense constellation of a past event in a pregnant relationship with the present. They sought to recover the "fullness of [the] past" for a "redeemed mankind," because "only for a redeemed mankind has its past become citable in all its moments. Each moment it has lived becomes a *citation a l'ordre du jour*—and that day is Judgment Day."[49] On one level, Benjamin's Judgment Day can be read as a transposition of Kant's categorical imperative into an apocalyptic key: one should act as if each deed stood before an ultimate judge. History, Benjamin believed, held within it the prospect of mankind's fulfillment, and the historian-artist's duty was to highlight—indeed activate—this potential. However inaccessible and metaphysical the standard of redemption and Judgment Day may seem, the injunction to confront unfulfilled history with the immanent possibility of its own fulfillment and transcendence affirmed a radical calling for the historian that dramatically expanded Riegl's vision.

Even Benjamin's uncompleted magnum opus of the 1930s, the Arcades project, his *Urgeschichte* of nineteenth-century capitalism and the fullest statement of his unique historical and philosophical perspective, bears the stamp of Riegl's influence. The art historian's themes echo through many of the most idiosyncratic passages of Benjamin's notes. Riegl's discontinuous model of temporal perception, which lit on surfaces in a flash and formed them into coherent objects and contexts, informed Benjamin's articulation of historical theory and his practice of historical method in the *Passagenwerk*. The discontinuity of Riegl's model, the interstices between its perceptual units, offered a revolutionary openness for possibility that countered the absolutism of ideological actuality. Methodologically, Benjamin came to share Riegl's taste for locating theory and philosophy in the "ruffle of a dress,"[50] the "small discarded objects" and "overlooked motifs" that were the art historian's stock in trade; these forgotten items contained their own material history and temporality.[51] Indeed, as part of the process of envisioning his Arcades project, Benjamin affirmed Riegl's preference not only for treating images as texts but also for including images of material objects within the written text to create a kind of philosophical picture book.[52] Benjamin's model in the *Passagenwerk* for the confrontation between natural history and cultural history also found a precursor in Riegl. In "Kunstgeschichte und Universalgeschichte," discussed in chapter 7, Riegl maintained that the "natural" substratum of art's development was always filtered through the historically determined perspective of the observer-historian. In the always uneasy, never completely harmonized convergence of these two temporalities, Riegl attempted to position his art histories as histories of perception. Benjamin, too, found fruitful this disruptive tension between a natural history of objects and a cultural/perceptual history of their reception.[53] Indeed, the concept of history informing Benjamin's *Passagenwerk* resembles the historical theory outlined by Riegl's *Kunstwollen.*[54] Citing the philosopher Hermann Lotze, Benjamin noted that progress was not found "in history longitudinally, but . . . rather in an upward direction at every single one of its points."[55] As discussed in chapter 9, Riegl's most renowned concept can also be rendered as a set of local teleologies that join the axis of progressive universal history at specific points. Perhaps Benjamin's "dialectics at a standstill," a static but historically fleeting convergence of visual elements mapped onto a set of coordinate axes, owes a debt to his fin-de-siècle forebears.[56]

It may not be too strong to say that Riegl's work taught Benjamin how to read images. Riegl offered a set of practices and procedures for reading history and temporality in apparently static visual constellations. These methods, however, eventuated in a vastly different scholarly project in Benjamin's hands than they had in Riegl's. In Benjaminian terms, Riegl the historian still demonstrated a "tranquil, contemplative attitude toward the object"[57] that prevented him from seeking or recognizing the sociocritical content his own methods offered. This lack of dimension allowed Riegl to cling to his dream of an autonomous and continuous art history despite countervailing signs of social influence and temporal discontinuity in art. His staunch defense of historical continuity prevented him from carrying forward the fruits of his own rigor: the perceptual cracks in time's visible surface were sealed up in the edifice of history.

Although Riegl's insight was to sever temporality from historical time and record its formality in art, he left his own discipline of art history fractured across incompatible temporal models—synchronic chronology on the one hand, diachronic continuity on the other. This separation accompanied a further unwillingness to connect art history effectively with broader historical developments. Riegl's autonomous artistic temporality isolated art from other human endeavors; it established the foundations for an independent art history by strictly severing it from other disciplines. Thus Riegl was forced by his own premises largely to ignore the impact of external context on the development of art. Benjamin's work recaptured Riegl's formal material temporality for broader historical analysis by reasserting its social context, demonstrating its wide historical relevance, and suggesting its radical political and redemptive potential.

Fin-de-Siècle Context

Twentieth-century scholarship on fin-de-siècle Vienna has produced several works of history remarkable for their groundbreaking impact and methodological innovation. Schorske's *Fin-de-Siècle Vienna* and Janik and Toulmin's *Wittgenstein's Vienna* not only delineated a cultural and historical era but also became standard-bearers for a contextualist approach to intellectual history, one that emphasized cultural, social, and political context as the key for understanding artistic and intellectual production. The political content of Freud's dreamwork, Schorske argues, can only be fully understood with reference to turn-of-the-century Viennese and Austrian politics. An account of Viennese intellectual preoccupations, write Janik and Toulmin, reveals that Wittgenstein's true purpose in writing the *Tractatus* was ethical.[58] In light of the methodological influence that these works have had within and beyond the field of modern Austrian cultural history, it is worth revisiting the question of context on both historical and theoretical levels.

To what degree did Riegl's context shape his work, and how do his ideas affect our understanding of the Austrian fin-de-siècle world? What does Riegl's thought suggest about the notion of historical context? These questions offer no easy answers. I have challenged recent intellectual histories of turn-of-the-century Austria for their tendency to depict Austrian modernist culture as antihistorical. This book demonstrates that references to history and temporality among at least one influential coterie of Austrian thinkers were simply too numerous, too varied, and too rich to suit the antihistoricist characterization. I examined Riegl's interest in artistic temporality and history and showed that it fit within a broad, transdisciplinary discourse on time and history carried on by scholars affiliated with the University of Vienna. Commentators on Austrian culture have noted a similar line of thinking in the work of other contemporaries.[59] It should be stressed, however, that while I attempt to recover a historiographical element missing from recent accounts of Austrian fin-de-siècle modernism, I do not offer a new characterization of the period as a whole. That there was a lively intellectual discourse surrounding the categories of temporality and history in Austria is clear; that there was a distinct Austrian philosophy of time and history, however, remains doubtful.

It is doubtful in part because Riegl's work calls into question the very notion of context as a set of fixed and bounded qualities. My investigation of Riegl's teachers and colleagues challenges the temporal and geographic boundaries posed by many accounts of fin-de-siècle Austrian culture. Although Riegl was raised in Austria, Büdinger, Brentano, and Sickel were German-born and German-educated. Sickel, a Saxon Protestant, studied in France as well. Both he and Brentano spent parts of their careers outside the German world in Italy, and they maintained allegiances to French and English scholarship. Pioneers in their respective disciplines, Brentano and Sickel experienced personal and professional frustrations in Vienna and bitterly criticized the educational bureaucracy, culture, and politics of their adopted home. Though both thinkers profoundly influenced Austrian thought, they can hardly be said to embody Austrian distinctiveness. Bohemians Thausing and Zimmermann also embraced the methodological ideas of non-Austrians. Thausing championed Morelli's work, Zimmermann the work of Herbart, a Saxon Protestant, and Bolzano, a fellow Bohemian. Thus, while Austrian political boundaries are analytically convenient, they can obscure questions of intellectual influence. The same can be said of temporal boundaries. Although it is valuable to compare Riegl with contemporary Austrian and European schools of thought such as Husserlian phenomenology, Nietzschean *Lebensphilosophie*, Bergsonian vitalism, and German historicism, full insight into his art history requires one to relax temporal boundaries and trace connections with earlier and later thinkers, from Leibniz and Augustine to Benjamin and modern cultural theorists. Culturally and intellectually, fin-de-siècle Austria was more of a crossroads than a crucible.

Nonetheless, it should be noted that the Austrian thinkers considered in this book often approached the study of history differently from their German academic counterparts. While one certainly finds the influence of Hegelian idealism and Rankean universalism in Austria, Riegl's contemporaries, drawing on an Austrian empirical tradition, tended to analyze history by probing its more fundamental building blocks: temporality, continuity, artifact, materiality. Instead of presuming that historical evolution defined the essential quality of social or artistic phenomena, Riegl and his colleagues asked how history and artifacts were related, how perception influenced our understanding of the past, and how presentist concerns affected history. In this tendency, Riegl's Viennese contemporaries anticipated post-structuralist concerns about the construction and uses of history and about the discipline's fundamental assumptions of temporal continuity, linear narrative, archival and artifactual legitimation, the priority of event and causality, and the standards of evidence and objectivity. These Austrian thinkers differed significantly enough from their Prussian School counterparts that scholars working within the historicist tradition could readily overlook their historiographical insights.

Today Riegl's work suggests to us that the nature of a historical context is intimately connected with our particular understanding of temporality and objectivity. He encourages us to understand context not in terms of either fixed boundaries or a semi-mystical *Zeitgeist*, but instead as an idea inherent in our perceptual relationship with the world. In this sense, historical context is not a "container" of objects and events that imparts to them a distinct set of qualities or imposes an appropriate interpretation; it is not a set of boundaries that demarcate characteristics, categorize differences, and confer significance. Nor is context a random collection of artifacts linked by the mere accidents of proximity and contemporaneity. Instead, Riegl's perceptual history of artifacts treated context as a set of nonexclusive correlates emerging from the artifacts themselves, found in perceptual forms as an intrinsic content, in the relationship between parts and whole, viewer and object. In other words, Riegl's work suggests that artworks embody their own temporal and historical context and that this immanent sense of context, not an idealized contextual framework comprising a set of hypostatized qualities, should enjoy priority in our study of the past. In Leibniz's words: "[I]n order to have an idea of *place*, and consequently of space, it is sufficient to consider these *relations* [among things], and the rules of their changes, without needing to face any absolute reality *outside* the things whose situation we consider."[60] Context, like place, can be seen as a relationship among objects rather than as a reified collection of historical qualities. Indeed, were we to conduct not a cultural history of fin-de-siècle Vienna but an *Urgeschichte* of modernism in Vienna (taking Benjamin's enterprise as a prototype), we would first have to discard stubborn notions of a context mystically unified around a set of cultural qualities and turn instead to the artifacts themselves, seeking origins in a juxtaposed arrangement of objects. A context such as fin-de-siècle Vienna, then, may be understood not as *res gestae*, a fixed light, but as only one among many possible constellations in the sky.

Notes

Introduction

1. Leibniz, letter to Colbert, quoted in David Landes, *Revolution in Time: Clocks and the Making of the Western World* (Cambridge, MA, 1983), 45.
2. Many recent books offer accounts of modern temporal consciousness. Some that I have found particularly useful are Stephen Kern, *The Culture of Time and Space 1880–1918,* (Cambridge, MA 1983); David Harvey, *The Condition of Postmodernity* (Cambridge, MA, 1989); and Marshall Berman, *All That Is Solid Melts into Air: The Experience of Modernity* (New York, 1982).
3. Charles Baudelaire, "The Painter of Modern Life," from *The Painter of Modern Life and Other Essays,* trans. Jonathan Mayne (Phaidon, 1964), 13.
4. Ernst Cassirer, *The Philosophy of the Enlightenment* (Princeton, 1951).
5. On instruments of time measurement, the calendar and clock, see E. G. Richards, *Mapping Time: The Calendar and its History* (Oxford, 1998) and David S. Landes, *Revolution in Time.* The latter in particular discusses a transformation in Western conceptions of time that occurred during the late Middle Ages with the invention of the mechanical clock. An equable, linear, commodifiable time measurement emerged from the structured schedules of monasteries and came to organize and regulate nascent capitalist production in the burgeoning towns of late medieval and early modern Europe. I learned of Landes's work from Moishe Postone, whose excellent *Time, Labor, and Social Domination: A Reinterpretation of Marx's Critical Theory* (Cambridge, 1996) includes a chapter on the social implications of abstract time. See chapter 5, 186–225.

See also Jacques Le Goff, *Time, Work, and Culture in the Middle Ages,* trans. Arthur Goldhammer (Chicago, 1980).

6. Hayden White, Dominick La Capra, Siegfried Kracauer, Paul Ricoeur, Michel de Certeau, Paul de Man, Frank Ankersmit, and Peter Novick are among the more renowned recent scholars to have focused their attention on the theoretical problems entailed in the concepts of time and historical representation. See also Kern, *The Culture of Time and Space;* Peter Osborne, *The Politics of Time: Modernity and the Avant-garde* (New York, 1995); Charles M. Sherover, *The Human Experience of Time: the Development of its Philosophic Meaning* (New York, 1975); Charles R. Bambach, *Heidegger, Dilthey, and the Crisis of Historicism* (Ithaca, 1995).
7. Both Michael Podro, *The Critical Historians of Art* (New Haven, 1982) and Michael Ann Holly, *Panofsky and the Foundations of Art History* (Ithaca, 1984) discuss the nineteenth-century emergence of an independent art historical discipline.
8. In *Abstraction and Empathy: A Contribution to the Psychology of Style,* trans. Michael Bullock (London, 1953), Wilhelm Worringer enlisted Riegl's dichotomies in his well-known, though now largely discredited theory of historico-anthropological types. Erwin Panofsky, in "Der Begriff des Kunstwollens" (*Aufsätze zu Grundfragen der Kunstwissenschaft* [Berlin, 1964], 33–47), offers a reading of Riegl's famously elliptical notion of *Kunstwollen* as an immanent *Sinnesgeschichte,* an attempt to grasp the internal symbolic structure of artworks. Paul Feyerabend credits Riegl's *Late Roman Art Industry* with breaking the "crude progressivism" of prior art historical accounts and recognizing that art had various purposes, intentions, and ideals of truth and beauty; Feyerabend likens Riegl's insight to his own beliefs in scientific relativism. See Feyerabend, "Science as Art: A Discussion of Riegl's Theory of Art and an Attempt to Apply It to the Sciences," *Art + Text* 12–13 (1984): 16–46; *Conquest of Abundance: A Tale of Abstraction versus the Richness of Being* (Chicago, 1999), 93–94; *Farewell to Reason* (New York, 1987), 294. At the same time, however, Feyerabend dismisses as "metaphysical speculation" Riegl's notion of *Kunstwollen* for its tendency to seek internal connections among all artistic products of a particular era. Gilles Deleuze and Félix Guattari use Riegl's distinction between haptic and optic art to elucidate their own distinction between the nomadic space of thought and the striated, or mapped and gridded space of state power. Deleuze and Guattari, *A Thousand Plateaus: Capitalism and Schizophrenia,* trans. Brian Massumi (Minneapolis, 1987), 492–93.

   I discuss Benjamin's complex and multi-faceted reception of Riegl in this book. For a passage exemplifying his enthusiasm for the Austrian art historian, see Walter Benjamin, "Bücher, die lebendig gewesen sei," in *Gesammelte Schriften* (Frankfurt am Main, 1972), 3:169–71, which celebrates Riegl's *Late Roman Art Industry* as one of the lasting works of the early twentieth century. In a recent issue of *American Historical Review,* Vanessa R. Schwartz ("Walter Benjamin for Historians," *AHR* 106, no. 5 [2001]: 1721–43) acknowledged Benjamin's elevation from a figure of merely specialized interest among philosophers to a theorist whose work has come to critically and widely inform historical practice. As interest in Benjamin crests, it becomes all the more important to examine those figures who shaped his ideas. As I argue in the conclusion, many insights Schwartz attributes to Benjamin can be traced to the influence of Riegl.

9. For the citations above, and articles by Riegl's New Vienna School followers, see *The Vienna School Reader: Politics and Art Historical Method in the 1930s,* ed. Christopher S. Wood (New York, 2000). Wood provides a list of Riegl's admirers on pages 14–15.
10. Rudolf Arnheim, "Victor Lowenfeld and Tactility" in *New Essays on the Psychology of Art* (Berkeley, 1986), 240–51.
11. Jacqueline E. Jung discusses the difficulty of Riegl's Viennese academic language and complex syntax in the preface to her translation of *Historische Grammatik der bildenden Künste.* Jung, "Übersetzungsfragen: Form, Communication, and Questions of Translating Riegl," in *Historical Grammar of the Visual Arts* (New York, 2004), 37–48.
12. Wolfgang Kemp, "Introduction" to Riegl's *The Group Portraiture of Holland,* trans. Evelyn M. Kain and David Britt (Los Angeles, 1999), 3. Elsewhere Kemp was less courteous, calling the system of binaries *Begriffsklapparatismus*—conceptual claptrap. See *Altmeister moderner Kunstgeschicte,* ed. Heinrich Dilly (Berlin, 1990), 41. I thank Benjamin Binstock's introduction to *Historical Grammar of the Visual Arts,* 34n. 19, for this citation.
13. Hans Sedlmayr, "Die Quintessenz der Lehren Riegls," in Alois Riegl, *Gesammelte Aufsätze* (Augsburg, 1928), xi–xxxiv.
14. St. Augustine's discussion in Confession 11 is probably the most illustrious, and certainly one of the most moving, philosophical considerations of the topic.
15. Hayden White, "Narrativity in the Representation of Reality," in *The Content of the Form: Narrative Discourse and Historical Representation* (Baltimore, 1987), 6–11.
16. See Margaret Olin, *Forms of Representation in Alois Riegl's Theory of Art* (University Park, PA, 1992), 3.
17. Judith Ryan, *The Vanishing Subject: Early Psychology and Literary Modernism* (Chicago, 1991), 10–11.

18. Despite Husserl's critique of a psychologism, a tendency that he attributed to Brentano as well as others, nineteenth-century phenomenology and psychology exhibited certain overlaps. Husserl's notion of phenomenological intuition, for example, was heavily indebted to Brentano's influential doctrine of intentionality. On Brentano's position in phenomenology and especially his important doctrine of intentionality, see Herbert Spiegelberg, *The Phenomenological Movement* (The Hague, 1975) and *The Context of the Phenomenological Movement* (The Hague, 1981). On nineteenth-century psychology and its critics, see Mitchell Ash, *Gestalt Psychology in German Culture, 1890–1967: Holism and the Quest for Objectivity* (Cambridge, 1995); Martin Kusch, *Psychologism: A Case Study in the Sociology of Philosophical Knowledge* (London, 1995); and Martin Jay, "Modernism and the Specter of Psychologism," in *Cultural Semantics* (Amherst, 1998), 165–80.

    Positivism, of course, had many variants, but these generally agreed on the possibility of a theoretically and metaphysically untainted access to facts and objects in the world. On the late nineteenth-century development of positivism, see David Lindenfeld, *The Transformation of Positivism: Alexius Meinong and European Thought, 1880–1920* (Berkeley, 1981).
19. This impulse became common in methodological debates of the late-nineteenth-century historical and human sciences. See Bambach, *Heidegger, Dilthey, and the Crisis of Historicism*; H. Stuart Hughes, *Consciousness and Society: The Reorientation of European Social Thought, 1890–1930* (New York, 1961).
20. Friedrich A. Lange, *The History of Materialism and Criticism of its Present Importance*, trans. Ernest Chester Thomas (London, 1950). On Lange, see Klaus Christian Köhnke, *The Rise of Neo-Kantianism: German Academic Philosophy between Idealism and Positivism*, trans. R. J. Hollingdale (Cambridge, 1991), 151–67.
21. Olin, 104–5.
22. Theodore Ziolkowski, *Virgil and the Moderns* (Princeton, 1993), 7.
23. Many scholars have grappled with the concept of historicism, its position in nineteenth-century German intellectual history, and the work of specific historians associated with the tradition. A standard although somewhat one-sided historical account of the tradition is Georg G. Iggers, *The German Conception of History: The National Tradition of Historical Thought from Herder to the Present* (Boston, 1968); see also Iggers, "Historicism: the History and Meaning of the Term," *Journal of the History of Ideas* 56, no. 1 (1995): 129–52; Hayden White, *Metahistory: The Historical Imagination in Nineteenth-Century Europe* (Baltimore, 1973); Carlo Antoni, *From History to Sociology: The Transition in German His-*

torical Thinking, trans. Hayden V. White (Detroit, 1959). For a much older but still helpful account of nineteenth-century German historians, see George P. Gooch, *History and Historians in the Nineteenth Century* (Boston, 1913). On the late nineteenth-century crisis of historicism, see Bambach, *Heidegger, Dilthey, and the Crisis of Historicism.* See also Hughes, *Consciousness and Society.*

24. For this section, I am heavily indebted to Ziolkowski, 6–12.
25. Ibid., 8.
26. Ibid., 9.
27. See Riegl, "Der moderne Denkmalkultus: sein Wesen und seine Entstehung," in *Gesammelte Aufsätze* (Augsburg, 1929), 144–93.
28. Diana Reynolds, "Vom Nutzen und Nachteil des Historismus für das Leben," in *Kunst und Industrie: Die Anfänge des Museums für angewandte Kunst in Wien,* ed. Peter Noever (Vienna, 2000), 20–29.
29. Heinrich Ritter von Srbik, *Geist und Geschichte vom deutschen Humanismus bis zur Gegenwart* (Salzburg, 1950), 98.
30. Quoted in Herbert Dachs, *Österreichische Geschichtswissenschaft und Anschluß, 1918–1930* (Vienna, 1974), 2. In a 1904 review of editor Emil von Ottenthal's anniversary history of the Institute for Austrian Historical Research, the journal *Historische Zeitschrift* commended Austrians on their strong research abilities but noted that they lacked the educational training to write history as effectively as Germans. See John Boyer's commentary on Fritz Fellner's essay about Heinrich Ritter von Srbik in *Paths of Continuity: Central European Historiography from the 1930s to the 1950s,* ed. Hartmut Lehmann and James van Horn Melton (Washington, DC, 1994), 190n. 7.
31. Alphons Lhotsky, *Österreichische Historiographie* (Vienna, 1962), 199.
32. These include Stefan Zweig's "world of security" or Hermann Broch's "value vacuum." See Stefan Zweig, *The World of Yesterday* (Lincoln, 1943) and Hermann Broch, *Hugo von Hoffmannstahl and His Time,* trans. Michael Steinberg (Chicago, 1984). Of course Robert Musil's *Mann Ohne Eigenschaften* is the forerunner and point of departure for most characterizations of turn-of-the-century Austria. On Musil, see David Luft, *Robert Musil and the Crisis of European Culture,* 1880–1942 (Berkeley, 1980).
33. Robert Kann's earlier *A Study in Austrian Intellectual History* (New York, 1960) offered a cyclical treatment of Austrian intellectual history and proposed a model of Austrian culture oscillating between Enlightenment rationalism and Baroque theatricality.
34. The major works in this revival of Austrian studies include the seminal essays of Carl Schorske, collected in Schorske, *Fin-de-Siècle Vienna: Politics and Culture* (New York, 1981); Allan Janik and Stephen Toulmin,

Wittgenstein's Vienna (New York, 1973); and the encyclopedic William M. Johnston, *The Austrian Mind: An Intellectual and Social History, 1848–1938* (Berkeley, 1972). For a later work in the field, see Jacques Le Rider, *Modernity and Crises of Identity,* trans. Rosemary Morris (New York, 1993). In his "Vienna 1900: Paradigms and Problems," Janik provided a handy summary of the state of the field as of 1995. Allan Janik, "Vienna 1900 Revisited: Paradigms and Problems" in *Austrian History Yearbook* 28 (1997): 1–27. Janik's essay was reprinted in *Rethinking Vienna 1900,* ed. Steven Beller (New York, 2001), which also contains a useful introductory survey of the field of Vienna 1900 by Beller.

35. Janik, "Vienna 1900," 7.
36. Schorske, *Thinking with History: Explorations in the Passage to Modernism* (Princeton, 1998), 125.
37. This is not to argue that Schorske's notion of context is either simplistic or uninterrogated. Responding to criticism of Schorske from Peter Gay and Dominick La Capra, Michael Roth has made a strong case for the self-conscious performativity of both context and history in *Fin-de-Siècle Vienna.* Michael Roth, "Performing History: Modernist Contextualism in Carl Schorske's *Fin-de-Siècle Vienna,*" in *American Historical Review* 9, no. 3 (1994): 729–45.
38. Janik, "Vienna 1900," 3.
39. Schorske, *Fin-de-Siècle Vienna;* Johnston, *The Austrian Mind;* Le Rider, *Modernity and Crises of Identity;* Janik and Toulmin, *Wittgenstein's Vienna.*
40. See, for example, Barry Smith, *Austrian Philosophy: The Legacy of Franz Brentano* (Chicago, 1994); Otto Neurath, *Le développement du Cercle de Vienne et l'avenir de l'empirisme logique* (Paris, 1935). J. C. Nyíri has published numerous books devoted to Austrian philosophy. See *Austrian Philosophy: Studies and Texts* (Munich, 1981); *From Bolzano to Wittgenstein: The Tradition of Austrian Philosophy* (Vienna, 1986); *Am Rande Europas: Studien zur österreichisch-ungarischen Philosophiegeschichte* (Vienna, 1988). On aestheticism and psychologism, see Schorske, *Fin-de-Siècle Vienna.* Aestheticism has long been a central component of Austria's historical identity. It appears, for example, in Johann Alexander von Helfert, *Über Nationalgeschichte und den gegenwärtigen Stand ihrer Pflege* (Prague, 1853). Austria, Helfert claimed, contributed to German culture through its music and art.
41. The field of Austrian studies, in fact, is full of monographs of individual figures used as lenses through which to see the wider Viennese cosmos. Janik and Toulmin, *Wittgenstein's Vienna,* and Smith, *Austrian Philosophy,* provide examples of this tendency. See also David Luft on Robert

Musil; Hermann Broch on Hugo von Hoffmannstahl.

42. On the ways in which Austrian literature and history have mythologized the Habsburg past, see Claudio Magris, *Der habsburgische Mythos in der österreichischen Literatur* (Salzburg, 1996); Ilsa Barea, *Vienna: Legend and Reality* (London, 1966).
43. Carl Schorske, "A Life of Learning," *American Council of Learned Societies,* Occasional Papers 1 (New York, 1987), 13. See his introduction to *Fin-de-Siècle Vienna* (xvii–xxx) for a full elaboration of the "death of history" (xvii) theme.
44. Recently, Schorske reiterated this theme in *Thinking with History.* Part 2 of that work is entitled "Clio Eclipsed: Toward Modernism in Vienna," and his introduction (3–16) addresses the prevalence of antihistoricism. Janik reminds us that Schorske's *Fin-de-Siècle Vienna* claimed to offer a case study in the rise of antihistoricism, not a comprehensive summary of Austrian culture. Janik, "Vienna 1900," 6.
45. Schorske's work does not utterly ignore the importance of temporality in the thought of Austrian modernists: after the decline of liberal politics and the intellectual withdrawal from social engagement and historical analysis, Schorske argues, a kind of historico-temporal thinking reemerged in the aestheticized and psychologized modernism of the early twentieth century, a tendency embodied most concretely in Schoenberg's focus on musico-logical history and music's sequential temporality. See *Fin-de-Siècle Vienna,* chapter 7, 322–66.
46. On Wittgenstein's ahistoricism, see Janik and Toulmin, 243–45.
47. In 1981, Johnston described Austrian attitudes to the past as cultural custodianship that preserved the past by setting it apart from the present. Johnston in Nyíri, *Austrian Philosophy,* 31–42.
48. See Lhotsky, *Österreichische Historiographie*; Dachs, *Österreichische Geschichtswissenschaft und Anschluß.* Günter Fellner has lamented the Austrian separation of *Geschichtsschreibung* from *Geschichtsforschung* and the emphasis on empiricism and positivism as an abdication of civic responsibility among historians. Günter Fellner, *Ludo Moritz Hartmann und die österreichische Geschichtswissenschaft* (Vienna, 1985), 87.
49. Steven Beller, *Vienna and the Jews, 1867–1938: A Cultural History* (Cambridge, 1989) is notable for its overt challenge to Schorske's image of Vienna, which, Beller claimed, overlooked the centrality of Jewish accomplishments in Austrian fin-de-siècle culture.
50. James Shedel, *Art and Society: The New Art Movement in Vienna* (Palo Alto, 1981), 3.
51. John Boyer, *Political Radicalism in Late Imperial Vienna* (Chicago, 1981); Boyer, *Culture and Political Crisis in Vienna* (Chicago, 1995).

52. Alfred Pfabigen, "Freud's 'Vienna Middle'" in Beller, *Rethinking Vienna 1900,* 154–170.
53. For Spiegelberg's take on Wittgenstein, see "The Puzzle of Wittgenstein's Phänomenologie," in Herbert Spiegelberg, *The Context of the Phenomenological Movement* (The Hague, 1981), 202–28. See also Allan Janik, *Essays on Wittgenstein and Weininger* (Amsterdam, 1985).
54. In recent decades, Riegl scholarship has produced several books and many essays. Recent English monographs include Margaret Olin, *Forms of Representation*; Margaret Iverson, *Alois Riegl: Art History and Theory* (Cambridge, MA, 1983); and Diana Reynolds, *Alois Riegl and the Politics of Art History* (Ph.D. diss., University of California, San Diego, 1997). Christopher S. Wood and Richard Woodfield have edited volumes of articles by Riegl's art historical contemporaries, successors, and commentators that help to contextualize his ideas in nineteenth and twentieth-century aesthetic discourses and examine the resurgent interest in his work. See Wood, *The Vienna School Reader: Politics and Art Historical Method in the 1930s* (New York, 2000); Woodfield, *Framing Formalism: Riegl's Work* (Amsterdam, 2001). See also Michael Podro, *Critical Historians of Art*, and Michael Ann Holly, *Panofsky and the Foundations of Art History*, cited above, for lengthy discussions of Riegl's impact.

    In German, essays on Riegl are also numerous, although, surprisingly, no monographs devoted exclusively to his work have, to my knowledge, been published. Lambert Wiesing, Thomas Zaunschirm, and Wolfgang Kemp are active expositors of his work. Lambert Wiesing, *Die Sichtbarkeit des Bildes: Geschichte und Perspektiven der formalen Ästhetik* (Reinbek bei Hamburg, 1997); Thomas Zaunschirm, *Distanz-Dialektik in der modernen Kunst: Bausteine einer Paragone-Philosophie* (Vienna, 1983); Wolfgang Kemp, "Fernbilder: Benjamin und die Kunstwissenschaft," in *"Links hatte noch alles sich zu enträtseln . . .": Walter Benjamin im Kontext*, ed. Burckhardt Lindner (Frankfurt am Main, 1978) all contain discussions of Riegl. One study exists in Italian: Sandro Scarrocchia, *Studi su Alois Riegl* (Emilia-Romagna, 1986). For an overview of the history of Riegl scholarship through the early 1980s, see Dietrich von Loh, *Alois Riegl und die Hegelsche Geschichtsforschung* (Ph.D. diss., University of Vienna), 83–128.
55. Pierre Bourdieu, *In Other Words: Essays Towards a Reflexive Sociology* (Cambridge, 1990), 143.
56. Michael Ann Holly notes that "[i]t is . . . as impossible for later commentators to unravel the braided strands of influence on Riegl's ideas as it would have been for Riegl himself to do so" (*Panofsky and the Foundations of Art History,* 76). She cites several instances of scholars trying to

speculate about what Riegl might have been reading around the time he wrote *Problems of Style*. Was it Ferdinand de Saussure as Iverson suggests? Or Adolf von Hildebrand as Henri Zerner proposes? (p. 75). Diana Graham Reynolds writes: "The contours of Riegl's professional life tell us little about the man, and there are few materials on his personal or intellectual development. Riegl's lecture notes . . . contain no information about his personal life and provide no insight into his intellectual development prior to 1889" (*Alois Riegl and the Politics of Art History,* 5).

57. Kemp, introduction to *The Group Portraiture of Holland,* 12–13.
58. See Podro, *Critical Historians of Art,* 71–97.
59. See Holly, *Panofsky.*
60. Reynolds, *Alois Riegl,* 24–46; William McGrath, *Dionysian Art and Populist Politics in Vienna* (New Haven, 1974).
61. Wiesing, *Die Sichtbarkeit des Bildes,* 72–76; Francesco dal Co, *Figures of Architecture and Thought: German Architecture Culture, 1880–1920* (New York, 1990), 83–169.
62. Roger Bauer in *La Réalité, Royaume de Dieu: Études sur l'originalité du théâtre viennois dans le premiére moitié du XIXe siècle* (Munich, 1965) connects Leibniz with an empiricist and Catholic intellectual tradition in Austria. William Johnston, in *The Austrian Mind,* echoes this theme.
63. See, for example, Robert Zimmermann, *Leibnitz' Monadologie* (Vienna, 1847), and Zimmermann, *Leibnitz und Herbart: Eine Vergleichung ihrer Monadologien* (Vienna, 1849).
64. Roger Bauer, *Der Idealismus und seine Gegner in Österreich* (Heidelberg, 1966), 55–57. See Albert Heinekamp, *Leibniz als Geschichtsforscher* (Wiesbaden, 1982), for a twentieth-century discussion of these issues.
65. Christopher S. Wood, for example, makes this argument in his introduction to *The Vienna School Reader.* See p. 15. Cf. Giles Peaker, "Works That Have Lasted . . .": Walter Benjamin "Reading Alois Riegl," in Woodfield, *Framing Formalism: Riegl's Work,* 303.
66. For Riegl's biographical sketch, I am indebted to Olin and Iverson, as well as to Max Dvořák, "Alois Riegl," in *Gesammelte Aufsätze zur Kunstgeschichte* (Munich, 1929); and Julius von Schlosser, "Die Wiener Schule der Kunstgeschichte" in *Mitteilungen des österreichischen Kunstgeschichte,* suppl. vol. 13 (Innsbruck, 1934). The *Universitätsarchiv* in Vienna contains a copy of the curriculum vita from his application for a teaching position at the University of Vienna; the application materials include a list of publications, lectures, and a handwritten biography, as well as recommendations from his professors Wickhoff and Sickel.
67. Among art historians, Max Dvořák, Julius von Schlosser, Erwin Panofsky, Edgar Wind, Meyer Schapiro, and others have cited his influence.
68. Alois Riegl, "Die mittelalterliche Kalenderillustration" in *Mitteilungen*

des Instituts für österreichische Geschichtsforschung (Innsbruck, 1889). His first article on calendars, "Die Holzkalender des Mittelalters und der Renaissance," also appeared in *Mitteilungen des Instituts für österreichische Geschichtsforschung,* 9 Band (Innsbruck, 1888).

69. Carl Schorske, *Thinking with History,* 16.
70. Throughout this book, I use the titles of the English translations of Riegl's work, though all quotations are translated from the original German volumes. Where no translation exists, I have left the title in German.

Chapter 1

1. Michel de Montaigne, "Of Cripples," in *The Complete Essays of Montaigne,* trans. Donald M. Frame (Stanford, 1957), 784–85.
2. A useful discussion of chronology can be found in Anthony Grafton's biography of Scaliger. See Grafton, *Joseph Scaliger: A Study in the History of Classical Scholarship* (Oxford, 1993), esp. 1–141. See also E. G. Richards, *Mapping Time: The Calendar and its History* (Oxford, 1998), 12–13, 102–3; and the introduction to Theodor Sickel, *Acta Regum et Imperatorum Karolinorum Digesta et enarrata: Die Urkunden der Karolinger* (Vienna, 1867).
3. Ludwig Ideler, *Handbuch der mathematischen und technischen Chronologie* (Berlin, 1825), 3–6.
4. Among other things, Böckh investigated the lunar cycles of ancient time measurement. George P. Gooch, *History and Historians in the Nineteenth Century* (Boston, 1913), 2.
5. Riegl thanked his professor Sickel for collecting a rich set of materials relating to medieval calendars. See Riegl, "Die Holzkalender des Mittelalters und der Renaissance," in *Mitteilungen des Instituts für oesterreichische Geschichtsforschung,* Band 9 (Innsbruck, 1888), 83n. 1. He also cited fellow Austrian art historian Josef Strzygowski for his work on calendar illustration. See Riegl, "Die mittelalterliche Kalenderillustration" in *Mitteilungen des Instituts für oesterreichische Geschichtsforschung,* 10 Band (Innsbruck, 1889), 74n. 2.
6. On the nineteenth-century Austrian historical discipline, see Alphons Lhotsky, *Österreichische Historiographie*; Von Srbik, *Geist und Geschichte vom deutschen Humanismus bis zur Gegenwart,* 2 Band, 75–122; Fellner, *Ludo Moritz Hartmann und die österreichische Geschichtswissenschaft*; Dachs, *Österreichische Geschichtswissenschaft und Anschluß.*
7. Riegl's concentration on a dominant European trajectory ignored the continued use of lunar calendars in the Jewish tradition and elsewhere.
8. "Die mittelalterliche Kalenderillustration," 1.

9. Ibid.
10. Ibid.
11. Ibid.
12. See Hayden White, "The Value of Narrativity in the Representation of Reality," in *The Content of the Form* (Baltimore, 1987), 1.
13. See White, "The Metaphysics of Narrativity: Time and Symbol in Ricoeur's Philosophy of History," in *The Content of the Form,* 181.
14. White discusses emplotment techniques in his now classic *Metahistory: The Historical Imagination in Nineteenth-Century Europe* (Baltimore, 1973).
15. The treatment of civilizations in terms of stages of development had widespread currency in the nineteenth century, and toward the end of the century anthropologists often focused their attentions on so-called primitive cultures. G. F. Klemm in Germany, Lewis Morgan in the United States, and E. B. Tylor in Britain were among the anthropologists to adopt this line of inquiry. In trying to situate historically several themes which Riegl left uncredited, I have benefited enormously from consulting Raymond Williams, *Keywords: A Vocabulary of Culture and Society*, rev. ed. (New York, 1983).
16. Riegl, "Die mittelalterliche Kalenderillustration," 2.
17. Ibid., 3.
18. Ibid., 2.
19. Ibid., 3.
20. Ibid. In the ancient Roman Republic, for example, patricians controlled the calendar and the scheduling of religious events.
21. Ibid.
22. Ibid.
23. Ibid.
24. "The new solar year for the needs of those on the land and the old lunar year for sacred function were allowed to remain alongside each other." Ibid.
25. On the *Kultur/Zivilisation* distinction, see Norbert Elias, *The Civilizing Process*, trans. Edmund Jephcott (Oxford, 1994).
26. See, for example, Winckelmann's essay "On the Imitation of the Painting and Sculpture of the Greeks," in *German Essays on Art History,* ed. Gert Schiff (New York, 1988), 1–17.
27. "Geschichte der Ornamentik 1," unpublished lecture, winter semester 1890/1891, 6–12, in Riegl Nachlaß, Schachtel I, Fakultat Kunstgeschichte, Universität Wien.
28. Riegl, "Die Holzkalender," 82.
29. Riegl, "Die mittelalterliche Kalenderillustration," 4.
30. Benjamin's discussion of Baudelairean correspondences in "On Some

Motifs in Baudelaire" shows interesting affinities with Riegl's discussion here. Correspondences, the "data of remembrance—not historical data, but data of prehistory" (182), remind us of the theological and ritualistic elements that infuse regular experience. In a passage that echoes Riegl's anthropology, Benjamin claims that a combination of regularity and theophany informs the work of the calendar: "Even though chronology places regularity above permanence, it cannot prevent heterogeneous, conspicuous fragments from remaining within it. To have combined recognition of a quality with the measurement of the quantity was the work of the calendars in which the places of recollection are left blank, as it were, in the form of holidays. The man who loses his capacity for experiencing feels as though he is dropped from the calendar" (184). Benjamin connects this discussion with Bergson's notion of *durée,* whose affinities with Riegl will be discussed later. See Benjamin, "On Some Motifs in Baudelaire" in *Illuminations,* trans. Harry Zohn (New York, 1969), 155–200.

31. The term "phantasie" was used by Franz Brentano to designate a kind of synthetic imagination that allowed people to move from immediate perceptions of time to a sense of durable temporal continuity. Husserl criticized the concept as lacking scientific rigor. See Franz Brentano, *Psychology from an Empirical Perspective;* Edmund Husserl, *The Phenomenology of Inner Time-Consciousness,* trans. James S. Churchill (Bloomington, 1964).
32. Walter Benjamin, "Epistemo-Critical Prologue" to *The Origin of German Tragic Drama,* trans. John Osborne (London, 1998), 34–35. On Benjamin's notion of constellation, see Richard Wolin, *Walter Benjamin: An Aesthetic of Redemption* (New York, 1982), 90–106; Martin Jay, "The Speed of Light and the Virtualization of Reality," in *The Robot in the Garden: Telerobotics and Telepistemology in the Age of the Internet,* ed. Ken Goldberg (Cambridge, MA, 2000), 154.
33. Lambert Wiesing, *Die Sichtbarkeit des Bildes: Geschichte und Perspektiven der formalen Ästhetik*, 76.
34. Riegl, "Die Holzkalender," 103.
35. Riegl, "Die mittelalterliche Kalenderillustration," 4.
36. Edmund Husserl, "The Origin of Geometry," trans. David Carr, in Jacques Derrida, *Edmund Husserl's Origin of Geometry: An Introduction,* trans. John P. Leavey, Jr. (Lincoln, 1978), 166, 174. In his introduction, Derrida notes Husserl's critique of the "empiricist cult of fact and causalist presumption" (26).
37. Ibid., 174.
38. The term "life-world" was developed by Husserl to describe the originary and intersubjective spatio-temporal horizon of human activity. See

his discussion of the term in *The Crisis of European Sciences and Transcendental Phenomenology,* trans. David Carr (Evanston, IL, 1970), 103–89.

39. One interesting claim arising from Husserl's phenomenological history is that the factual world is only one of the conceptual possibilities of history, an idea that Walter Benjamin would exploit more fully. Benjamin explored the potential for rearranging the debris of history in new constellations that would release the latent redemptive possibilities of the past.
40. Riegl, "Die mittelalterliche Kalenderillustration," 4.
41. Ibid., 14.
42. Ibid., 6.
43. Ibid., 8.
44. Olin, 9–14.
45. Riegl, "Die mittelalterliche Kalenderillustration," 12.
46. This discussion foreshadowed Erwin Panofsky's thesis about the uneven historical relationship between form and content in medieval art, a theory put forth in his well-known work, *Renaissance and Renascences in Western Art* (New York, 1960). Panofsky also considered zodiac images among his evidence.
47. Riegl, "Die mittelalterliche Kalenderillustration," 14.
48. Ibid., 22.
49. Ibid., 21.
50. Ibid., 24.
51. Ibid., 25.
52. Ibid.
53. Ibid.
54. Ibid., 27.
55. Ibid., 29.
56. Ibid., 30. This reference to inner necessity prefigured the concept of *Kunstwollen.*
57. Ibid., 30–31.
58. Ibid., 27.
59. Ibid., 33.
60. Ibid., 32.
61. Ibid., 33, 30.
62. Ibid., 34–35.
63. See Riegl, *Late Roman Art Industry* (*Spätrömische Kunstindustrie*) (Darmstadt, 1973), 394–95n. 2.
64. Riegl, "Die mittelalterliche Kalenderillustration," 34.
65. "Geschichte der Ornamentik 1," unpublished lecture, winter semester 1890/1891, 2–3, in the Riegl Nachlaß, Schachtel I, Fakultat Kunst-

geschichte, Universität Wien.

66. Ibid.
67. In part 2 of this book I examine the relationship between temporal continuity and visual form.
68. Riegl, "Die mittelalterliche Kalenderillustration," 38.
69. Ibid., 39.
70. Ibid.
71. Ibid., 38–39.
72. Ibid., 40–43. Perhaps Riegl knew that his former instructor Theodor von Sickel would be reading "Die mittelalterliche Kalenderillustration" in his application for habilitation, for the incorporation of chronology and paleography was bound to please him. In his evaluation of Riegl's materials, Sickel noted that "Die mittelalterliche Kalenderillustration" showed a command of the development of time measurement that put Riegl in a position to evaluate scientifically the artworks in question. Nonetheless, Sickel did not consider the essay an exemplary application of the diplomatic method because of its lack of empirical foundations. (See comment from Sickel on Riegl's *Habilitationsschrift, Universitätsarchiv;* letter from Riegl to Wickhoff [undated, late 1880s], Wickhoff Nachlaß, Institut für österreichische Geschichtsforschung archives.) Although Sickel considered Riegl's conclusions of limited empirical relevance, partly because of the small number of calendars surveyed, he granted that the author had demonstrated his scholarly credentials and should be approved for *Habilitation*. The art historian Franz Wickhoff was more generous in his praise of Riegl's merits. (See Sickel's and Wickhoff's comments on Riegl's *Habilitation* in the Riegl file at the Vienna *Universitätsarchiv.*) The epistolary exchanges among Wickhoff, Sickel, and Riegl, held by the Institut für österreichische Geschichtsforschung, contain clues that help to illuminate the relationship between the three men. Wickhoff, it seems, was something of a confidant for Riegl, who was not always sure that Sickel appreciated his work.

    Riegl's mention of a decorative acanthus motif on the Wandalbert-Martyrolog foreshadowed his work in *Problems of Style* (*Stilfragen*).
73. Riegl, "Die mittelalterliche Kalenderillustration,"47.
74. Ibid., 61.
75. Ibid., 51–61.
76. Ibid., 67, 68.
77. Ibid., 71.
78. Ibid., 72.
79. Ibid., 50.
80. Ibid.
81. In his later writings, Riegl increasingly disavowed arguments stressing the

influence of external factors on the development of art in favor of internalist arguments emphasizing the formal imperatives of artistic change.

82. Again, Riegl's use of the fairly vague concept of "spirit" to denote the cultural attributes of particular eras can be seen as a precursor to his notion of *Kunstwollen*.
83. Reigl, "Die mittelalterliche Kalenderillustration," 43, 50.
84. Ibid., 49.
85. In this regard, Olin's description of Riegl as a conservative revolutionary who used radical innovations in order to preserve an art historical tradition applies equally to his scholarly approach and his understanding of the workings of history. This theme is the preface and premise of Olin's book, the best scholarly monograph on Riegl. Olin writes: "[Riegl's] theories . . . attempted to rescue the highly valued notion of representation from the onslaught of modern challengers and, as such, occupy a precarious position between the values he upheld and the anti-representational theories that his work would later help others to support." Margaret Olin, *Forms of Representation in Alois Riegl's Theory of Art* (University Park, PA, 1992), xvii.
86. Paul Ricoeur, *Husserl: An Analysis of his Phenomenology,* trans. Edward G. Ballard and Lester E. Embree (Evanston, IL, 1967), 110.

Introduction to Part 1

1. Franz Wickhoff, *Römische Kunst* (Soest, 1974), 25–26; Alois Riegl, "Kunstgeschichte und Universalgeschichte," in *Festgaben zu Ehren Max Büdinger's von seinen Freunden und Schülern* (Innsbruck, 1898), 455.
2. The lecture notes for a later, expanded version of the seminar Riegl attended were published as *Grundlegung und Aufbau der Ethik,* ed. Franziska Meyer-Hillebrand (Bern, 1952). The English translation by Elizabeth Hughes Schneewind is entitled *The Foundation and Construction of Ethics* (London, 1973).
3. See Roger Bauer, *Der Idealismus und seine Gegner in Österreich*; Bauer, *La Réalité, Royaume de Dieu*; Johnston, *The Austrian Mind.*
4. The term "flexible positivism" is used by David Lindenfeld to characterize the thought of Alexius Meinong, also one of Riegl's professors. See David Lindenfeld, *The Transformation of Positivism.* Lindenfeld challenges H. Stuart Hughes's notion of a late nineteenth-century "revolt against positivism," noting that figures such as Freud and Weber, heroes of Hughes's *Consciousness and Society,* expressed commitment to the positivist ideals of scientific empiricism and rational explanation even as they expanded the narrow psychological models of mid-century positivism by

acknowledging the influence of intuition, emotion, and irrationalism. In practice, Freud's method was perhaps more hermeneutic than positivist. See Lindenfeld, 7–8; H. Stuart Hughes, *Consciousness and Society* (New York, 1961).

5. For recent histories of nineteenth-century formalist aesthetics and perceptual theory, see *Empathy, Form, and Space: Problems in German Aesthetics, 1873–1893,* ed. Harry Francis Mallgrave and Eleftherios Ikonomou (Santa Monica, 1994), and Jonathan Crary, *Techniques of the Observer: On Vision and Modernity in the Nineteenth Century* (Cambridge, MA, 1990). See also Michael Podro, *The Manifold of Perception: Theories of Art from Kant to Hildebrand* (Oxford, 1972), and *The Critical Historians of Art* (New Haven, 1982); and Ernst K. Mundt "Three Aspects of German Aesthetic Theory," *The Journal of Aesthetics and Art Criticism* 17, no. 3 (1959): 287–310.
6. On Baumgarten, see Terry Eagleton, *The Ideology of the Aesthetic* (Cambridge, 1990), 13–17.
7. On Kant's aesthetics, see Eagleton, *Ideology*; Martin Jay, "'The Aesthetic Ideology' as Ideology: or What Does It Mean to Aestheticize Politics?" in *Force Fields: Between Intellectual History and Cultural Critique* (New York, 1993), 79–80; S. Körner, *Kant* (Bristol, 1955).

   In his Third Critique, Immanuel Kant argues that the purpose of an aesthetic effort was fulfilled in the integrated realization of its component parts; art did not have an instrumental or utilitarian connection with the world. See Immanuel Kant, *Critique of Judgment*, trans. J. H. Bernard (New York, 1951); S. Körner, *Kant* (Great Britain, 1955). For Kant's influence on the emergence of modern aesthetic theory and art history, see Andrew Bowie, *Aesthetics and Subjectivity: from Kant to Nietzsche* (Manchester, 1990); Terry Eagleton, *The Ideology of the Aesthetic* (Cambridge, 1990); Podro, *The Manifold of Perception* and *The Critical Historians of Art.*
8. Arthur Schopenhauer, *The World as Will and Representation,* trans. E.F.J. Payne (New York, 1958), 2:191.
9. On Müller, see Crary, *Techniques of the Observer,* 88–95.
10. Unlike Kant and Schopenhauer, Herbart has been the subject of only very limited scholarship, especially in English. For the most extended recent discussion, see Michael Podro, *The Manifold of Perception,* 61–79. Mallgrave and Eleftherios, 10–14, and Crary, 100–102 provide briefer considerations of his significance in the history of nineteenth-century aesthetic philosophy.
11. The term *Vorstellung* presents some difficulties for translation. It is most precisely rendered as "presentation," although I have sometimes used the term "idea" to avoid awkwardness. This synonym should not sug-

gest, however, that I intend any distinction between ideas and presentations in Herbart.

12. One of Herbart's earliest published works was the *Psychologische Bemerkungen zur Tonlehre* (1811), which outlined a musical model of mental activity based on the harmonies and dissonances of presentations.
13. These efforts were subjected to strenuous criticism by philosophers such as Gottlob Frege in *The Foundations of Arithmetic* (1894) and Edmund Husserl in *Logical Investigations* (1900). On nineteenth-century psychology and anti-psychologism, see Mitchell Ash, *Gestalt Psychology in German Culture, 1890–1967: Holism and the Quest for Objectivity* (Cambridge, 1995); Martin Kusch, *Psychologism: A Case Study in the Sociology of Philosophical Knowledge* (London, 1995); and Martin Jay, "Modernism and the Specter of Psychologism," in *Cultural Semantics: Keywords of Our Time* (Amherst, 1998), 166–67.
14. Diana Graham Reynolds, *Alois Riegl and the Politics of Art History: Intellectual Traditions and Austrian Identity in Fin-de-siècle Vienna* (San Diego, 1997), makes a sharp distinction between historicism and Hegelian idealism on the one hand and Riegl's thought on the other. Alphons Lhotsky, *Österreichische Historiographie* (Vienna, 1962), and Heinrich Ritter von Srbik, *Geist und Geschichte vom deutschen Humanismus bis zur Gegenwart* (Munich, 1951), assert a strong anti-idealist strain in Austrian historiography.
15. Alois Riegl, *Das holländische Gruppenporträt* (Vienna, 1931), 4.
16. Ibid., 280–81.
17. On the history of the University of Vienna, see Rudolf Kink, *Geschichte der kaiserlichen Universität zu Wien* (Vienna, 1954); on Thun's reforms, see S. Frankfurter, *Graf Leo Thun-Hohenstein, Franz Exner und Hermann Bonitz* (Vienna, 1893); Hans Lentze, "Die Universitätsreform des Graf Leo Thun-Hohenstein," in *Österreichische Akademie der Wissenschaft, Philosophisch-Historische Klasse, Sitzungsberichte 239* (Vienna, 1962).
18. Richard Woodfield, "Reading Riegl's *Kunst-Industrie*," in *Framing Formalism: Riegl's Work*, ed. Richard Woodfield (Amsterdam, 2001), 60.

Chapter 2

1. For Brentano's biography, see Oskar Kraus, "Biographical Sketch of Franz Brentano," in *The Philosophy of Franz Brentano*, ed. Linda L. McAlister (London, 1976), 1–9; Antos C. Rancurello, *A Study of Franz Brentano: His Psychological Standpoint and His Significance in the History of Psychology* (New York, 1968).

2. Brentano's dissertation, *Von der mannigfachen Bedeutung des Seienden nach Aristoteles* (Freiburg, 1862), a reconsideration of Aristotelian ontology, was published in 1862. It was translated by Rolf George as *On the Several Senses of Being in Aristotle* (Berkeley, 1975).
3. Brentano, *Die Psychologie des Aristoteles, insbesondere seine Lehre von Nous Poietikos* (Mainz, 1867); trans. by Rolf George as *The Psychology of Aristotle: In Particular His Doctrine of the Active Intellect* (Berkeley, 1977).
4. Edmund Husserl, "Reminiscences of Franz Brentano," in McAlister, *The Philosophy of Franz Brentano,* 49.
5. Kraus, "Biographical Sketch," 5.
6. Rancurello, 6. Brentano was certainly aware of the debates and arguments preceding the declaration; he wrote a position paper attacking the proposed doctrine of infallibility.
7. See Franz Brentano, *On the Existence of God: Lectures Given at the Universities of Würzburg and Vienna, 1868–1891,* trans. Susan F. Krantz (Dordrecht, 1987); see also Eugen Seiterich, *Die Gottesbeweise bei Franz Brentano* (Freiburg im Breisgau, 1936), 17–25.
8. In a letter written to Carl Stumpf in the winter of 1870–71, Brentano insisted: "I have no close connection with the partisans of the anti-infallibility movement. You know how much I disagree with the doctrine of infallibility. However, I have no trust in these men." Rancurello, *A Study,* 9. See also Kraus, "Biographical Sketch." On the Altkatholiker, see Victor Conzemius, *Katholizismus ohne Rom: Die altkatholische Kirchengemeinschaft* (Zürich, 1969); see also Gertrude Himmelfarb, *Lord Acton: A Study in Conscience* (Chicago, 1952).
9. Both Austrian and Church law rejected the marriage of priests, but several court cases had extended the law to apply even to former priests. In fact, Brentano had faced heavy opposition in both Würzburg and Vienna for other reasons leading up to his marriage crisis. Husserl notes that Brentano had been labeled "a Scholastic, a Jesuit, a rhetorician, a monger, [and] a Sophist" by opponents. Quoted in Rancurello, *A Study,* 9.
10. See Franz Brentano, *Meine letzten Wünsche für Österreich* (Stuttgart, 1895), for his criticisms of the Austrian academic and political establishment.
11. This relative obscurity is in marked contrast to Brentano's acknowledged impact on Anglo-American philosophy and cognitive science, where the concept of intentionality has revolutionized the understanding of cognition. See in McAlister, *The Philosophy of Brentano*; Rancurello, *A Study*; *The School of Franz Brentano,* ed. Liliana Albertazzi, Massimo Libardi, and Robert Poli (Dordrecht, 1996); Barry Smith, *Austrian Philosophy: The Legacy of Franz Brentano* (Chicago, 1994); *The Brentano Puzzle,* ed. Roberto Poli (Aldershot, 1998); and to some extent the edited volumes

of J. C. Nyíri. See also the numerous works on Austrian philosophy by Rudolf Haller, such as *Studien zur österreichischen Philosophie* (Amsterdam, 1979) and *Fragen zu Wittgenstein und Aufsätze zur österreichischen Philosophie* (Amsterdam, 1986).

12. On Brentano's position in logical positivism, see Smith, *Austrian Philosophy*; Albertazzi et al., *The School*; and Otto Neurath, *La développement du Cercle de Vienne et l'avenir de l'empirisme logique* (Paris, 1935). On phenomenology, see Herbert Spiegelberg, *The Phenomenological Movement* (The Hague, 1975); Oskar Kraus, *Franz Brentano's Stellung zur Phänomenologie und Gegenstandstheorie* (Leipzig, 1924).

    Brentano disputed the accusation that his theories fell prey to psychologism by reducing categories of logic to those of psychology. He insisted that his evident perceptions had a certainty and universality that was distinct from mere feelings of conviction. Franz Brentano, *The Foundation and Construction of Ethics,* trans. Elizabeth Hughes Schneewind (London 1973), 140.

13. "The first philosophical text through which I worked my way, again and again from 1907 on, was Franz Brentano's "Von der mannigfachen Bedeutung des Seienden nach Aristoteles," wrote Heidegger. In Brentano's work, Heidegger discovered the "being of beings in its difference from beings." See Heidegger's Preface to *Heidegger: Through Phenomenology to Thought,* by William J. Richardson (The Hague, 1963), XI, 631.
14. William McGrath, *Freud's Discovery of Psychoanalysis: The Politics of Hysteria* (Ithaca, 1986), 122; James R. Barclay, "Franz Brentano and Sigmund Freud," *Journal of Existentialism* 5 (1964): 1–36.
15. Barry Smith, in a notable exception to this trend, considers Brentano's impact on Carl Menger's economics. See Smith, *Austrian Philosophy,* 299–332.
16. Franz Brentano, *Psychology from an Empirical Standpoint,* trans. Antos Rancurello, D. B. Terrell, Linda McAlister (London, 1973), 29–30.

    Cf. Edmund Husserl, *Experience and Judgment,* trans. James Churchill and Karl Ameriks (Evanston, IL, 1973), 80–81:"In general, attention is a tending of the ego toward an intentional object, toward a unity which 'appears' continually in the change of the modes of its givenness and which belongs to the essential structure of a specific act of the ego . . . ; it is a tending-toward in realization."

17. Brentano, *Descriptive Psychology,* trans. Benito Müller (London, 1995), 7.
18. Ibid., 31–79.
19. Ibid., 23.
20. Franz Brentano, *Psychology from an Empirical Standpoint,* 88.

21. Barry Smith, *Austrian Philosophy,* 37.
22. Brentano, *Descriptive Psychology,* 24–27.
23. Brentano, *On the Existence of God.* Roderick Chisholm cites a fundamental shift in Brentano's ontology that occurred in the 1880s and 1890s, perhaps as a reaction to accusations of psychologism. Chisholm noted that in his early career Brentano accepted the correspondence between mental objects and physical objects, whereas toward the end of his life he insisted that only concrete things, not concepts or qualities, could be objects of thought. His strict reism suspended the question of correspondence between mental objects and an external world, and denied the existence of fictitious objects of thought. See Roderick Chisholm, "Introduction to Brentano," *Descriptive Psychology,* xxii. See also Dale Jacquette, ed., *The Cambridge Companion to Brentano* (Cambridge, 2004).
24. The term mereology, designating the study of the relationship between parts and whole, is most closely associated with the work of the Polish philosopher Stanislaw Lesniewski, who studied under one of Brentano's philosophical heirs, Kasimir Twardowski. Several commentators, however, have noted Brentano's own predilection for explaining phenomena in terms of the description of their parts and thus fit him into the history of mereology. See Barry Smith, *Austrian Philosophy*; and Peter Simons, *Parts: A Study in Ontology* (Oxford, 1987).
25. Brentano, *On the Several Senses of Being in Aristotle,* trans. Rolf George, 109.
26. Ibid., 113.
27. Brentano, *Philosophical Investigations on Time, Space, and the Continuum,* trans. Barry Smith (London, 1988), 49–50.
28. Ibid., 79.
29. Husserl criticized Brentano for failing to include time among the objects of intentionality and falling prey to what he described as an implicit psychologism in the modal theory of time. Brentano, Husserl argued, believed that time was a mode of "phantasie" that attached to every perception, a quality distinct from perceived objects and generated in the mind. Brentano's theory of the "primordial association" of past, present, and future modes presented time as a series of discrete perceptual qualities linked together successively in the mind; it therefore could not account for the perception of continuity uniting the distant past, the not-so-distant past, and the present. Brentano's time, said Husserl, was nonreal (*irreale*), not an object. Against this, Husserl contended that the pure data of sense perception were themselves temporally constituted; phenomenological time was observable as the intentional object of time consciousness, witnessed in the sensory data itself. Edmund Husserl, *The Phe-*

nomenology of Inner Time Consciousness, trans. James S. Churchill (Bloomington, 1964), 29–40.

30. Brentano, *Philosophical Investigations on Time, Space, and the Continuum*, 9.
31. These were published posthumously as Brentano, *Geschichte der griechischen Philosophie* (Hamburg, 1988); Brentano, *Geschichte der mittelalterlichen Philosophie im christlichen Abendland* (Hamburg, 1980); Brentano, *Geschichte der Philosophie der Neuzeit* (Hamburg, 1987). Brentano's histories of philosophy were partly inspired by Johann Adam Möhler's church history. Oskar Kraus, "Franz Brentano," in *Neue Österreichische Biographie* (Vienna, 1926), 3:106.
32. Brentano, "Über die Gründe der Entmutigung auf philosophischem Gebiet," in *Über die Zukunft der Philosophie* (Leipzig, 1929).
33. Brentano, "Die vier Phasen der Philosophie und ihr augenblicklicher Stand," in *Die vier Phasen der Philosophie und ihr augenblicklicher Stand* (Leipzig, 1926). (This volume was first translated into English in 1998 by Balsz M. Mezei and Barry Smith, who provide an extensive introduction; see *The Four Phases of Philosophy* [Amsterdam, 1998].) Many essays in the volume serve to illuminate Brentano's theory of cyclical phases in the history of philosophy, his disdain for idealism, and his positivist allegiances. See, for example, "Plotinus" for a discussion of ancient philosophical mysticism and "Schopenhauer" for its modern counterpart. "Auguste Comte" celebrates the work of the French thinker. See also Josef Werle, *Franz Brentano und die Zukunft der Philosophie: Studien zur Wissenschaftsgeschichte und Wissenschaftssystematik im 19. Jahrhundert* (Amsterdam, 1989).
34. Franz Brentano, "Zur Methode aristotelischer Studien, und zur geschichtlicher Forschung auf philosophischem Gebiet überhaupt," in *Über Aristoteles*, ed. Rolf George (Hamburg, 1986), 10.
35. Brentano's attack is directed against Eduard Zeller's *Philosophie der Griechen* (1879) and *Grundriß der Geschichte der Griechischen Philosophie* (1893).
36. Brentano, "Zur Methode," 12–13.
37. Brentano, *Psychology from an Empirical Standpoint*, 42.
38. Ibid., 72–73.
39. Ibid.
40. Brentano, *The Foundation and Construction of Ethics*, 123.
41. Ibid., 62–77.
42. Smith, *Austrian Philosophy*, 45–51. This tripartite classification, as Brentano noted in his 1889 lecture *On the Origin of Our Knowledge of Right and Wrong*, can be found in similar form in Descartes's Third Meditation. See E. S. Haldane and G. R. T. Ross, *Philosophical Works of*

Descartes (Cambridge, 1931), 1:159; Brentano, *Vom Ursprung sittlicher Erkenntnis* (Hamburg, 1969), 17; Roderick M. Chisholm, *Brentano and Intrinsic Value* (Cambridge, 1986), 1–2.

43. Brentano, quoted in Roderick Chisholm, "Brentano's Descriptive Psychology," in McAlister, ed., *The Origin of Our Knowledge of Right and Wrong,* trans. Roderick M. Chisholm and Elizabeth H. Schneewind (London, 1969), 24n. 33.
44. Franz Brentano, *The Foundation and Construction of Ethics,* 130.
45. Ibid., 265–66.
46. Ibid., 266–67.
47. See *The Essential Descartes,* ed. Margaret D. Wilson (New York, 1969), 190–91.
48. Franz Brentano, *Philosophical Investigations on Time, Space, and the Continuum,* 54.
49. Indeed, he passed it on to Husserl, who used Brentano's and Descartes's programs as a springboard for his phenomenology. See Edmund Husserl, *Cartesian Meditations: An Introduction to Phenomenology* (The Hague, 1977).
50. See Franz Brentano, *On the Existence of God.*
51. Smith, *Austrian Philosophy,* 81.
52. Ibid.
53. Roger Bauer, *La Réalité, Royaume de Dieu.*
54. Alexius Meinong, "Über Gegenstände höherer Ordnung und deren Verhältniss zur inneren Wahrnehmung," in *Gesamtausgabe,* Band 2 (Graz, 1973); Meinong, *Über die Erfahrungsgrundlagen unseres Wissens,* in *Gesamtausgabe,* Band 5 (Graz, 1973), 367–481.
55. Recent commentators have tended to dismiss Meinong's position as simplistic. On Meinong's views on time, see Paolo Bozzi, "Higher-Order Objects," in Albertazzi, et al., 296–303; David Lindenfeld, *The Transformation of Positivism: Alexius Meinong and European Thought, 1880–1920* (Berkeley, 1980), 124–29.

Chapter 3

1. For Sickel's biography, see Theodor von Sickel, *Römische Erinnerungen,* introduced and edited by Leo Santifaller (Vienna, 1947).
2. On Thun, see S. Frankfurter, *Graf Leo-Thun Hohenstein, Franz Exner und Hermann Bonitz* (Vienna, 1893); Hans Lentze, "Die Universitätsreform des Ministers Graf Leo Thun-Hohenstein," in *Sitzungsberichte der Philosophisch-Historischen Klasse österreichischen Akademie der Wissenschaft* 239 (1962); and for a briefer account, Robert Kann, *A History of the Habsburg Empire, 1526–1918* (Berkeley, 1974).

3. Joseph Alexander von Helfert, *Über Nationalgeschichte und den gegenwärtigen Stand ihrer Pflege in Österreich* (Prague, 1853), 2.
4. Ibid.
5. The historian Alphons Lhotsky began his 1954 history of the Institute of Austrian Historical Research with a quotation from Wilhelm Dilthey that echoed Helfert's statement: "One of the hardest of all steps taken by the human spirit is that in which fantasy is subordinated to reality." Quoted in Lhotsky, *Geschichte des Instituts für österreichische Geschichtsforschung, 1854–1954* (Graz, 1954), 11. For a brief account of the Institute, see James van Horn Melton, "From Folk History to Structural History: Otto Brunner (1898–1982) and the Radical-Conservative Roots of German Social History" in Lehmann and Melton, *Paths of Continuity: Central European Historiography from the 1930s to the 1950s.*
6. Helfert, Über Nationalgeschichte, 2–4.
7. Quoted in Emil von Ottenthal, *Das k.k. Institut für österreichische Geschichtsforschung, 1854–1904: Festschrift zur Feier des fünfzigjährigen Bestandes* (Innsbruck, 1904), 84.
8. On Jäger, see Hans Voltelini, "Albert Jäger," in *Neue Österreichische Biographie, 1815–1918*, Band 8 (Vienna, 1935), 162–73.
9. For a discussion of the types of German nationalism, see Leonard Krieger, *The German Idea of Freedom* (Boston, 1957), 303–14, 358–70.
10. Austria's resistance to German nationalism and German unification, as well as its official Catholicism, were among the chief reasons why North German liberals considered the Habsburg state reactionary and espoused a *kleindeutsch* position. Austria's illiberal reputation lasted even into the 1860s and 1870s, the period of Liberal predominance in Parliament. Liberalism in Austria was, of course, conflict ridden, as many histories have shown. For works that discuss Austrian liberalism, see Carl Schorske, *Fin-de-Siècle Vienna* (New York, 1981); Alan Sked, *The Decline and Fall of the Habsburg Empire* (London, 1989); Oscar Jaszi, *The Dissolution of the Habsburg Monarchy* (Chicago, 1929); and John Boyer, *Political Radicalism in Late Imperial Vienna: Origins of the Christian Social Movement, 1848–1897* (Chicago, 1981). Istvan Deak offers a more progressive image of the monarchy and its institutions in his *Beyond Nationalism: a Social and Political History of the Habsburg Army Corps, 1848–1914* (New York, 1990).

    Sickel always remained ill at ease in Vienna and complained frequently about professional hindrances. His position as a Saxon (Saxony was the most Protestant of northern German states) in Austria may have necessitated a certain political and religious reserve. In the late 1850s, when he was dissatisfied over his post in Vienna and perhaps about the post-1848 political situation as well, he was encouraged by his German colleagues to apply for a teaching position in Bavaria that ultimately went to someone else. During his early student days in Paris around 1850, Sickel wrote articles for a Prussian journal, *Der Tagebucheintrag,* where he described revolutionary events in Paris and lamented the return to monarchy in December 1851. See Theodor Sickel, *Denkwürdigkeiten aus der Werdezeit eines deutschen Geschichtsforschers,* ed. Wilhelm Erben (Munich, 1926), 33. See also his "Jugendgedichte" and his article "Die gothischen Thürme in Deutschland und Frankreich," which includes the familiar distinction between German depth and French superficiality, for other early examples of Sickel's German nationalism. In Sickel, *Denkwürdigkeiten,* see 26–27, 40–46.

11. See Lhotsky, *Geschichte des Instituts für österreichische Geschichtsforschung,* 51; see also Sickel, *Denkwürdigkeiten,* 229–30.
12. Sickel, letter to Heinrich Sybel, reproduced in Lhotsky, *Geschichte des Instituts für österreichische Geschichtsforschung,* 120.
13. He reported Sickel as saying that, in one ten-year period, the Spanish Inquisition immolated a million Jews! Ibid., 121.
14. See the mandates of 1874, written by Sickel, in ibid., 131–34.
15. Jean Mabillon, quoted in *Versions of History from Antiquity to the Enlightenment,* ed. Donald R. Kelley (New Haven, 1991), 414.

    Blandine Barret-Kriegel, in *La defaite de l'histoire* (Paris, 1988) describes Mabillon's battles against the church and against public opinion to defend his source-based historical *erudition.* By the mid-eighteenth century, she argues, the battle was largely lost, and French historians laid greater stress on form, style, and presentation—what she calls *savoir*—than they did on rigorous empirical research. The rehabilitation of Mabillon's project by nineteenth-century scholars such as Sickel forms a subsequent chapter in this story.

    Arnaldo Momigliano traces the history of antiquarian research and *erudition* from ancient times through the nineteenth century; he shows the surprising persistence of this often neglected and maligned step-sibling of Western historiography. See Momigliano, "The Rise of Antiquarian Research," in *The Classical Foundations of Modern Historiography* (Berkeley, 1990), 54–79.

    On Mabillon and the history of diplomatic documentary analysis, see also Donald R. Kelley, *Faces of History: Historical Inquiry from Herodotus to Herder* (New Haven, 1998) and Sickel, Introduction to *Acta Regum et Imperatorum Karolinorum: Digesta at Enarrata—Die Urkunden der Karolinger* (Vienna, 1867).
16. Leo Santifaller, *Das Institut für österreichische Geschichtsforschung: Festgabe zur Feier des zweihundertjährigen Bestandes des Wiener Haus-, Hof, und Staatsarchivs* (Vienna, 1950), 13.

17. From the Institute's 1874 statutes. Quoted in Sickel, "Das k. k. Institut für österreichische Geschichtsforschung," *Mitteilungen des Instituts für österreichische Geschichtsforschung* 1 (1880): 14.

The Institute's new orientation can be partly attributed to changing needs of the times, to the growing prominence of archives and museums—each conspicuously represented among the buildings of the Ringstraße—in late Imperial Austria and the need for curators, librarians, and archivists. For works on late nineteenth-century museum culture, see Schorske, *Fin-de-Siècle Vienna;* James J. Sheehan, *Museums in the German Art World: From the End of the Old Regime to the Rise of Modernism* (Oxford, 2000); and Suzanne Marchand, *Down from Olympus: Archaeology and Philhellenism in Germany, 1750–1970* (Princeton, 1996). For an article discussing Riegl's conception of the museum as producing, not simply classifying, scientific knowledge, see Ignasi de Solà-Morales, "Toward a Modern Museum: From Riegl to Giedion," *Oppositions* 25 (Fall 1982): 69–77.

18. Sickel, *Acta,* 1–63. See also Richard Rosenmund, *Die Fortschritte der Diplomatik seit Mabillon* (Munich, 1897), 59–72. See Sickel's memorandum reproduced in Lhotsky, *Geschichte,* 68–70.
19. Sickel, *Acta,* 55.
20. Ibid., 55–56.
21. Ibid., 56–60, 106–356; see also Sickel, *Beiträge zur Diplomatik* (Hildesheim, 1975), 335–37.
22. Sickel, *Acta,* 40–42.
23. Sickel, "Die Urkunden Ludwig's des Deutschen bis zum Jahre 859," in *Beiträge zur Diplomatik,* 337.
24. Sickel, *Acta,* 62–63.
25. Sickel memorandum, reprinted in Lhotsky, *Geschichte,* 68.
26. These essays were initially published in the *Sitzungsberichte der Philosophisch-Historischen Classe der kaiserlichen Akademie der Wissenschaften,* Bände 39, 47, 49, 85, 93, 101 (Vienna, 1861–1882). They were collected and reprinted in 1975, at times retaining their old page numbers. See Sickel, *Beiträge Zur Diplomatik.*
27. Sickel, *Beiträge Zur Diplomatik,* 329.
28. Ibid., 331.
29. Ibid., 332–33.
30. Sickel, *Acta,* 58–60.
31. Throughout Metternich's time, government-owned archives and document collections operated under extreme restrictions on accessibility. Censorship was the norm, especially in Austria, and histories generated from archival materials were expected to conform to the monarchical image of the state. Distance also hampered research; documents scat-

tered around many archives could be reached only through time-consuming and often treacherous journeys. The document collections that appeared with increasing frequency in late nineteenth-century Austria demonstrated the relaxed restrictions in archives throughout the Empire and Europe more widely. See George P. Gooch, *History and Historians in the Nineteenth Century* (Boston, 1913), chapter 1.

See also Sickel's 1857 memorandum about his methodological concerns, in which he complained of the lingering restrictions and authorizations needed to enter archives and gather documents. Reprinted in Lhotsky, *Geschichte,* 68–70.

32. Sickel, *Beiträge zur Diplomatik,* 330.
33. Sickel was a director and contributor to the "Monumenta Graphica Medii Aevi." Gooch, *History and Historians,* 149.
34. For details of events related to the photoduplication of documents, see Lhotsky, *Geschichte,* 57–61. For a later chapter in this debate, dealing with the 1870s and 1880s, see Leo Santifaller, "Über Pause und Photographie und über Sickels Kontroverse mit Pflugk-Harttung," in Theodor von Sickel, *Römische Erinnerungen,* 92–96.
35. Albert Jäger, "Graf Leo Thun und das Institut für österreichische Geschichtsforschung," *Österreichisch-Ungarische Revue* (Vienna, October 1889–March 1990), 18.
36. Quoted in Lhotsky, *Geschichte,* 58.
37. "This technique for manufacturing documentary facsimiles, developed through patriotic [*vaterländische*] inventiveness and means," read the imperial verdict, "demonstrated its accuracy and above all its security, and every doubt about the damaging or return of originals has been left behind." Quoted in Lhotsky, *Geschichte,* 60.
38. Theodor von Sickel, "Die Lunarbuchstaben in den Kalendarien des Mittelalters," in *Sitzungsberichte der Philosophische-Historischen Classe der kaiserlichen Akademie der Wissenschaften* (Vienna, 1862).
39. Ibid., 153.

Chapter 4

1. Alois Riegl, review of *Die Krypta in St. Florian: Ein Beitrag zur Baugeschichte der Stiftskirche St. Florian* by Alphons Müllner, *Mitteilungen des Instituts für österreichische Geschichtsforschung* 6 (1885): 319.
2. Margaret Olin, *Forms of Representation in Alois Riegl's Theory of Art* (University Park, PA, 1992), 6.
3. On Büdinger, see Adolf Bauer, "Büdinger, Max," *Biographisches Jahrbuch und Deutscher Nekrolog* 7 (1902), 223–31; Oswald Redlich, "Max

Büdinger," *Neue Österreichische Biographie* 6 (1929), 9–14.

4. For brief overviews of Büdinger's teachers, see Gooch, *History and Historians in the Nineteenth Century*; Georg Iggers, *The German Conception of History: The National Tradition of Historical Thought from Herder to the Present* (New Hampshire, 1968).
5. See, for example, Büdinger, *Die Universalhistorie im Alterthume* (Vienna, 1985). On Augustinian notions of history, see in Kelley, *Versions of History,* 142–54, 371; Kelley, *Faces of History,* 75–98.
6. Quoted in Kelley, *Versions of History,* 434–35.
7. Ibid., 435.
8. Ibid.
9. Quoted in *The Varieties of History from Voltaire to the Present,* ed. Fritz Stern, 2d ed. (New York, 1973), 59.
10. Ibid., 61.
11. Ibid., 60.
12. Oswald Redlich, "Max Büdinger," 2.
13. See Büdinger, *Vom Bewußtsein der Kulturübertragung* (Zürich, 1864).
14. Adolf Bauer, "Büdinger, Max," 27.
15. Srbik, *Geist and Geschichte,* 94–95.
16. Ibid.
17. On this incident, see Redlich, "Max Büdinger"; Bauer, "Büdinger," 223–24; Victor L. Tapie, *The Rise and Fall of the Habsburg Monarchy,* trans. Stephen Hardman (New York, 1971), 260.
18. See Büdinger, *Die Königenhofer Handschrift und ihre Schwestern* (Munich, 1859); Büdinger, *Die Königenhofer Handschrift und ihr neuester Vertheidiger* (Vienna, 1859); Johann Alexander von Helfert, *Max Büdinger und die Königenhofer Geschwister* (Prague, 1859). On Hanka, see Robert Kann, *A History of the Habsburg Empire, 1526–1918,* 385. By the 1880s, Büdinger's claims were vindicated, and even Czech nationalists acknowledged that the documents were clever forgeries by Hanka.
19. Max Büdinger, "Zeit und Raum bei dem indogermanischen Volke: eine universalhistorische Studie," in *Sitzungsberichte der Philosophisch-Historischen Classe der kaiserlichen Akademie der Wissenschaften* (Vienna, 1881), 512.
20. Ibid., 494.
21. Ibid., 495.
22. Ibid.
23. Ibid., 496.
24. Ibid.
25. Ibid., 503
26. Ibid., 508.
27. Ibid., 506.

28. Ibid.
29. Max Büdinger, "Zeit und Schicksal bei Römern und Westariern: eine universalhistorische Studie," in *Sitzungsberichte der Philosophisch-Historischen Classe der kaiserlichen Akademie der Wissenschaften* (Vienna, 1887), 3.
30. Büdinger, "Zeit und Raum," 503.
31. Büdinger, "Zeit und Schicksal," 5.
32. Ibid., 10.
33. See "Zoroastrian Dualist Cosmogony: Ohrmazd and Ahriman" in Mircea Eliade, *Essential Sacred Writings from around the World* (New York, 1967), 117–18.
34. Max Büdinger, "Zeit und Schicksal," 28.
35. Ibid., 28–30.
36. Alphons Lhotsky noted Büdinger's influence on art historians in particular and the vogue for Rankean universal history that German scholars launched in Vienna. See Lhotsky, *Österreichische Historiographie,* 176–77.

Chapter 5

1. On Zimmermann, see Lionello Venturi, "Robert Zimmermann et les origines de la science de l'art," *Deuxième Congrès international d'esthétique et de science de l'art* (Paris, 1937), 2:35–38; Johnston, *The Austrian Mind.* Podro, *The Critical Historians of Art*, 70–72, mentions Zimmermann in connection with Riegl, a link that Lambert Wiesing develops more fully in *Die Sichtbarkeit des Bildes: Geschichte und Perspektiven der formalen Ästhetik.*
2. Johnston, *Austrian Mind,* 289; see also Podro, *Critical Historians*, 71.
3. Wiesing, 45.
4. Zimmermann, *Leibnitz' Monadologie* and Zimmermann, *Leibnitz und Herbart: Eine Vergleichung ihrer Monadologien* (Vienna 1849).
5. On Bolzano, Herbart, Zimmermann, and their reception of Leibnizian thought, see Johnston, *Austrian Mind*, 274–90. On Zimmermann and Herbart, see Margaret Dana Iverson, "Alois Riegl's Historiography" (Ph.D. diss., University of Essex, 1980), 19–21.
6. Herbart was a dedicated musician, and Zimmermann was one of the first to point out that harmonic theory provided an apt model for Herbart's philosophical system. Robert Zimmermann, "Über die Einfluss der Tonlehre auf Herbart's Philosophie," *Sitzungsberichte der kaiserlichen Akademie der Wissenschaften-Wien, Phil.-Hist Klasse 73* (1873), 33–74.
7. Bolzano referred to Zimmermann as his "Herzensjunge." See "Bernard

Bolzano," in *Neue Österreichische Biographie ab 1815,* Band 16 (Vienna, 1965), 180. On Bolzano, see the works of Eduard Winter, *Der böhmische Vormärz in Briefen B. Bolzanos an F. Přihonsky, 1824–48* (East Berlin, 1956), and Winter, *Wissenschaft und Religion im Vormärz: Der Briefwechsel Bernard Bolzanos mit Michael Josef Fesl, 1822–1848* (Berlin, 1965).

8. A free thinker in Metternich's post-Josephinist Austria, Bolzano encountered considerable political and professional opposition to his religious views. His heterodox ideas contributed to his dismissal from the university in Prague, where he had a wide following, and to his trial for heresy in the 1820s. After 1819, he never again held a teaching post. He was able to continue his studies because of protection from Count Leo Thun. See Johnston, *Austrian Mind,* 275; "Bernard Bolzano," 176–77; Peter Demetz, *Prague in Black and Gold: Scenes in the Life of a European City* (New York, 1997), 275–78.
9. Bernard Bolzano, *Paradoxes of the Infinite,* trans. Frantisek Přihonsky (New Haven, 1950), 70.
10. Johnston, *Austrian Mind,* 286, describes Zimmermann as a "faithful interpreter of Herbart." Barry Smith, in *Austrian Philosophy,* 155–56, has indicated Zimmermann's debt to Bolzano. Lambert Wiesing also fits Zimmermann's aesthetic formalism within the rubric of Herbart's philosophical school. Wiesing, *Die Sichtbarkeit des Bildes,* chapter 1. On Zimmermann's extension of Herbartian aesthetic principles, see also Lionello Venturi, "Robert Zimmermann," 35–38.
11. Robert Zimmermann, *Aesthetik* (Vienna, 1858), 1:797.
12. Ibid., 804.
13. Zimmermann, *Aesthetik* (Vienna, 1865), 2:3.
14. See Mallgrave and Ikonomou, *Empathy, Form, and Space,* 15–17.
15. Zimmermann, *Aesthetik* 2:3.
16. Ibid., 4.
17. Despite their collegiality, Brentano and Zimmermann diverged radically when it came to the severing of philosophy from psychology. Brentano devoted his career to establishing the scientific credentials of philosophy by grounding it in a descriptive psychology. Although he shared with Zimmermann the belief that mental presentations provided access to philosophical concepts, Brentano rejected the Platonism and idealism latent in Zimmermann's thought.
18. Zimmermann, *Aesthetik,* 1:vi–vii.
19. Wiesing, *Die Sichtbarkeit des Bildes,* 43.
20. Ibid., 45.
21. In this regard, Wiesing (ibid., p. 43) asserts the affinities between Zimmermann's formalism and the linguistic concerns of Wittgenstein. Zim-

mermann's emphasis on surface analysis, on the immanence of form in physiognomy, and on form as relationship all found echoes in Wittgenstein's theories of language.

22. Johnston, *Austrian Mind,* 288.
23. Zimmermann, *Aesthetik,* 1:797.
24. Ibid., 799.
25. Ibid., 798.
26. Ibid., 799.
27. Zimmermann, *Aesthetik,* 2:222.

Chapter 6

1. For a history of the Vienna School as chronicled by one of its members, see Julius von Schlosser, "Die Wiener Schule der Kunstgeschichte," in *Mitteilungen des österreichischen Instituts für Geschichtsforschung,* Ergänzungsband 13 (Innsbruck, 1934). See also Thomas Zaunschirm, "Kunstgeschichte als Geistesgeschichte: Eine andere Wiener Schule," in *Das Grössere Österreich: Geistiges und Soziales Leben von 1880 bis zur Gegenwart* (Vienna, 1982); Udo Kultermann, *Geschichte der Kunstgeschichte* (Munich, 1996), 149–61; Christopher S. Wood, ed., *The Vienna School Reader: Politics and Art Historical Method in the 1930s* (New York, 2000).
2. Artur Rosenauer has recently tried to rehabilitate Thausing by demonstrating his seminal impact on the theoretical and methodological program associated with Wickhoff, Riegl, and other Vienna School luminaries. Artur Rosenauer, "Moriz Thausing und die Wiener Schule der Kunstgeschichte," in *Wiener Jahrbuch für Kunstgeschichte,* Band 36 (Vienna, 1983), 135–39. On Thausing, see Anton Springer, "Moriz Thausing," in *Repertorium für Kunstwissenschaft* (1885) 8:142–47; Theodor von Frimmel, "Thausing, Moritz Th.," in *Allgemeine Deutsche Biographie* (1894) 37:660–64.
3. On Böhm, see Kultermann, *Geschichte der Kunstgeschichte,* 150; Schlosser, "Die Wiener Schule," 146–47.
4. On Eitelberger, see Taras von Borodajkewicz, "Aus der Frühzeit der Wiener Schule der Kunstgeschichte: Rudolf Eitelberger und Leo Thun," in *Festschrift für Hans Sedlmayr* (Munich, 1962), 321–48; see also Hubert Janitschek, "Rudolf Eitelberger," in *Repertorium für Kunstwissenschaft* (1885) 8:398–404; J. Folnesics, "Eitelberger, Rudolf E. von Edelberg," in *Allgemeine Deutsche Biographie* (1910) 55:734–38.
5. According to Diana Graham Reynolds, Eitelberger hoped through his curatorship to promote Austrian handicrafts and design by demonstrat-

ing their commercial relevance. See Reynolds, *Alois Riegl and the Politics of Art History,* 72–77.

6. Jan Bialostocki asserts a direct connection between museum work and art historical method in Vienna. "In the Viennese tradition the museum . . . immediately confronted a young student with the basic problems of materials, tools, pigments, technics, iconography. It furnished the more mature student and the scholar with the original works of art—often not yet explained, enigmatic and puzzling—which constitute the primary material of any research. Volumes of the bulky Yearbook of the art collections of the highest Imperial House with their excellent articles bear witness to the concentration of the Vienna professors on the works of art kept in the museums." Quoted in Woodfield, *Framing Formalism,* 59–60. James Sheehan notes a connection between museums and scholarship in the wider German art world. Sheehan, *Museums in the German Art World: From the End of the Old Regime to the Rise of Modernism,* 90.
7. Gottfried Semper, *Der Stil in den technischen und tektonischen Künsten* (Mittenwald, 1977), translated as *Style in the Technical and Tectonic Arts, or, Practical Aesthetics, a Handbook for Technicians, Artists, and Friends of the Arts,* by Harry Francis Mallgrave and Malcolm Francis Baker (Los Angeles, 2003).
8. Reynolds, *Alois Riegl,* 85–88. Reynolds notes that Riegl's rejection of the dogmatic materialism of Semper's disciples in *Stilfragen* may have had Falke as its unnamed target.
9. Schlosser, "Die Wiener Schule," 160.
10. Thausing, *Dürer: Geschichte seines Lebens und seiner Kunst* (Leipzig, 1876).
11. See Thausing's article entitled "Iwan Lermoliew," Morelli's German *nom de plume,* in *Wiener Kunstbriefe,* 183–90.
12. On Morelli, see Kultermann, *Geschichte der Kunstgeschichte,* 105–9; Edgar Wind, *Art and Anarchy* (Great Britain, 1963), 30–46; and for an intriguing modern day application of Morelli's methods to cultural history, see Carlo Ginzburg, *Clues, Myths, and the Historical Method* (Baltimore, 1989), 96–102.
13. Morelli, from *Italian Painters,* quoted in Wind, *Art and Anarchy,* 38.
14. For the analogy with detective work, see Ginzburg, *Clues.* Edgar Wind described Morelli's method as a kind of "visual dissociation" of the objects on the canvas. See Wind, *Art and Anarchy,* 32.
15. Quoted in Kultermann, *Geschichte der Kunstgeschichte,* 107. Max Friedländer and Hermann Grimm also voiced skepticism about Morelli's methods. See Wind, *Art and Anarchy,* 35.
16. Of his admirer Franz Wickhoff, who was Thausing's student and Riegl's colleague, Morelli wrote, "I'm sorry for him because I can see that he

takes the study of art much too lightly, and that he wants to run before he has learned to walk. But so it is with most of these art students." Kultermann, *Geschichte der Kunstgeschichte,* 105.

17. In addition to Thausing and Wickhoff, Morelli's admirers included Gustavo Frizzoni and Bernard Berenson.
18. Olin, *Forms of Representation,* 7.
19. Moritz Thausing, "Die Stellung der Kunstgeschichte als Wissenschaft," in *Wiener Kunstbriefe* (Leipzig, 1884), 1–20.
20. See Winckelmann, "On the Imitation of the Painting and Sculpture of the Greeks," in *German Essays on Art History* (New York, 1988), 1–17.
21. For an excellent history of German classical archaeology, see Suzanne Marchand, *Down from Olympus: Archaeology and Philhellenism in Germany, 1750–1970* (Princeton, 1996). The classic account of German philhellenism is by Edith May Butler, *The Tyranny of Greece over Germany* (Cambridge, 1935).
22. On Conze, see Marchand, *Down from Olympus,* 92–103.
23. This attitude was already evident in responses to eighteenth-century excavations at Pompeii and Herculaneum, which helped to inspire the passionate German admiration for things Greek and Roman. Hugh Honour writes: "Whereas the site had at first been regarded as no more than a mine from which precious objects might be extracted, it was now [by the late eighteenth and early nineteenth centuries] seen as an historical terrain to be explored and mapped out in detail, with as much regard for broken pots and fallen stones as works of art. The distinction is similar to that between the Neo-classical artist's selection from Antiquity and the Romantic's attempt to retrieve a moment of the past. Both looked back, but in different ways and for different purposes." See Honour, *Romanticism* (New York, 1979), 208.
24. Marchand, *Down from Olympus,* 98.
25. See Riegl, "Der moderne Denkmalkultus," in *Gesammelte Aufsätze* (Augsburg, 1928), for the most explicit example of this approach. Conze identified the Geometric Style of ancient art that Riegl would later analyze in art historical depth.
26. Thausing, "Die Stellung der Kunstgeschichte als Wissenschaft," 2.
27. Ibid., 7–8.
28. Ibid., 5.
29. Ibid., 5–6.
30. Ibid., 9.
31. Ibid.
32. Ibid.
33. Ibid., 19–20.
34. Ibid., 13.

35. Ibid., 15.
36. See Thausing, *Dürer.* The categories of optical and tactile reappear in Riegl's historical analysis.
37. Olin, *Forms of Representation,* 7.

Chapter 7

1. Schlosser, "Die Wiener Schule," 121; Kultermann, *Geschichte der Kunstgeschichte,* 152. On Wickhoff, see Julius Schlosser, "Franz Wickhoff," in *Neue Österreichische Biographie,* Band 8 (Vienna, 1935), 190–98.
2. Franz Wickhoff, *Römische Kunst: Die Wiener Genesis* (Soest, 1974). The English translation is entitled *Roman Art,* trans. S. Arthur Strong (New York, 1900).
3. On Hartel's defense of modern art and the *Sezession* movement, see Schorske, *Fin-de-Siècle Vienna,* 238–39.
4. Wickhoff, *Römische Kunst,* 3.
5. The use of various narrative strategies to represent distinct temporal modes in literature is a theme that Erich Auerbach explores in *Mimesis: The Representation of Reality in Western Literature*, trans. Willard R. Trask (Princeton, 1953). His reflections on literary style and historical continuity touch on many of the themes I discuss.
6. Wickhoff, *Römische Kunst,* 124.
7. Ibid., 16.
8. Ibid., 14, 16.
9. Ibid., 16.
10. Ibid.
11. Ibid., 136.
12. Ibid.
13. Ibid., 135–36.
14. Ibid., 20.
15. Wickhoff was not alone at the turn of the century in using the categories of isolated perception and illusionism. The classical archaeologist Emanuel Löwy described pictorial memory [*Erinnerungsbild*] as presenting isolated forms against an abstract backdrop. Moreover, the history of art, Löwy believed, was progressing toward ever more perfect illusionism, what he called a retinal image, in which individual forms and clear borders gradually disappeared. Their complete disappearance would mark the end of visual art. See Margaret Olin's remarks on Löwy's *Die Naturwiedergabe in der älteren griechischen Kunst* (1900) in Olin, *Forms of Representation,* 222n. 39, 223n. 72.
16. On the Klimt controversy, see Schorske, *Fin-de-Siècle Vienna,* 208–78;

Hermann Bahr, *Gegen Klimt* (Vienna, 1903); Margaret Iverson, *Alois Riegl: Art History and Theory* (Cambridge, MA, 1993), 35–37.

17. Schorske, *Fin-de-Siècle Vienna,* 231–34; Alice Strobl, "Zu den Fakultätsbildern von Gustav Klimt," in *Albertina Studien 2,* 1964.
18. Bahr, *Gegen Klimt,* 31–34. The manuscript of Wickhoff's lecture no longer exists, so we must rely on Bahr's secondary account.
19. The characterization of the nineteenth century as a quintessentially historical era recurred in Riegl's work and has become a common trope in analyses of nineteenth-century intellectual history. Many of Wickhoff's themes in this lecture—of the relation between nature and art, of the antagonism between old and new—reappear in Riegl's oeuvre.
20. Wickhoff, like Riegl, no doubt drew this theme from the early Nietzschean writings that captivated many intellectuals in late nineteenth-century Vienna. For the now classic account of the influence of Nietzsche and Schopenhauer in Austria, see William McGrath, *Dionysian Art and Populist Politics in Vienna.* Diana Graham Reynolds has recently highlighted this point in her dissertation, *Alois Riegl and the Politics of Art History.*
21. Wickhoff, *Römische Kunst,* 25–26.
22. Franz Wickhoff, "Ueber die historische Einheitlichkeit der gesammten Kunstentwicklung," in *Festgaben zu Ehren Max Büdinger's von seinen Freunden und Schülern,* 461–69. An English translation can be found in *German Essays on Art History,* ed. Gert Schiff (New York, 1988), 165–72.
23. Wickhoff, "Ueber die historische Einheitlichkeit der gesammten Kunstentwicklung," 466. Wickhoff noted the influence of Japanese art on nineteenth-century European painting in *Römische Kunst* as well, 63–65.
24. Wickhoff, "Ueber die historische Einheitlichkeit der gesammten Kunstentwicklung," *Römische Kunst,* 469.
25. Riegl, *Spätrömische Kunstindustrie,* 109.
26. Ibid., 9–11.
27. Ibid., 108–18.
28. Riegl, "Der moderne Denkmalkultus, sein Wesen, seine Entstehung" (1903), in *Gesammelte Aufsätze,* 188.
29. Riegl, *Historische Grammatik der bildenden Künste* (Graz, 1966), 261–62, 282.
30. Riegl, *Spätrömische Kunstindustrie,* 111–12.
31. Ibid., 10.
32. Ibid., 11.
33. Riegl, "Kunstgeschichte und Universalgeschichte," in *Festgaben zu Ehren Max Büdinger's von seinen Freunden und Schülern* (Innsbruck, 1898), 452. Introducing the second version of *Historical Grammar of*

the Visual Arts, Riegl told a similar history of art history using an architectural metaphor. Riegl, *Historische Grammatik der bildenden Künste,* 207–8.

34. "It is a scientist," Riegl complained, who questioned the universal applicability of the "careful inductive method" that his own discipline pioneered, the method that "examines single appearances and only with the utmost caution ventures the next step toward direct cause and effect." Riegl, "Kunstgeschichte und Universalgeschichte," 452.
35. As the twentieth century demonstrated, even the natural sciences would not trust such unproblematic empiricism for long.
36. Riegl, "Kunstgeschichte und Universalgeschichte," 452–53.
37. Ibid., 453.
38. Ibid.
39. Ibid., 454.
40. Ibid., 455.
41. Ibid.
42. Ibid.
43. Ibid.
44. "Zwischen Wellenberg und Wellenthal liegt ein todter Punkt, in welchem die Extreme sich berühren." Ibid., 456.

Introduction to Part 2

1. Alois Riegl, "Review of Joseph Neuwirth, Studien zur Geschichte der Miniaturmalerei in Oesterreich," in *Mitteilungen des Instituts für österreichische Geschichtsforschung* (Innsbruck, 1887), 663.
2. Donald Preziosi notes that the metaphor of art object as readable text has pervaded the modern art historical discipline since its inception. See Preziosi, *Rethinking Art History* (New Haven, 1989), 44. I have found the whole of chapter 2 (21–54) quite helpful.
3. Riegl, Review of David R. v. Schönherr, *Alexander Colin und seine Werke,* 1562–1612, in *Mitteilungen des Instituts für österreichische Geschichtsforschung* (Innsbruck, 1890), 343–44.
4. Henri Zerner, "Alois Riegl: Art, Value, and Historicism," *Daedalus* 105, no. 1 (1996): 185.
5. See especially Olin, *Forms of Representation*; Reynolds, *Alois Riegl*; Iverson, *Alois Riegl.*
6. Hans Sedlmayr, "Die Quintessenz der Lehren Riegls," Introduction to Riegl, *Gesammelte Aufsätze,* xxxiii.
7. Dietrich von Loh, "Alois Riegl und die Hegelsche Geschichtsphilosophie," in *Kunstjahrbuch der Stadt Linz* (1986), 16; cf. von Loh, "Alois

Riegl und die Hegelsche Geschichtsforschung," Ph.D. diss., Freie Universität.

8. Wolfgang Kemp, Introduction to Alois Riegl, *The Group Portraiture of Holland,* trans. Evelyn M. Kain and David Britt (Los Angeles, 1999); Kemp, "Alois Riegl," in *Altmeister Moderner Kunst,* ed. Heinrich Dilly (Berlin, 1990), 37–60; Schorske, *Fin-de-Siècle Vienna.*
9. Olin, *Forms of Representation,* 113–27.
10. Ibid., 113.
11. Commentators who fit Riegl into a broad historical narrative include Podro, *The Critical Historians of Art*; Holly, *Panofsky and the Foundations of Art History*; Wiesing, *Die Sichtbarkeit des Bildes* (Reinbek bei Hamburg, 1997).
12. Riegl's lecture seminars at the University of Vienna from 1890 to 1903 also covered topics, such as German art, Spanish art, and Baroque art, that barely made it into his published work.

Chapter 8

1. Olin, *Forms of Representation,* 6.
2. Riegl, "Der moderne Denkmalkultus: sein Wesen und seine Entstehung," in *Gesammelte Aufsätze,* 144–93. For writings by and about Riegl on the subject of monument preservation and renovation, see *Kunstwerk oder Denkmal? Alois Riegls Schriften zur Denkmalpflege,* ed. Ernst Bacher (Cologne, 1995).
3. After the mid-century reconstruction of the Ring, several proposals were submitted for the renovation of historical monuments in Vienna, including a plan to restore the Giant Portal of St. Stephen's Cathedral to its original Romanesque style by removing Gothic additions. See Thausing, "Phylloxera Renovatrix" and "Das Riesenthor des St. Stephansdom, wie es ist und wie es war" in his *Wiener Kunstbriefe* (Leipzig, 1884).
4. See Olin, *Forms of Representation,* 20–22, 175–77; see also Olin, "The Cult of Monuments as a State Religion in Late Nineteenth-century Austria," in *Wiener Jahrbuch für Kunstgeschichte* 38 (1985): 177–98.
5. Riegl, "Der moderne Denkmalkultus," 145.
6. Cf. Hans Georg Gadamer, *Truth and Method* 2d rev. ed., trans. Joel Weinsheimer and Donald G. Marshall (New York, 1991). Gadamer argued that a scholar overcame the distance between past and present by "fusing horizons" with a historical text in the act of interpreting the past. The human sciences in his model aimed at understanding the reception of past meaning, not at recovering the past as it allegedly was.
7. Riegl, "Der moderne Denkmalkultus," 153.

8. Ibid., 145–46.
9. Ibid.
10. Ibid., 146.
11. Ibid.
12. Ibid., 149.
13. Ibid., 172.
14. Ibid., 150.
15. Ibid., 186. Riegl's designation of age value as a modern aesthetic-*cum*-religious cult [*Kultus*] recalled his discussion of the ritual cult of time measurement in antiquity and prefigured Benjamin's discussion of the cult value of art in the well-known "Work of Art" essay.
16. Ibid., 156.
17. Ibid., 162
18. Max Dvořák uses the term rhythm in discussing Riegl's art history. See Dvořák, "Alois Riegl," in *Gesammelte Aufsätze zur Kunstgeschichte* (Munich, 1929), 294. I consider the term's conceptual relevance in chapter 12.
19. Riegl, "Der moderne Denkmalkultus," 150.
20. Although "Der moderne Denkmalkultus" was Riegl's fullest exposition of the value attached to age and decay, it was not the first time he argued in favor of letting age effect its physical erosion. In *Volkskunst, Hausfleiß, und Hausindustrie* (Mittenwald, 1978), Riegl argued against those devotees of handicrafts who sought to promote rural folk art by marketing its products as consumer goods. With the best of intentions, they sought to preserve arts and crafts by making them competitive in a modern industrial marketplace. However, as modern economic processes, commodification and mass production actually sped up the disappearance of rural art by transforming it into something it was not: an exchange commodity on the modern market. The best a latter-day admirer could hope to do was study, classify, and appreciate folk art before it gradually vanished in the face of industrial life. Although we may apprehend the perceptual tendencies of bygone cultures in their art and artifacts, we cannot reproduce their authentic works or their modes of temporality using modern techniques. This message also figured into the end of Riegl's *Altorientalische Teppiche* (Mittenwald, 1979). For a further examination of the changing nature of craft production in history, see the notes of Riegl's lecture entitled "Die Zukunft des Handwerks," delivered in Prague on January 27, 1895. ("Die Zukunft des Handwerks," unpublished notes in folder marked "Frühennotizen," Riegl Nachlaß, Institut für Kunstgeschichte, Universität Wien.) The most thorough treatment of *Volkskunst, Hausfleiß, und Hausindustrie* that I have found is in chapter 5 of Diana Graham Reynolds's disserta-

tion on Riegl, which shows that his concern for folk arts and crafts grew out of his employment at the Museum für Kunst und Industrie in the late 1880s. Reynolds, 129–80.

Walter Benjamin carried forward the connection between modern perception and folk art. In a fragment from 1929, he claimed that folk art embodied its own genre-specific characteristics. Equating it to kitsch as evocative of "the world of primitives," Benjamin averred that folk art opened up realms of experience for modern observers that they could "wrap themselves up in," experiences that were at once lost to modern life and yet strangely familiar. These experiences, he noted, could serve as masks recovered from unconscious moments. "Art," Benjamin wrote, "teaches us to look into objects. Folk art and kitsch allow us to look outward from within them." Benjamin, "Some Remarks on Folk Art," in *Selected Writings,* ed. Marcus Bullock and Michael W. Jennings (Cambridge, 1996), 2: 278–79.

21. Riegl, "Der moderne Denkmalkultus," 179.
22. Ibid., 180.
23. Ibid., 172.
24. Ibid., 173.
25. Although he never responded directly to Nietzsche's writings on history, Riegl was exposed to Nietzschean thought through the *Leseverein der deutsche Studenten Wiens.* See McGrath, *Dionysian Art and Populist Politics in Vienna.*

Chapter 9

1. See Riegl, *Historische Grammatik der bildenden Künste.* An English translation by Jacqueline E. Jung was published in 2004.
2. Riegl, "Der moderne Denkmalkultus," 147.
3. Riegl, *Das holländische Gruppenporträt,* 189.
4. Riegl, "Der moderne Denkmalkultus," 149.
5. Zerner, "Alois Riegl," 183.
6. In *Spätrömische Kunstindustrie,* Riegl distinguished among the visual arts by organizing the work into chapters devoted to the different genres of sculpture, architecture, painting, and handicrafts. Although the basic laws of the *Kunstwollen* were common to all genres, they appeared with greater clarity in architecture and crafts than in figurative sculpture and painting, in which content tended to distract from pure form (19).
7. Riegl, *Das holländische Gruppenporträt,* 4.
8. See von Loh, *Alois Riegl und die Hegelsche Geschichtsforschung,* 83–132, for a survey of the literature on Riegl's reception. See also Iverson, *Alois*

Riegl, 2–18; Binstock, the foreword to *Historical Grammar of the Visual Arts,* 19–25.

9. Riegl's main attack on Semper's technical materialist theories came at the beginning of *Stilfragen,* v–xix. The architect Gottfried Semper attempted to place art history on a scientific basis by arguing that artistic form resulted from three factors—raw material, technique, and function—each of which could be studied empirically. Riegl dismissed this approach as reductive materialism and described Semper's factors as merely the "coefficients of friction" in an art history driven by an autonomous creative will. (See Riegl, *Spätrömische Kunstindustrie,* 9.) He noted, however, that Semper, like Darwin, needed to be distinguished from his followers, who applied his theories in oversimplified ways. He also made the same point in his lecture notes for the seminar "Geschichte der Ornamentik," praising Semper while criticizing his epigoni. See his unpublished lecture notes, Riegl Nachlaß, Institut für Kunstgeschichte, Universität Wien, 17–18.

   Semper's classic statement of the technical and functionalist origins of style appear in *Der Stil in den technischen und tektonischen Künsten.* On the relationship between Semper and Riegl, see especially Olin, *Forms of Representation,* 39–50.

10. Riegl, *Das holländische Gruppenporträt,* 261.

11. Dvořák, "Alois Riegl," 294. In the obituary for his former teacher, Dvořák celebrated Riegl's *Kunstwollen* as a new, flexible, and specifically artistic paradigm for art historians to follow, a concept that helped art history escape three impasses in which it was stuck at the turn of the century. The "kulturgeschichtliche" impasse, exemplified by the work of Burckhardt, "emerged from Romanticism and the patriotic study of antiquity, and remained satisfied arranging its depictions of the cultural and artistic life of the past chronologically." The "ästhetisch-dogmatisch" cul-de-sac, demonstrated in the work of Semper, "finds its origins in a naive application of the theories of English rationalists to cultural strivings, and attributes the origin and development of art to mechanistic laws." And the "historisch dogmatische" dead-end, typified by Schnaase, "in whose soil the self-adulation of the humanists, the teachings of classicism, and Hegel's religion of the absolute idea are rooted, views the history of art from the standpoint of evident and eternal values." Dvořák, "Alois Riegl," 282–83.

12. Wilhelm Worringer, *Abstraction and Empathy: A Contribution to the Psychology of Style,* trans. Michael Bullock (London, 1953).

13. Ibid., 9.

14. Hans Sedlmayr, "Die Quintessenz der Lehren Riegls" in Alois Riegl, *Gesammelte Aufsätze,* xvii–xviii.

15. E. H. Gombrich, *Art and Illusion: A Study in the Psychology of Pictorial Representation* (Princeton, 1960), 19. See also Gombrich, *The Sense of Order: A Study in the Psychology of Decorative Art* (Ithaca, 1979), 197–202.
16. Erwin Panofsky, "Der Begriff des Kunstwollens," in *Aufsätze zu Grundfragen der Kunstwissenschaft* (Berlin, 1964), 33–47.
17. See Wiesing, *Die Sichtbarkeit des Bildes,* 57–91.
18. Zerner, "Alois Riegl," 183.
19. Ibid., 182.
20. Riegl, "Naturwerk und Kunstwerk 1," in Riegl, *Gesammelte Aufsätze,* 59–60.
21. Ibid, 60.
22. Zerner, "Alois Riegl," 183.
23. Riegl, *Das holländische Gruppenporträt,* 189. The passage cited here refers to the empiricist/nativist debate among psychologists, a debate that involved Brentano. Heinrich von Helmholtz distinguished between nativists and empiricists in the field of psychology. The former argued that qualities such as color did not have autonomous existence but adhered to spatial phenomena; all color sensations were simultaneously sensations of space. The latter disputed the necessity of this spatial element and allowed for the autonomy of colors in perception. Brentano's position drifted toward nativism in the second half of his career. Brentano, *Untersuchungen zur Sinnespsychologie* (Hamburg, 1979), 66–70; Rancurello, *A Study of Franz Brentano,* 55.
24. Riegl, *Spätrömische Kunstindustrie,* 401.
25. Ibid. Riegl's somewhat ambiguous notion of *Weltanschauung* seems to share certain characteristics with Wilhelm Dilthey's more renowned theory of worldviews, although it is not clear that he ever read the latter's work. In publications such as "The Essence of Philosophy" (1907) and *The Types of Worldview and their Development in the Metaphysical Systems* (1911), Dilthey challenged the conventional distinction between a subjective *Weltanschauung* and an objective *Wissenschaft.* Although worldviews were historically conditioned, they were not merely subjective norms but contained within them certain objective structures corresponding to other *Weltanschauungen.* All worldviews shared a set of objective, homologous structures, thus establishing the epistemological possibility for a rigorous human science. Dilthey urged historians to study these "objective facts of life" in given eras. See Charles R. Bambach, *Heidegger, Dilthey, and the Crisis of Historicism,* 169–76.
26. Riegl, *Spätrömische Kunstindustrie,* 9.
27. Francesco dal Co, *Figures of Architecture and Thought,* 120. Dal Co is correct to note that Riegl's historiography rejects a regular, rhythmic

oscillation between flowering and decadence, but his contention that Riegl's historiography "imposes it own will, which is fulfilled outside of time" ignores the inherent temporality of viewing and signifying that Riegl analyzed in works such as "The Modern Cult of Monuments."

28. Leibniz described monads as entelechies "because they have in themselves a certain perfection. There is in them a sufficiency which makes them the source of their internal activities." Leibniz, "Monadology," in *Basic Writings,* trans. George R. Montgomery (La Salle, IL, 1968), 254–55.
29. Sergio Bettini, "Nota introduttiva," in *Industria artistica tardo romana,* xliv. Quoted in dal Co, *Figures of Architecture and Time,* 118.
30. Riegl, *Das holländische Gruppenporträt,* 64.
31. Riegl, *Stilfragen,* v.
32. Bergson, *Creative Evolution* (Mineola, NY, 1998), 87.
33. Ibid., 30.
34. Ibid., 1–2.
35. Ibid., 6–7.
36. Ibid., 10–11.
37. Riegl admired the remarkable accuracy of photographs and shared Sickel's optimism about the role the new medium could play in historical research. With technological improvement, he conjectured, photography might offer wholesale substitutes for original documents. (Riegl, "Der moderne Denkmalkultus," 172.) By the time he wrote *Late Roman Art Industry* and *The Group Portraiture of Holland,* Riegl was relying more heavily on photographs to make up for the expenses of distance and travel than he had in *Problems of Style.* (See his references to photographs in *Das holländische Gruppenporträt,* 26nn. 2, 56.) Although he lamented the shortcomings of photographic copies, he was also aware of the interpretive laxity that even the best drawing encouraged. (See Riegl, *Stilfragen,* 224–28, for interpretive problems related to drawings; see also p. 291 for remarks on photographs of Syrian artworks.) But like Sickel, he recognized the limitations of the medium. Riegl complained that incomplete or inadequate copies hampered his analysis of certain artworks. (See, for example, *Das holländische Gruppenporträt,* 56.) A copy could not entirely replace the original document because certain techniques of historical analysis were simply impossible unless one had access to original script and parchment, fragile though they may be. Furthermore, Riegl dismissed the artistic pretensions of at least one genre of photography, modern group photography; it served only a mnemonic function and made little contribution to the artistry of group portraiture. (*Das holländische Gruppenporträt,* 176, 233.)
38. Roland Barthes, *Camera Lucida: Reflections on Photography,* trans.

Richard Howard (New York, 1981), 88.

39. Ibid., 76.
40. Martin Jay, *Downcast Eyes: The Denigration of Vision in Twentieth-Century French Thought* (Berkeley, 1993), 435–56.

Chapter 10

1. Seminar notes dating from 1895 demonstrate that Riegl's interest in seventeenth-century Dutch painting was more than half a decade old by 1902. See "Geschichte der niederländische Malerei im 17. Jahrhundert" (Summer semester 1896), "Holländische Malerei" (winter semester 1896/1897), and "Holländische Malerei des 17. Jahrhunderts" (winter semester 1900/1901). I benefited from conversations with Georg Vasold in Vienna, who wrote a master's thesis on Riegl's lectures on Dutch art at the University of Vienna.
2. Riegl, *Das holländische Gruppenporträt,* 261–62.
3. Ibid., 262.
4. Jonathan Crary has documented the tremendous interest in attention found among late nineteenth-century humanistic scholars and social scientists. He includes Riegl briefly in his account, describing the art historian's concept of attention as a hushed communion between an elite observer and an artistic/historical community, the "secular equivalent of a religious experience." Jonathan Crary, *Suspensions of Perception: Attention, Spectacle, and Modern Culture* (Cambridge, 1999), 51–52.
5. Wolfgang Kemp, introduction to Riegl, *The Group Portraiture of Holland,* trans. Kain and Britt (Los Angeles, 1999), 15.
6. Riegl, *Das holländische Gruppenporträt,* 14.
7. Margaret Olin, "Forms of Respect: Alois Riegl's Concept of Attentiveness," *Art Bulletin* 71 (1989). See also chapter 8 of Olin's *Forms of Representation in Alois Riegl's Theory of Art,* 155–70.
8. Riegl, *Das holländische Gruppenporträt,* 61–62.
9. See Kemp, introduction to Riegl, *The Group Portraiture of Holland,* 1–57.
10. Riegl, *Das holländische Gruppenporträt,* 213.
11. Ibid., 188.
12. Riegl, "Salzburg's Stellung in der Kunstgeschichte," in *Gesammelte Aufsätze,* 111–32. See the analysis by Olin, *Forms of Representation,* 174. Riegl discusses Salzburg as a gateway for cross-cultural influences in his lecture notes for an 1894 seminar on the "Geschichte der deutschen Baukunst in die neueren Zeit," Summer semester, Riegl Nachlaß, Institut für Kunstgeschichte, Universität Wien. These lecture notes distin-

guish among cultural regions of the German-speaking lands, and they credit Austria with specific and often overlooked contributions to decorative art during the German Renaissance.

13. "Terborch is the painter of a striking brand of egoism that uses the knowledge of the others' weaknesses not in order to clarify human commonalities [*gemeinmenschlich*] but in order to exploit them and gain a sense of triumphant superiority. It is commonly known that this is the psychological attitude of people from the north of France. And thus, when we see the last great independent artist of Holland turning toward the French conception, the fate of painting in Holland as it declined during the last third of the seventeenth century becomes understandable: its own logical development rendered it irrelevant [*unanwendbar.*]" Riegl, *Das holländische Gruppenporträt,* 274. See his discussions of Italian, French, and Hollandish (North and South, Haarlem and Amsterdam) tendencies on pages 180, 278.
14. Svetlana Alpers, in *The Art of Describing: Dutch Art in the Seventeenth Century* (Chicago, 1983), makes surprisingly little reference to Riegl's analysis of the same topic. Like Riegl, she relies on a strong division between Italian and Dutch art, or, more precisely, Albertian and non-Albertian art. As opposed to Italian art, Dutch painting is an "art of space, not of time," a delight for the eyes, not *-istoria* (xxi). Dutch art, she argues, did not "constitute itself as a progressive tradition. It did not make a history in the sense that Italian art did." For Alpers, Italian, not Dutch art, was unusual in this regard. "Most artistic traditions mark what persists and is sustaining, not what is changing, in a culture" (xxv). Although Alpers largely ignores the issue of temporality that Riegl highlighted, she expands his discussion by connecting it with a broader visual culture.
15. For this development, see Riegl's discussion of Geertgen van Haarlem's "Legend of John the Baptist." Riegl, *Das holländische Gruppenporträt,* 8–25.
16. See Ibid., 40–50, for explicit comparisons between Italian and early Dutch painting.
17. Ibid., 61.
18. Perhaps for fear of compromising his internalist art history, Riegl never went into detail regarding the socio-historical context of Dutch civic democratization. See Ibid., 1–6, 40. See also Kemp's introduction to the English translation of *The Group Portraiture of Holland.*
19. For the image, see Riegl, *The Group Portraiture of Holland,* 107.
20. Riegl, *Das holländische Gruppenporträt,* 42.
21. Ibid., 44–45.
22. Ibid., 55–56.

23. Ibid., 52.
24. Ibid., 105. As we have seen, the relationship between the everyday and the eternal had appeared as a theme in Riegl's analysis of calendar illustrations in the late 1880s.
25. Ibid., 105.
26. Ibid., 85.
27. Ibid., 85–93.
28. Ibid., 28.
29. Ibid., 20.
30. Ibid., 261.
31. Ibid., 20. Riegl also stressed, to a lesser extent, the role of the hands in expressing the relationship between soul and action, inner and outer life.
32. Ibid., 15–16.
33. Ibid., 16. Following this discussion, Riegl echoed the work of his teacher Büdinger when he surmised that perhaps the Christian dualism was connected with an influx of Indo-European tribes in the late Roman Era. Like Büdinger, Riegl traced the purest form of this dualism to the primeval worldview of India, an early destination of Aryan migrants.
34. Ibid., 20.
35. Riegl, *The Group Portraiture of Holland*, 79–80. Wolfgang Kemp discusses the terms in his introduction.
36. Norman Bryson, *Vision and Painting: The Logic of the Gaze* (New Haven, 1983), 93. Cf. Bergson's notion of *durée* in *Creative Evolution.*
37. Bryson, *Vision and Painting*, 94.
38. Ibid., 95. See the discussion of the concept of constellation in Chapter 1 of this book.
39. See Martin Jay, "The Speed of Light and the Virtualization of Reality," in *The Robot in the Garden: Telerobotics and Telepistemology in the Age of the Internet*, ed. Ken Goldberg (Cambridge, MA, 2000), 144–62.
40. Bryson, *Vision and Painting*, 94.
41. Ibid., 95.
42. There are, of course, important differences between Bryson's and Riegl's conceptions of art's temporality. Bryson distinguishes between the durational time of production and the abstract and detemporalized time of punctuality. He contends that Western painting has systematically effaced what he calls the *deictic* aspect of art—the self-reference to duration and place of production. Unlike Eastern painting, which highlights "the work of production" by emphasizing such features as the brushwork, Western art sought to depict an arrested moment, lifted from temporal *durée,* to a viewing subject abstracted from both time and space. "The act of viewing is constructed as the removal of the dimensions of space and time, as the

disappearance of the body: the construction of an *acies mentis,* the punctual viewing subject" (Bryson 96). Western painting and viewing idealized an atemporal punctuality not in Riegl's sense of the historical and chronological punctum but as pure unspecified abstraction (Bryson 89). Despite his tendency to speak in terms of national and epochal blocks, Riegl's art history did not use characterizations as sweeping as Bryson's; the *Kunstwollen* progressed through subtle differentiations and combinations, not homogeneous blocks. For Riegl, Western art history revealed a wealth of artistic *Wollen* that could not be reduced to a single quality as Bryson's categorical indictment suggests. And whereas Bryson seeks to recover for art the incarnate, corporeal subject, Riegl privileged the psychological subject.

43. Riegl, *Das holländische Gruppenporträt,* 55.
44. Ibid., 161.
45. Ibid., 169–282.
46. Ibid., 260. Elsewhere in this passage, Riegl noted the difference between Rembrandt's *Kunstwollen* and its modern counterpart. While Hollandish group portraiture anticipated modern subjectivity in important ways, seventeenth-century artists preserved aspects of objectivity that disappeared by the nineteenth century. The modern *Kunstwollen* "required a deepening of the subject and his soulful experience of consciousness [*seelischen Erfahrungsbewußtseins*] as he became involved in the inner psychological coherence of the scene; through this process, the outer, objective aspect of the work is transformed into an inner experience of the viewer. As is well known, this psychological method of depiction is one of the means modern art uses to subjectivize the objective treatment of figures in an artwork" (201). Though Rembrandt's "Anatomy Lesson of Dr. Tulp" exhibited this strikingly modern tendency, the artist was ahead of his time.

    This passage can be compared with Wickhoff's discussion of illusionistic art, which also involved the subject in completing the objective depiction.
47. For a similar line of argument about eighteenth-century French painting, see Michael Fried, *Absorption and Theatricality: Painting and Beholder in the Age of Diderot* (Berkeley, 1980). Fried argues that painters like Greuze tried to represent the pure absorption of figures on the canvas by making them oblivious to the beholder, but at the same time tried to "attract," "arrest," and "enthrall" the viewer, to hold him transfixed before the canvas. The painting of figures absorbed in action became the key to effecting this seemingly paradoxical relationship to an observer who was both excluded and enthralled.

48. Bryson, *Vision and Painting,* 131.
49. Husserl, *The Phenomenology of Inner Time Consciousness,* 43.
50. Ibid., 42.

Chapter 11

1. Riegl, *Stilfragen,* 3.
2. Ibid., 20. He sometimes referred simply to the "künstlerische" or "schöpferische" drive.
3. Ibid., 22.
4. See the introduction to "Geschichte der dekorativen Kunst 1," unpublished lecture notes, winter semester 1896/1897, Riegl Nachlaß, Institut für Kunstgeschichte, Universität Wien.
5. Ultimately, Riegl's purpose in writing *Altorientalische Teppiche* was presentist: he sought to trace the independent source of a European rug tradition back to household production during Roman and Hellenistic times. The modern arts and crafts movement, which tried to preserve ancient artistic practices, could only simulate the household rug production of antiquity because it could not commit the requisite time to handicraft production. In nomadic tribes, Riegl wrote, women and slaves made handicrafts; modern social and economic circumstances prevented this recourse. Handicraft production could be appreciated but not reproduced in modern times.
6. Riegl, *Stilfragen,* 24.
7. Riegl "Geschichte der Ornamentik I," unpublished lecture notes, winter semester 1890/1891, 4.
8. Riegl, *Stilfragen,* 22.
9. Dal Co, *Figures of Architecture and Thought,* 118–21.
10. Riegl, *Stilfragen,* 23.
11. As noted previously, Riegl's empiricism was not restricted to pure sensory observation or constrained by a fetishism of date and material fact. Julián Marías, in his *History of Philosophy,* trans. Stanley Appelbaum and Clarence C. Strowbridge (New York, 1941), 371–77, ascribes this flexible notion of empiricism to Franz Brentano.
12. Riegl, *Stilfragen,* 107.
13. Ibid., 1.
14. Ibid., 3.
15. Ibid.
16. Ibid.
17. Riegl, *Historische Grammatik der bildenden Künste,* 75.
18. Ibid., 76.

19. Riegl, *Stilfragen,* 2.
20. Riegl, *Spätrömische Kunstindustrie,* 5–6.
21. Ibid., 4.
22. Ibid., 229.
23. Riegl, "The Place of the Vapheio Cups in the History of Art," trans. Tawney Becker, in Christopher S. Wood, *The Vienna School Reader: Politics and Art Historical Method in the 1930s* (New York, 2000), 105. See Riegl, "Zur kunsthistorischen Stellung der Becher von Vafio," in *Gesammelte Aufsätze,* 71.
24. Riegl, *Spätrömische Kunstindustrie,* 395n. Cf. Conrad Fiedler's *Über die Beurtheilung von Werken der bildenden Kunst* (1876): "interest in art begins only when interest in literary content vanishes." Quoted in Woodfield, "Reading Riegl's *Kunst-Industrie,*" in *Framing Formalism: Riegl's Work,* ed. Richard Woodfield, 52. Woodfield discusses the impact on Riegl of late nineteenth-century aesthetic theories of pure visibility (52–55).
25. Riegl, *Spätrömische Kunstindustrie,* 9.
26. Riegl, *Stilfragen,* viii.
27. Riegl, *Spätrömische Kunstindustrie,* 11. Riegl claimed that the recently discovered Dordogne cave paintings disproved materialist theories that the earliest art was geometric patterning derived from weaving and wickerwork technique. His rant against German scholarship cannot help but remind one of Nietzsche.
28. Riegl, *Stilfragen,* 4.
29. Ibid., xvii.
30. Ibid., xii.
31. Riegl, *Spätrömische Kunstindustrie,* 7.
32. Riegl, *Stilfragen,* vi.
33. Even when Riegl noted the relevance of external social developments on the course of art history, as for example in *The Group Portraiture of Holland,* he did so in a brief and perfunctory, almost evasive fashion.
34. This criticism might be read partly as a jab at Theodor Sickel's overemphasis on the auxiliary disciplines in history, and his subordination of art history to auxiliary status.
35. Wolfgang Kemp, "Fernbilder: Benjamin und die Kunstwissenschaft," in "*Links hatte noch alles sich zu enträtseln . . ." Walter Benjamin im Kontext,* 224–57.
36. Riegl, *Spätrömische Kunstindustrie,* 8.
37. Aristotle's star shone brightly in the Austrian philosophical firmament, and the influence of his notion of form as entelechy, perhaps inherited through Brentano, can be detected in Riegl's formalism.
38. Riegl, *Stilfragen,* 154.

Chapter 12

1. Riegl, *Stilfragen,* 11, 3.
2. Ibid., 39.
3. Ibid., 40.
4. Ibid., 89–90.
5. Ibid., 99.
6. Ibid., chapter 3, pt. B.
7. Ibid., 197.
8. Ibid., 259–346.
9. Riegl, *Spätrömische Kunstindustrie,* 80; see the whole section, 73–80.
10. Ibid., 27; see 25–27. This claim was the starting point of *Late Roman Art Industry,* from which Riegl traced the gradual emergence of space as a bounded object in late imperial times.
11. "The [Near Eastern] artist exchanged an original, vegetal motif that followed specific, living natural laws for a lifeless, geometric motif: he subdivided it and transformed it as he saw fit, depending upon the requirements of the geometrically and symmetrically defined space to be filled. . . . As a rule, one element provided the entire decorative conception: whether by division or duplication, a continuous and permanent interrelationship [*fortwährender Rapport*] is set up. Indeed, in geometrical design, this rule had long been known and practiced: patterns of squares and diamonds are the earliest examples of this kind. The achievement of the Saracens was to establish this law of infinite rapport as the leading principle in their vegetal tendril ornament." Riegl, *Stilfragen,* 307–8.
12. Riegl, *Spätrömische Kunstindustrie,* 80.
13. When Francesco dal Co indicates that "analogous methodological presumptions" underlie both artistic and historical practices in Riegl, he acknowledges a key principle in art historian's work. Dal Co, *Figures of Architecture and Thought,* 117–24.

    It is worthwhile here to recall the concepts of rhythm and temporality proposed by the philosopher Henri Bergson. In 1889, Bergson published his early *Essai sur les données immédiates de la conscience,* in which he described the effects of rhythm in dance—"the regularity of the rhythm establishes a kind of communication between him [the dancer] and us [the audience], and the periodic returns of the measure are like so many invisible threads by means of which we set in motion this imaginary puppet" (Bergson, *Time and Free Will: An Essay on the Immediate Data of Consciousness,* trans. F. L. Pogson [New York, 1960], 12)—and in music—"the rhythm and measure suspend the normal flow of our sensations and ideas by causing our attention to swing to and fro between fixed points" (14–15). In the temporal arts, rhythm organizes a work around clear points by conferring regularity and establishing a relationship between the artwork (the dance, the musical performance) and the viewer—a relationship of communication and of reciprocal control. The art object becomes predictable and comprehensible without relinquishing its objectivity entirely to the viewing subject. Rhythm governs both the artwork and viewer perception, which would otherwise remain an undifferentiated *durée.* Bergson compared aesthetic rhythm to the passage of states of mind, and noted the apparent conflict between an experience of undifferentiated *durée* and an awareness of time that seeks to apprehend by demarcation.

Riegl too believed that history moved in seemingly incompatible ways. History progressed by vacillating between recognizable and relatively definable poles; such was the tendency of art history to oscillate between abstract geometry and naturalism, pure decoration and figuration, "the two poles between which all artistic creation moves" (Riegl, *Stilfragen* 241). However, the internal movement of artistic forms themselves, barely perceptible and hardly measurable as such, drove art progressively forward by offering new problems, new goals, and new forms. Rhythm organized this visual history by regulating the relationship between artistic temporality and historical time and by connecting a localized *Kunstwollen* with a progressive historical continuity.

14. The section is entitled "The leading characteristics of the late Roman Kunstwollen." Riegl, *Spätrömische Kunstindustrie,* 389–405.
15. Ibid., 389–90.
16. Ibid., 391.
17. Ibid., 398.
18. Riegl recognized the apparent contradiction of turning to a contemporaneous literary text after his attacks on iconography, but insisted that he was merely testing and not proving his hypotheses with external sources. He used as his main source for citations Auguste Berthaud's *Sancti Augustini doctrinam de pulchro ingenuisque artibus e variis illius operibus excerptam* (Pictavii, 1891). See *Spätrömische Kunstindustrie,* 393–94n. 1. For our purpose, what is most important is Riegl's interpretation of Augustine, not the accuracy of his reading.
19. Riegl, *Spätrömische Kunstindustrie,* 394–95. The title of one of Augustine's early lost works—*de pulchro et apto*—also seemed to affirm Riegl's division between *Kunstzweck* and *äußerem Zweck,* between the inner imperatives of art and external nonartistic influences. Ibid., 393.
20. Ibid., 398–99.
21. Augustine, *De Ordine,* selection reprinted in *Philosophies of Art and Beauty: Selected Readings in Aesthetics from Plato to Heidegger,* ed. Albert Hofstadter and Richard Kuhns (Chicago, 1964), 175.
22. Augustine, *De Musica,* in Ibid., 191, 201.

23. Riegl, *Spätrömische Kunstindustrie,* 396–97, 400. In *The Group Portraiture of Holland,* chiaroscuro, a modernized concern for the coloristic manipulation of light and dark, played an important role in Riegl's analysis of free space.
24. Augustine, *De Musica,* in Hofstadter and Kuhns, *Philosophies of Art and Beauty,* 202.
25. Ibid., 201.
26. Ibid., 186.
27. See Kelley, *Versions of History from Antiquity to the Enlightenment,* 118, 142–48.
28. Riegl, *Spätrömische Kunstindustrie,* 396.
29. Ibid., 23–36.
30. Ibid., 26.
31. Ibid., 27–28.
32. Cf. Adolf Hildebrand, "The Problem of Form in the Fine Arts," in *Empathy, Form, and Space: Problems in German Aesthetics, 1873–1893,* ed. Harry Francis Mallgrave and Eleftherios Ikonomou (Santa Monica, 1994), 227–79. Hildebrand, a sculptor and visual theorist, also emphasized tactility and empathy in his discussion of form. See also Woodfield, 53–54.
33. Riegl, *Spätrömische Kunstindustrie,* 28–29.
34. Ibid., 402–3.
35. Riegl, "Die Stimmung als Inhalt der modernen Kunst," in *Gesammelte Aufsätze,* 28–39. In his seminar notes on Dutch group portraiture, Riegl used the term *Stimmung* to express both the heightened subjectivity of modern man and a pantheistic sense of the divinity of objects [*Gottheit der Dinge*]. The term described a modern version of the temporal link between subject and object that Riegl analyzed as articulated form in late antiquity. See seminar notes for "Holländische Malerei" (winter semester 1896/1897) and "Holländische Malerei des 17. Jahrhunderts" (winter semester 1900/1901), Riegl Nachlaß, Institut für Kunstgeschichte, Universität Wien. For the cultural background of the term *Stimmung,* see Olin, *Forms of Representation,* 122–27.
36. Crary, *Techniques of the Observer,* 73, 91. "The image," as Goethe put it, "now belongs to the eye." Quoted in Ibid, 69.
37. Ibid., 97–104. Crary ties the notion of retinal continuity to Johann Friedrich Herbart's model of presentations in consciousness. 100–104.
38. Crary's latest work, *Suspensions of Perception,* helps to illuminate a blind spot in Riegl's analysis. Crary argues that attention became a problem for the human and natural sciences in the late nineteenth century as the presence of the world receded into images. Men and women were called to pay attention to increasingly disjunct, abstract, and commodified simu-

lacra of experience that were open for colonization by external agents. Crary's argument points out political and social implications of changing notions of attention that Riegl, in his zeal to defend a purely autonomous art history, never acknowledged.

39. Crary, *Techniques of the Observer,* 60. Crary used this phrase to describe a seventeenth and eighteenth-century visual culture that the nineteenth century supposedly abandoned.

    The term "haptic," from the Greek word for touch, was used by Wilhelm Wundt in his laboratory experiments on physical psychology. Rudolf Arnheim makes a useful distinction between two senses of touch: the tactile, conveyed by receptors on the body surface, and the kinesthetic, conveyed my movements and tensions of the body. Riegl's term "haptic" emphasized the former. Arnheim, "Victor Lowenfeld and Tactility" in *New Essays on the Psychology of Art,* 240–51.
40. Crary, *Techniques of the Observer,* 82.
41. Ibid., 64.
42. In his *New Theory of Vision,* the eighteenth-century philosopher George Berkeley prefigured Riegl's analysis by arguing that man's knowledge of space came from isolated sensations of touch and corporeal movement that the mind fused into coherent perceptual wholes. See Ernst Gombrich, *Art and Illusion* (Princeton, 1960), 15, 297.
43. Leibniz, "Monadology," 263. Quoted in Crary, *Techniques of the Observer,* 52, as exemplifying eighteenth-century visual culture.
44. Olin, *Forms of Representation,* 171–87. Olin argues that Riegl's historical researcher engaged in an enterprise modeled on tactile isolation.

Conclusion

1. Stephen Kern, *The Culture of Time and Space, 1880–1918* (Cambridge, MA, 1983), 1.
2. Georg Lukàcs, *History and Class Consciousness,* trans. Rodney Livingstone (Cambridge, MA, 1971), 153; quoted in Woodfield, *Framing Formalism,* 57.
3. Theodor W. Adorno, *Aesthetic Theory,* trans. Robert Hullot-Kentor (Minneapolis, 1997), 60, 146, 169.
4. On Benjamin's reception of Riegl, see Wolfgang Kemp, "Benjamin's Beziehungen zur Wiener Schule," in *Kritische Berichte* 1, 1973; Kemp, "Benjamin und die Kunstwissenschaft," in Lindner, *Links hatte noch alles sich zu enträtseln . . . : Walter Benjamin in Kontext;* Michael P. Steinberg, "The Collector as Allegorist: Goods, Gods, and the Objects of History," in *Walter Benjamin and the Demands of History* (Ithaca, 1996); Thomas

Y. Levin, "Walter Benjamin and the Theory of Art History," *October* 47 (Winter 1988); and Giles Peaker, "Works that Have Lasted . . . : Walter Benjamin Reading Alois Riegl," in Woodfield, *Framing Formalism,* 291–309. See also references in Howard Caygill, *Walter Benjamin: The Color of Experience* (London, 1998).

5. Benjamin, "Review of Oskar Walzel, *Das Wortkunstwerk,*" in *Gesammelte Schriften* 3 (Frankfurt, 1972), 50. Translation from Giles Peaker, "Works that Have Lasted . . ." in Woodfield, *Framing Formalism,* 293.
6. A reference to the *Vienna Genesis* credited Wickhoff's contributions in this regard as well. See Benjamin's "Karl Kraus," in *Reflections,* trans. Edmund Jephcott (New York, 1978), 441.
7. Benjamin, "The Rigorous Study of Art," in *Selected Writings* (Cambridge, MA, 1999), 2: 669.
8. Benjamin, "Bücher, die lebendig geblieben sind," in *Gesammelte Schriften* III (Frankfurt a.M., 1972), 169–70.
9. Benjamin, "Curriculum Vitae of 1928," in *Gesammelte Schriften* VI (Frankfurt a.M., 1972), 217–19.
10. Benjamin, "Curriculum Vitae (3)," in *Selected Writings* 2: 78. In offering this interpretation, Benjamin repudiated scholars such as Worringer who invoked Riegl to support nationally or racially essentialist theories.
11. Benjamin, *The Origin of German Tragic Drama,* trans. John Osborne (London, 1998), 99.
12. Ibid., 55.
13. Ibid., 99, 59; See Alois Riegl, *Die Entstehung der Barockkunst in Rom* (Vienna, 1908).
14. Benjamin, "A Berlin Chronicle," in *Reflections,* 30–34.
15. Benjamin, "News about Flowers," in *Selected Writings* 2: 156. In "A Berlin Chronicle," he also mentioned the vegetal laws of fate, growing imperceptibly into the fabric of reality. See *Reflections,* 33.
16. Karl Blossfeldt, *Art Forms in the Plant World* (New York, 1985); Blossfeldt, *Natural Art Forms* (Mineola, NY, 1998).
17. Quoted in Richard Wolin, *Walter Benjamin: An Aesthetic of Redemption* (New York, 1982), 97. See chapter 3, 79–106. On Benjamin's notion of ideas, see Wolin's chapter 1.
18. See Martin Jay, *The Dialectical Imagination* (Berkeley, 1973), 200. See also Jay, *Marxism and Totality,* 247–52; Wolin, *Walter Benjamin,* chapter 2.

    The art historian Christopher S. Wood noted that Benjamin's recognition of "the unmediated eloquence of the isolated object" derives from multiple sources: "the late Renaissance concept of allegory; Goethe's biological *Urform* as explicated by the philosopher Georg Simmel; Riegl's art history." Wood, *The Vienna School Reader: Politics and Art*

Historical Method in the 1930s, 45.

19. See "Historical Nature: Ruins," in Susan Buck-Morss, *The Dialectics of Seeing: Walter Benjamin and the Arcades Project* (Cambridge, 1989), 159–201.
20. Benjamin, *The Origin of German Tragic Drama,* 55.
21. Ibid., 28.
22. Ibid., 29. Benjamin also employed the term "rhythm" in discussing the related concept of "origin." Origin described "that which emerges from the process of becoming and disappearance. . . . Its rhythm is apparent only to a dual insight. On the one hand it needs to be recognized as a process of restoration and reestablishment, but, on the other hand, and precisely because of this, as something imperfect and incomplete" (45). In his "Theologico-Political Fragment" (*Reflections,* 312–13), Benjamin used the term to describe the convergent quality of worldly existence and Messianic nature as happiness: "To the spiritual *restitutio in integrum,* which introduces immortality, corresponds a worldly restitution that leads to the eternity of downfall, and the rhythm of this eternally transient worldly existence, transient in its totality, in its spatial but also in its temporal totality, the rhythm of Messianic nature, is happiness. For nature is Messianic by reason of its eternal and total passing away."

    Benjamin's references to the term "rhythm" were themselves too transient to justify a full comparison with Riegl's use of the term. The passage cited above, with its description of decay and worldly temporal rhythm, however, at least suggests a conceptual similarity.
23. Benjamin, *The Origin of German Tragic Drama,* 29.
24. Ibid.
25. Ibid., 43.
26. Ibid., 47–48.
27. Ibid., 34.
28. Ibid., 37–38.
29. Benjamin, "Little History of Photography," in *Selected Writings* 2:518–19.
30. Ibid., 519.
31. Zerner, 186–87. Cf. Riegl, "Der moderne Denkmalkultus: sein Wesen und seine Entstehung," in *Gesammelte Aufsätze,* 160–65.
32. Benjamin, "The Work of Art in the Age of Mechanical Revolution," in *Illuminations,* trans. Harry Zohn (New York, 1969), 222.
33. Benjamin, "Little History of Photography," 523.
34. Benjamin, "The Work of Art in the Age of Mechanical Revolution," 220–21.
35. Ibid., 221.
36. Ibid., 236.

37. Ibid., 230.
38. Bergson too used cinematography as a metaphor for temporal duration and organic continuity. "He who installs himself in becoming sees in duration the very life of things, the fundamental reality. The Forms, which the mind isolates and stores up in concepts, are then only snapshots of the changing reality. They are moments gathered along the course of time; and, just because we have cut the thread that binds them to time, they no longer endure. They tend to withdraw into their own definition, that is to say, into the artificial reconstruction and symbolical expression which is their intellectual equivalent. They enter into eternity, if you will; but what is eternal in them is just what is unreal. On the contrary if we treat becoming by the cinematographical method, the Forms are no longer snapshots taken of the change, they are its constitutive elements, they represent all that is positive in Becoming. Eternity no longer hovers over time, as an abstraction; it underlies time, as a reality." Time, to use a phrase borrowed from Plato, became "a moving image of eternity." Bergson, *Creative Evolution,* 317–18.
39. In an essay on film, Erwin Panofsky wrongly equated the "spatialization of time" with the "dynamization of space." I contend that they are distinct processes. Erwin Panofsky, "Style and Medium in the Motion Pictures," in *Film: An Anthology,* ed. Daniel Talbot (Berkeley, 1959), 18.
40. Benjamin, "The Work of Art in the Age of Mechanical Revolution," 224.
41. Ibid., 238.
42. Ibid.
43. Ibid., 240.
44. Ibid., 239.
45. Benjamin, "Theses on the Philosophy of History," in *Illuminations,* 255.
46. Ibid., 262.
47. Ibid., 255.
48. Ibid., 256.
49. Ibid., 254.
50. Quoted in Susan Buck-Morss, 23; see Benjamin, *The Arcades Project,* trans. Howard Eiland and Kevin McLaughlin (Cambridge, MA, 1999), 463.
51. Phrases quoted from Buck-Morss, 93–95.
52. Ibid., 71.
53. Ibid., 59.
54. Ibid., 205–15.
55. Quoted in Ibid., 243; see Benjamin, *The Arcades Project,* 479.
56. Buck-Morss, 210–11.
57. Quoted in Ibid., 289–90.
58. Michael Roth and Dominick LaCapra have discussed the influence and

shortcomings of contextualist paradigms in Schorske, Janik, and Toulmin. See LaCapra, "Reading Exemplars: *Wittgenstein's Vienna* and Wittgenstein's *Tractatus*," in *Rethinking Intellectual History: Texts, Contexts, Language* (Ithaca, 1983), 84–117; Roth, "Performing History: Modern Contextualism in Carl Schorske's *Fin-de-Siècle Vienna*," *American Historical Review* 99, no. 3 (1994): 729–45.

59. Both Howard Eaton and David Lindenfeld, for example, point out that Austrian logical positivists rejected the belief in fixed objects in favor of object-relationships, asserting the fundamental temporality of all perception (though not necessarily of all objects). Howard Eaton, *The Austrian Philosophy of Values* (Norman, OK, 1930); David Lindenfeld, *The Transformation of Positivism: Alexius Meinong and European Thought 1880–1920.*

60. From Leibniz's Fifth Paper, quoted in Sherover, *The Human Experience of Time*, 141.

Bibliography

Archives

Universitätsarchiv, Vienna, Austria
Institut für österreichische Geschichtsforschung, Vienna, Austria
Riegl Nachlaß at the Institut für Kunstgeschichte, University of Vienna, Austria
Forschungsstelle für österreichische Philosophie, Graz, Austria
Houghton Library, Harvard University, Cambridge, MA

Books and Articles

Adorno, Theodor W. *Aesthetic Theory.* Translated by Robert Hullot-Kentor. Minneapolis: University of Minnesota, 1997.

Albertazzi, Liliana, Massimo Libardi, and Roberto Poli, eds. *The School of Franz Brentano.* Dordrecht: Kluwer Academic Press, 1996.

Alpers, Svetlana. *The Art of Describing: Dutch Art in the Seventeenth Century.* Chicago: University of Chicago Press, 1983.

Antoni, Carlo. *From History to Sociology: The Transition in German Historical Thinking.* Translated by Hayden V. White. Detroit, MI: Wayne State University Press, 1959.

Arnheim, Rudolf. *New Essays on the Psychology of Art.* Berkeley: University of California Press, 1986.

Ash, Mitchell. *Gestalt Psychology in German Culture, 1890–1967: Holism and the Quest for Objectivity.* Cambridge: Cambridge University Press, 1995.

Auerbach, Erich. *Mimesis: The Representation of Reality in Western Literature.*

Translated by Willard R. Trask. Princeton, NJ: Princeton University Press, 1953.

Bacher, Ernst, ed. *Kunstwerk oder Denkmal? Alois Riegls Schriften zur Denkmalpflege*. Vienna: Böhlau, 1995.

Bachmeier, Helmut, ed. *Paradigmen der Moderne*. In the series "Viennese Heritage." Amsterdam: John Benjamin, 1990.

Bahr, Hermann. *Gegen Klimt*. Vienna: Eisenstein, 1903.

Bambach, Charles. *Heidegger, Dilthey, and the Crisis of Historicism*. Ithaca: Cornell University Press, 1995.

Barclay, James R. "Franz Brentano and Sigmund Freud." *Journal of Existentialism* 5 (1964): 1–36.

Barea, Ilsa. *Vienna: Legend and Reality*. London: Secker and Warburg, 1966.

Barret-Kriegel, Blandine. *La défaite de l'érudition*. Paris: Presses Universitaires de France, 1988.

Barthes, Roland. *Camera Lucida: Reflections on Photography*. Translated by Richard Howard. New York: Hill and Wang, 1981.

Baudelaire, Charles. *The Painter of Modern Life and Other Essays*. Translated by Jonathan Mayne. New York: Phaidon, 1964.

Bauer, Adolf. "Büdinger, Max." In *Biographisches Jahrbuch und Deutscher Nekrolog*. 7 Band. Berlin: Reimer, 1905, 223–231.

Bauer, Roger, Eckhard Heftrich, Helmut Koopmann, Wolfdietrich Rasch, Willibald Sauerländer, and J. Adolf Schmoll, eds. *Fin-de-Siècle: Zu Literatur und Kunst der Jahrhundertwende*. Frankfurt am Main: Vittorio Klostermann, 1977.

Bauer, Roger. "Der Idealismus und seine Gegner in Österreich." In *Beihefte zum Euphorion: Zeitschrift für Literaturgeschichte*, edited by Rainer Gruenter and Arthur Henkel, 3. Heidelberg: Carl Winter Universitätsverlag, 1966.

———. *La Réalité, Royaume de Dieu: Études sur l'originalité du théâtre viennois dans la première moitié du XIXe siécle*. Munich: Hueber Verlag, 1965.

Beiträge zur Kunstgeschichte: Franz Wickhoff gewidmet. Von einem Kreise von Freunden und Schülern. Vienna: Anton Schroll, 1903.

Beller, Steven. *Vienna and the Jews, 1867–1938: A Cultural History*. Cambridge: Cambridge University Press, 1989.

Beller, Steven, ed. *Rethinking Vienna 1900*. New York: Berghahn, 2001.

Benedikt, Michael. *Kunst und Wurde*. Vienna: Turia & Kant, 1994.

Benesch, Otto. *Collected Writings*. Vol. 4. Edited by Eva Benesch. London: Phaidon, 1973.

Benjamin, Walter. *The Arcades Project*. Translated by Howard Euland and Kevin McLaughlin. Cambridge, MA: Harvard University Press, 1999.

———. *Der Begriff der Kunstkritik in der deutschen Romantik*. Frankfurt:

Suhrkamp, 1973.
———. *Gesammelte Schriften* 3 and 6. Frankfurt am Main: Suhrkamp, 1972.
———. *Illuminations.* Translated by Harry Zohn. New York: Schocken, 1969.
———. *Reflections.* Translated by Edmund Jephcott. New York: Schocken, 1978.
———. *The Origin of German Tragic Drama.* Translated by John Osborne. London: Verso, 1998.
———. *Selected Writings.* Vols. 1 and 2. Edited by Michael W. Jennings. Cambridge, MA: Belknap, 1996, 1999.
Bergson, Henri. *Creative Evolution.* Translated by Arthur Mitchell. Mineola, NY: Dover, 1998.
———. *Time and Free Will.* Translated by F. L. Pogson. New York: Harper, 1960.
Berman, Marshall. *All That Is Solid Melts into Air: The Experience of Modernity.* New York: Penguin, 1982.
"Bernard Bolzano." In *Neue Österreichische Biographie ab 1815,* Band 16. Vienna: Amalthea, 1965.
Berner, Peter, Emil Brix, Wolfgang Mantl, eds. *Wien um 1900: Aufbruch in die Moderne.* Vienna: Verlag für Geschichte und Politik, 1986.
Berthaud, Auguste. *Sancti Augustini doctrinam de pulchro ingenuisque artibus e variis illius operibus excerptam.* Pictavii: Apud P. Oudin, 1891.
Bloch, Ernst. *A Philosophy of the Future.* Translated by John Cumming. New York: Herder & Herder, 1970.
Blossfeldt, Karl. *Art Forms in the Plant World.* Mineola, NY: Dover, 1985.
———. *Natural Art Forms.* Mineola, NY: Dover, 1998.
Bolzano, Bernard. *Paradoxes of the Infinite.* Translated by Frantisek Prihonsky. New Haven, CT: Yale University Press, 1950.
———. *Wissenschaftslehre.* Leipzig: Verlag Felix Meiner, 1929.
Borodajkewycz, Taras von. "Aus der Frühzeit der Wiener Kunstgeschichte Rudolf Eitelberger und Leo Thun." In *Festschrift für Hans Sedlmayr.* Munich: Verlag C. H. Beck, 1962, 321–48.
Bourdieu, Pierre. *In Other Words: Essays towards a Reflexive Sociology.* Cambridge: Polity Press, 1990.
Bowie, Andrew. *Aesthetics and Subjectivity: from Kant to Nietzsche.* Manchester, UK: Manchester University Press, 1990.
Boyer, John. *Culture and Political Crisis in Vienna: Christian Socialism in Power, 1897–1918.* Chicago: University of Chicago Press, 1995.
———. *Political Radicalism in Late Imperial Vienna: Origins of the Christian Social Movement, 1848–1897.* Chicago: University of Chicago Press, 1981.
Brentano, Franz. *Aristoteles Lehre vom Ursprung des Menschlichen Geistes.* Leipzig: Veit & Comp., 1911.

———. *Descriptive Psychology.* Translated by Benito Müller. London: Routledge, 1995.

———. *Die Abkehr vom Nichtrealen.* Bern: Francke Verlag, 1966.

———. *The Foundation and Construction of Ethics.* Translated by Elizabeth Hughes Schneewind. London: Routledge and Kegan Paul, 1973.

———. *The Four Phases of Philosophy.* Edited by Balsz M. Mezei and Barry Smith. Amsterdam: Rodopi, 1998.

———. *Das Genie.* Leipzig: Duncker and Humblot, 1892.

———. *Geschichte der griechischen Philosophie.* Hamburg: Felix Meiner Verlag, 1988.

———. *Geschichte der mittelalterlichen Philosophie im christlichen Abendland.* Hamburg: Meiner, 1980.

———. *Geschichte der Philosophie der Neuzeit.* Hamburg: Feliz Meiner Verlag, 1987.

———. *Grundzüge der Ästhetik.* Bern: Francke Verlag, 1959.

———. *Meine letzten Wünsche für Österreich.* Stuttgart: Cottaschen Buchhandlung, 1895.

———. *On the Existence of God: Lectures given at the Universities of Würzburg and Vienna (1868–1891).* Translated by Susan F. Krantz. Dordrecht: Nijhoff, 1987.

———. *On the Several Senses of Being in Aristotle.* Translated by Rolf George. Berkeley: University of California Press, 1975.

———. *The Origin of our Knowledge of Right and Wrong.* Translated by Roderick Chisholm and Elizabeth Schneewind. London: Routledge and Kegan Paul, 1969.

———. *Philosophical Investigations on Space, Time, and the Continuum.* Translated by Barry Smith. London: Croom Helm, 1988.

———. *Psychology from an Empirical Standpoint.* Translated by Antos Rancurello, D. B. Terrell, and Linda McAlister. London: Routledge, 1973.

———. *The Psychology of Aristotle: In Particular His Doctrine of the Active Intellect.* Translated by Rolf George. Berkeley: University of California Press, 1977.

———. *Das Schlechte als Gegenstand dichterische Darstellung.* Leipzig: Duncker & Humblot, 1892.

———. *Sensory and Noetic Consciousness: Psychology from an Empirical Standpoint III.* Translated by Margarete Schättle and Linda L. McAlister. London: Routledge and Kegan Paul, 1981.

———. *Über Aristoteles.* Edited by Rolf George. Hamburg: Felix Meiner, 1986.

———. *Über die Zukunft der Philosophie.* Leipzig: Meiner, 1929.

———. *Untersuchungen zur Sinnespsychologie.* Edited by Roderick Chisholm and Reinhard Fabian. Hamburg: Feliz Meiner Verlag, 1979.

———. *Die Vier Phasen der Philosophie und ihr augenblicklicher Stand.* Leipzig: Meiner, 1926.

Bresslau, Harry. *Geschichte der Monumenta Germaniae Historica im Auftrag ihrer Zentraldirektion.* Leipzig: Hahnsche Buchhandlung, 1921.

Brix, Emil, and Patrick Werkner, eds. *Die Wiener Moderne.* Vienna: Verlag für Geschichte und Politik, 1990.

Broch, Hermann. *Hugo von Hoffmannstahl and His Time.* Translated by Michael Steinberg. Chicago: University of Chicago Press, 1984.

Bronner, Stephen Eric, and F. Peter Wagner, eds. *Vienna: The World of Yesterday, 1889–1914.* Atlantic Highlands, NJ: Humanities Press, 1997.

Brunner, Otto. "Das österreichische Institut für Geschichtsforschung und seine Stellung in der deutschen Geschichtswissenschaft." In *Mitteilungen des österreichischen Instituts für Geschichtsforschung.* Innsbruck: Universitäts-Verlag Wagner, 1938, 385–416.

Büdinger, Max, ed. *Untersuchungen zur Römischen Kaisergeschichte.* Leipzig: Teubner Verlag, 1870.

Büdinger, Max. *Die Königinhoferhandschrift und ihr neuester Vertheidiger.* Vienna: C. Gerold, 1859.

———. *Die Königinhoferhandschrift und ihre Schwestern.* Munich, 1859.

———. *Die Universalhistorie im Alterthume.* Vienna: C. Gerold, 1985.

———. *Vom Bewußtsein des Kulturübertragung.* Zürich, 1864.

———. "Zeit und Raum bei dem indogermanischen Volke: eine universalhistorische Studie." In *Sitzungsberichte der philosophisch-historischen Classe der kaiserlichen Akademie der Wissenschaften.* Vienna: Carl Gerold's Sohn, 1881, 493–512.

———. *Zeit und Schicksal bei Römern und Westariern: eine universalische Studie.* Vienna: Carl Gerold's Sohn, 1887.

Butler, Edith May. *The Tyranny of Greece over Germany.* Boston: Beacon, 1958.

Campos, Eliam. *Die Kantkritik Brentanos.* Bonn: Bouvier Verlag Herbert Grundmann, 1979.

Cassirer, Ernst. *The Philosophy of the Enlightenment.* Boston: Beacon, 1951.

Caygill, Howard. *The Color of Experience.* London: Routledge, 1998.

Chisholm, R. M., and R. Haller, eds. *Die Philosophie Franz Brentanos.* Amsterdam: Editions Rodopi, 1978.

Chisholm, Roderick. *Brentano and Intrinsic Value.* Cambridge: Cambridge University Press, 1986.

———. *Brentano and Meinong Studies.* Atlantic Highlands, NJ: Humanities Press, 1982.

Chmel, Joseph, ed. *Fontes Rerum Austriacum.* Vienna: K. K. Hof- und Staatsdrückerei, 1849.

———, ed. *Monumenta Habsburgica.* Vienna: K. K. Hof- und Staatsdrückerei, 1854.

———. *Der österreichische Geschichtsforscher.* Vienna: Beckschen Universitäts Buchhandlung, 1838.

Coffa, J. Alberto. *The Semantic Tradition from Kant to Carnap: To the Vienna Station.* Cambridge: Cambridge University Press, 1991.

Colquhoun, Alan. "Thoughts on Riegl." *Oppositions* 25 (Fall 1982): 79–83.

Conzemius, Victor. *Katholizismus ohne Rom: Die altkatholische Kirchengemeinschaft.* Zürich: Benziger, 1969.

Crary, Jonathan. *Suspensions of Perception: Attention, Spectacle, and Modern Culture.* Cambridge, MA: MIT Press, 1999.

———. *Techniques of the Observer: On Vision and Modernity in the Nineteenth Century.* Cambridge, MA: MIT Press, 1992.

Dachs, Herbert. *Österreichische Geschichtswissenschaft und Anschluß, 1918–1930.* Vienna: Geyer, 1974.

Dal Co, Francesco. *Figures of Architecture and Thought: German Architecture Culture, 1880–1920.* Translated by Stephen Sartarelli. New York: Rizzoli, 1990.

Deak, Istvan. *Beyond Nationalism: A Social and Political History of the Habsburg Army Corps, 1848–1914.* New York: Oxford University Press, 1990.

Deleuze, Gilles, and Félix Guattari. *A Thousand Plateaus: Capitalism and Schizophrenia.* Translated by Brian Massumi. Minneapolis: University of Minnesota Press, 1987.

Demetz, Peter. *Prague in Black and Gold: Scenes in the Life of a European City.* New York: Hill and Wang, 1997.

Descartes, Rene. *The Essential Descartes.* Edited by Margaret D. Wilson. New York: Mentor, 1969.

Die Universität Wien: Ihre Geschichte, ihre Institute und Einrichtungen. Edited by Akademischen Senat. Düsseldorf: Lindner Verlag, 1929.

Dilly, Heinrich, ed. *Altmeister moderner Kunstgeschichte.* Berlin: D. Reimer, 1990.

Dilly, Heinrich. *Kunstgeschichte als Institution: Studien zur Geschichte einer Disziplin.* Frankfurt: Suhrkamp, 1979.

Duranti, Luciana. "*Diplomatics: New Uses for an Old Science.*" Lanham, MD: Scarecrow Press, 1998.

Dvořák, Max. "Alois Riegl" and "Franz Wickhoff." In *Gesammelte Aufsätze zur Kunstgeschichte.* Munich: R. Piper & Co., 1929, 279–312.

Eagleton, Terry. *The Ideology of the Aesthetic.* Cambridge: Basil Blackwell, 1990.

Eaton, Howard. *The Austrian Philosophy of Values.* Norman: University of Oklahoma Press, 1930.

Eliade, Mircea. *Essential Sacred Writings from around the World.* San Francisco: Harper, 1967.

Elias, Norbert. *The Civilizing Process.* Translated by Edmund Jephcott.

Oxford: Blackwell, 1994.

Fellner, Günter. *Ludo Moritz Hartmann und die österreichische Geschichtswissenschaft*. Vienna: Geyer Edition, 1985.

Feulner, Adolf. *Kunst und Geschichte: Eine Anleitung zum Kunstgeschichtlichen Denken*. Leipzig: Verlag Karl W. Hiersemann, 1942.

Feyerabend, Paul. *Conquest of Abundance: A Tale of Abstraction versus the Richness of Being*. Chicago: University of Chicago Press, 2001.

———. *Farewell to Reason*. New York: Verso, 1987.

———. "Science as Art: A Discussion of Riegl's Theory of Art and an Attempt to Apply it to the Sciences." *Art + Text* 12–13 (1984): 16–46

Fischer, Kurt R. *Philosophie aus Wien*. Vienna: Geyer-Edition, 1991.

Folnesics, J. "Eitelberger, Rudolf E. von Edelberg." In *Allgemeine Deutsche Biographie* 55. Leipzig: Duncker und Humblot, 1910, 734–38.

Forster, Kurt. "Monument/Memory and the Morality of Architecture," *Oppositions* 25 (Fall 1982): 2–19.

Frankfurter, S. *Graf Leo Thun-Hohenstein, Franz Exner und Hermann Bonitz*. Vienna: Alfred Hölder, 1893.

Fried, Michael. *Absorption and Theatricality: Painting and Beholder in the Age of Diderot*. Berkeley: University of California Press, 1980.

Friedjung, Heinrich. *Österreich von 1848 bis 1860*. J. G. Stuttgart: Cottasche Buchhandlung Nachfolger, 1911.

Frimmel, Theodor von. "Thausing, Moriz." In *Allgemeine Deutsche Biographie* Band 37. Leipzig: Duncker & Humblot, 1894.

Gadamer, Hans-Georg. *Truth and Method*. 2d rev. ed. New York: Crossroad, 1991.

Ginzburg, Carlo. *Clues, Myths, and the Historical Method*. Translated by John and Anne C. Tedeschi. Baltimore, MD: Johns Hopkins University Press, 1989.

Gombrich, E. H. *Art and Illusion: The Study of Psychology in Pictorial Representation*. Princeton, NJ: Princeton University Press, 1960.

———. *The Sense of Order: A Study in the Psychology of Decorative Art*. Ithaca: Cornell University Press, 1979.

Gooch, George. *History and Historians in the Nineteenth Century*. Boston: Beacon Press, 1913.

Grafton, Anthony. *Joseph Scaliger: A Study in the History of Classical Scholarship*. Volume 2. Oxford: Clarendon, 1993.

Haller, Rudolf. *Fragen zu Wittgenstein und Aufsätze zur österreichischen Philosophie*. Amsterdam: Rodopi, 1986.

———. *Studien zur österreichischen Philosophie*. Amsterdam: Rodopi, 1979.

Hanák, Peter. *The Garden and the Workshop: Essays on the Cultural History of Vienna and Budapest*. Princeton, NJ: Princeton University Press, 1998.

Harvey, David. *The Condition of Modernity.* Cambridge, MA: Blackwell, 1989.

Heinekamp, Albert, ed. *Leibniz als Geschichtsforscher.* Wiesbaden: Franz Steiner Verlag, 1982.

Helfert, Josef Alexander. *Max Büdinger und die Königenhofer Geschwister.* Prague: Fr. Tempsky, 1859.

———. *Über Nationalgeschichte und den gegenwärtigen Stand ihrer Pflege.* Prague: J. G. Calveschen Buchhandlung, 1853.

Herbart, Johann Friedrich. *The Science of Education.* Translated by Henry M. and Emmir Felkin. London: Routledge and Sons, 1924.

Himmelfarb, Gertrude. *Lord Acton: A Study in Conscience and Politics.* Chicago: University of Chicago Press, 1952.

Hirsch, Hans. "Das österreichische Institut für Geschichtsforschung 1854–1934." In *Mitteilungen des österreichischen Instituts für Geschichtsforschung.* Innsbruck: Universitäts-Verlag Wagner, 1935, 1–14.

Hofstadter, Albert, and Richard Kuhns, ed. *Philosophies of Art and Beauty: Selected Readings in Aesthetics from Plato to Heidegger.* Chicago: University of Chicago Press, 1964.

Holly, Michael Ann. *Panofsky and the Foundations of Art History.* Ithaca: Cornell University Press, 1984.

Honour, Hugh. *Romanticism.* New York: Harper & Row, 1979.

Hughes, H. Stuart. *Consciousness and Society: The Reorientation of European Social Thought, 1890–1930.* New York: Vintage, 1961.

Husserl, Edmund. *Cartesian Meditations: An Introduction to Phenomenology.* Translated by Dorion Cairns. The Hague: Nijhoff, 1977.

———. *The Crisis of European Sciences and Transcendental Phenomenology: An Introduction to Phenomenological Philosophy.* Translated by David Carr. Evanston, IL: Northwestern University Press, 1970.

———. *Experience and Judgment: Investigations in a Genealogy of Logic.* Translated by James S. Churchill and Karl Ameriks. Evanston, IL: Northwestern University Press, 1973.

———. *Logical Investigations.* Translated by J. N. Findlay. London: Routledge, 1970.

———. "The Origin of Geometry." In *Edmund Husserl's Origin of Geometry: An Introduction*, edited by Jacques Derrida, 157–80. Translated by David Carr. Lincoln: University of Nebraska Press, 1978.

———. *The Phenomenology of Inner Time Consciousness.* Translated by James S. Churchill. Bloomington: Indiana University Press, 1964.

Ideler, Ludwig. *Handbuch der mathematischen und technischen Chronologie.* Berlin: August Rücker, 1825.

Iggers, Georg. *The German Conception of History: The National Tradition of Historical Thought from Herder to the Present.* Boston: Wesleyan University Press, 1968.

International Bibliography of Austrian Philosophy 1984/5. Edited by Thomas Binder, Reinhard Fabian, and Jutta Valent. Amsterdam: Rodopi, 1992.

Iversen, Margaret. "Style as Structure: Alois Riegl's Historiography." *Art History* 2, no. 1 (1979): 62–72.

———. *Alois Riegl's Historiography*. Ph.D. diss. University of Essex, 1980.

———. *Alois Riegl: Art History and Theory*. Cambridge, MA: MIT Press, 1983.

Jacquette, Dale, ed. *The Cambridge Companion to Brentano*. Cambridge: Cambridge University Press, 2004.

Jäger, Albert. "Graf Leo Thun und das Institut für österreichische Geschichtsforschung." *Österreichisch-Ungarische Revue* 8 (October 1889–March 1890): 1–22.

Janik, Allan, and Stephen Toulmin. *Wittgenstein's Vienna*. New York: Simon and Schuster, 1973.

Janik, Allan. *Essays on Wittgenstein and Weininger*. Amsterdam: Rodopi, 1985.

———. *Style, Politics, and the Future of Philosophy*. Dordrecht: Kluwer Academic Press, 1989.

———. "Vienna 1900 Revisited: Paradigms and Problems." *Austrian History Yearbook* 28 (1997): 1–27.

Janitschek, Hubert. "Rudolf Eitelberger." In *Repertorium für Kunstwissenschaft* 8. Vienna: Gerold, 1885. 398–404.

Jaszi, Oscar. *The Dissolution of the Habsburg Monarchy*. Chicago: University of Chicago Press, 1929.

Jay, Martin. *Cultural Semantics: Keywords of Our Time*. Amherst: University of Massachusetts Press, 1998.

———. *The Dialectical Imagination: A History of the Frankfurt School and the Institute of Social Research, 1923–1950*. Berkeley: University of California Press, 1973.

———. *Downcast Eyes: The Denigration of Vision in Twentieth-Century French Thought*. Berkeley: University of California Press, 1993.

———. "The Speed of Light and the Virtualization of Reality." In *The Robot in the Garden: Telerobotics and Telepistemology in the Age of the Internet*. Cambridge, MA: MIT Press, 2000.

Johnston, William M. *The Austrian Mind*. Berkeley: University of California Press, 1972.

Kann, Robert. *A History of the Habsburg Empire, 1526–1918*. Berkeley: University of California Press, 1974.

———. *A Study in Austrian Intellectual History: From Baroque to Romanticism*. New York: Praeger, 1960.

Kant, Immanuel. *Critique of Judgment*. Translated by J. H. Bernard. New York: Hafner, 1951.

Kaschnitz-Weinberg, Guido. Review of "Alois Riegl: Spätrömische Kunstindustrie." *Gnomon* 5, no. 4/5 (1929): 195–213.

Kastil, Alfred. *Die Philosophie Franz Brentanos: Eine Einführung in seine Lehre.* Bern: Francke Verlag, 1951.

Kelley, Donald R. *Faces of History: Historical Inquiry from Herodotus to Herder.* New Haven, CT: Yale University Press, 1998.

Kelley, Donald, ed. *Versions of History from Antiquity to the Enlightenment.* New Haven, CT: Yale University Press, 1991.

Kemal, Salim, and Ivan Gaskell. *The Language of Art History.* Cambridge: Cambridge University Press, 1991.

Kemp, Wolfgang. "Fernbilder: Benjamin und die Kunstwissenschaft." In "*Links hatte noch alles sich zu enträtseln . . .": Walter Benjamin im Kontext.* Edited by Burckhardt Lindner. Frankfurt am Main: Syndikat, 1978.

———. "Introduction." *The Group Portraiture of Holland* by Alois Riegl. Los Angeles: Getty Research Institute, 1999.

Kern, Stephen. *The Culture of Time and Space, 1880–1918.* Cambridge, MA: Harvard University Press, 1983.

Kink, Rudolf. *Geschichte der kaiserlichen Universität zu Wien.* Minerva GMBH (1969) Vienna: Unveränderter Druck, 1954.

Kleinbauer, W. Eugene. *Modern Perspectives in Western Art History.* New York: Holt, Reinhart, and Winston, 1971.

Köhnke, Klaus Christian. *The Rise of Neo-Kantianism: German Academic Philosophy between Idealism and Positivism.* Translated by R. J. Hollingdale. Cambridge: Cambridge University Press, 1991.

Körner, S. *Kant.* Bristol: Penguin Books, 1955.

Kraus, Oskar. *Franz Brentano's Stellung zur Phänomenologie und Gegenstandstheorie.* Leipzig: Felix Meiner, 1924.

Krieger, Leonard. *The German Idea of Freedom.* Boston: Beacon, 1957.

Kultermann, Udo. *Geschichte der Kunstgeschichte.* Munich: Prestel, 1996.

Kusch, Martin. *Psychologism: A Case Study in the Sociology of Philosophical Knowledge.* London: Routledge, 1995.

LaCapra, Dominick. *Rethinking Intellectual History: Texts, Contexts, Language.* Ithaca: Cornell University Press, 1983.

Landes, David. *Revolution in Time: Clocks and the Making of the Modern World.* Cambridge, MA: Harvard University Press, 1983.

Lange, Friedrich Albert. *The History of Materialism and Criticism of its Present Importance.* Translated by Ernest Chester Thomas. London: Routledge & Kegan Paul, 1950.

Le Rider, Jacques. *Modernity and Crises of Identity.* Translated by Rosemary Morris. New York: Continuum, 1993.

Lehmann, Hartmut, and James van Horn Melton, eds. *Paths of Continuity: Central European Historiography from the 1930s to the 1950s.* Washington, DC: German Historical Institute, 1994.

Leibniz, Gottfried Wilhelm von. *Basic Writings.* Translated by George R. Montgomery. La Salle, IL: Open Court, 1968.

Lentze, Hans. "Die Universitätsreform des Ministers Graf Leo Thun-Hohenstein." Österreichische Akademie der Wissenschaft, Philosophisch-Historische Klasse, Sitzungsberichte, 239. Vienna: Hermann Böhlaus Nachfassung, 1962.

Lhotsky, Alphons. *Aufsätze und Vorträge* in 5 Bände. Vienna: Verlag für Geschichte und Politik, 1974.

———. *Geschichte des Instituts für österreichische Geschichtsforschung 1854–1954.* Graz: Hermann Böhlaus Nachf, 1954.

———. *Österreichische Historiographie.* Vienna: Verlag für Geschichte und Politik, 1962.

Lindenfeld, David. *The Transformation of Positivism: Alexius Meinong and European Thought, 1880–1920.* Berkeley: University of California Press, 1980.

Luft, David. *Robert Musil and the Crisis of European Culture, 1880–1942.* Berkeley: University of California, 1980.

Magris, Claudio. *Der habsburgische Mythos in der österreichischen Literatur.* Salzburg: Otto Müller Verlag, 1966.

Mallgrave, Harry Francis, and Eleftherios Ikonomou, eds. *Empathy, Form, and Space: Problems in German Aesthetics, 1873–1893.* Santa Monica: Getty Center, 1994.

Mannheim, Karl. *Essays on the Sociology of Knowledge.* Edited by Paul Kecskemeti. London: Routledge and Kegan Paul Ltd., 1952.

Mariás, Julián. *History of Philosophy.* Translated by Stanley Applebaum and Clarence W. Strowbridge. New York: Dover, 1967.

Marchand, Suzanne. *Down from Olympus: Archaeology and Philhellenism in Germany, 1750–1970.* Princeton, NJ: Princeton University Press, 1996.

McAlister, Linda L., ed. *The Philosophy of Franz Brentano.* London: Duckworth, 1976.

McAlister, Linda. *The Development of Franz Brentano's Ethics.* Amsterdam: Rodopi, 1982.

McGrath, William. *Dionysian Art and Populist Politics in Vienna.* New Haven, CT: Yale University Press, 1974.

———. *Freud's Discovery of Psychoanalysis: The Politics of Hysteria.* Ithaca: Cornell University Press, 1986.

Meinong, Alexius. "Über die Erfahrungsgrundlagen unseres Wissens." In *Gesamtausgabe* 5. Graz: Akademische Druck und Verlagsanstalt, 1973.

———. "Über Gegenstände höher Ordnung und deren Verhältniss zur inneren Wahrnehmung." In *Gesamtausgabe* 2. Graz: Akademische Druck und Verlagsanstalt, 1971. 377–480.

Momigliano, Arnaldo. *The Classical Foundations of Modern Historiography.*

Berkeley: University of California Press, 1990.

Mundt, Ernst K. "Three Aspects of German Aesthetic Theory." *The Journal of Aesthetics and Art Criticism* 17, no. 3 (1959): 287–310.

Neurath, Otto. *La développement du Cercle de Vienne et l'avenir de l'empirisme logique*. Paris: Hermann, 1935.

Nietzsche, Friedrich. *The Birth of Tragedy* and *The Genealogy of Morals*. Translated by Francis Golffing. Garden City, NY: Doubleday, 1956.

———. *Untimely Meditations*. Edited by Daniel Breazeale. Cambridge: Cambridge University Press, 1997.

Noever, Peter, ed. *Kunst und Industrie: Die Anfänge des Museums für Angewandte Kunst in Wien*. Vienna: MAK and Hatje Kantz Verlag, 2000.

Nyíri, J. C. *Am Rande Europas: Studien zur österreichisch-ungarischen Philosophiegeschichte*. Vienna: Böhlau Verlag, 1988.

Nyíri, J. C., ed. *Austrian Philosophy: Studies and Texts*. Munich: Philosophia Verlag, 1981.

———. ed. *From Bolzano to Wittgenstein: The Tradition of Austrian Philosophy*. Vienna: Verlag Hölder-Pichler-Tempsky, 1986.

Oberhaidacher, Jörg. "Riegls Idee einer theoretischen Einheit von Gegenstand und Betrachter und ihre Folgen für die Kunstgeschichte." *Wiener Jahrbuch für Kunstgeschichte* 38 (1985): 199–218.

Olin, Margaret. *Forms of Representation in Alois Riegl's Theory of Art*. University Park: Pennsylvania State University Press, 1992.

———. "The Cult of Monuments as a State Religion in Late 19th Century Austria." *Wiener Jahrbuch für Kunstgeschichte* 38 (1985): 177–198.

Osborne, Peter. *The Politics of Time: Modernity and the Avant-garde*. New York: Verso, 1995.

Österreichische Philosophie. Katalog zur Ausstellung aus den Beständen der Graz: Forschungsstelle und Dokumentationszentrum für österreichische Philosophie, 1992.

Ottenthal, Emil von. *Das K. K. Institut für österreichische Geschichtsforschung 1854–1904*. Vienna: Adolf Holzhausen, 1904.

———. "Theodor v. Sickel Nekrolog." In *Mitteilungen des österreichischen Instituts für Geschichtsforschung*. Innsbruck: Universitäts-Verlag Wagner, 1908. 545–59.

Pächt, Otto. *Methodisches zur kunsthistorischen Praxis*. Munich: Prestel Verlag, 1977.

Panofsky, Erwin. *Aufsätze zu Grundfragen der Kunstwissenschaft*. Berlin: Verlag Bruno Hessling, 1964.

———. *Renaissance and Renascences in Western Art*. New York: Harper, 1960.

Podro, Michael. *The Critical Historians of Art*. New Haven, CT: Yale University Press, 1982.

———. *The Manifold of Perception: Theories of Art from Kant to Hildebrand*.

Oxford: Clarendon Press, 1972.

Poli, Roberto, ed. *The Brentano Puzzle.* Aldershot, UK: Ashgate, 1998.

Postone, Moishe. *Time, Labor, and Social Domination: A Reinterpretation of Marx's Critical Theory.* Cambridge: Cambridge University Press, 1996.

Preziosi, Donald. *Rethinking Art History: Meditations on a Coy Science.* New Haven, CT: Yale University Press, 1989.

Quellen und Forschungen zur vaterländischen Geschichte Literatur und Kunst. Vienna: Wilhelm Braumüller, 1849.

Rancurello, Antos C. *A Study of Franz Brentano: His Psychological Standpoint and his Significance in the History of Psychology.* New York: Academic Press, 1968.

Redlich, Oswald. "Max Büdinger." In *Neue Österreichische Biographie, 1815–1918.* 6 Band. Vienna: Amalthea, 1929.

Reynolds, Diana Graham. *Alois Riegl and the Politics of Art History: Intellectual Traditions and Austrian Identity in Fin-de-siècle Vienna.* Ph.D. diss. University of California, San Diego, 1997.

Ricoeur, Paul. *Husserl: An Analysis of his Phenomenology.* Evanston, IL: Northwestern University Press, 1967.

———. *Time and Narrative.* Translated by Kathleen McLaughlin and David Pellauer. 3 vols. Chicago: University of Chicago Press, 1984–1988.

Riegl, Alois. *Altorientalische Teppiche.* Mittenwald: Mäander, 1979.

———. *Aufsätze in Tageszeitungen, 1898–1905.* Facsimile collection in stacks of the library at the Institut für Kunstgeschichte, University of Vienna.

———. *Die Entstehung der Barockkunst in Rom.* Vienna: Anton Schroll & Co., 1908.

———. *Gesammelte Aufsätze.* Augsburg: Filser Verlag, 1928.

———. *The Group Portraiture of Holland.* Translated by Evelyn M. Kain and David Britt. Los Angeles: Getty Research Institute, 1999.

———. *Historical Grammar of the Visual Arts.* Translated by Jacqueline E. Jung. New York: Zone, 2004.

———. *Historische Grammatik der bildenden Künste.* Graz: Hermann Böhlaus Nachf, 1966.

———. *Das holländische Gruppenporträt.* Vienna: Österreichischen Staatsdruckerei, 1931.

———. "Die Holzkalendar des Mittelalters und der Renaissance" in *Mitteilungen des Instituts für österreichische Geschichtsforschung.* 9 Band. Innsbruck: Verlag Wagnerschen Universität, 1888. 82–103.

———. "Kunstgeschichte und Universalgeschichte." In *Festgaben zu Ehren Max Büdingers von seinen Freunden und Schülern.* Innsbruck: Wagnerschen Universitäts-Buchhandlung, 1898. 451–57.

———. *Late Roman Art Industry.* Translated by Rolf Winkes. Rome: Giorgio Bretschneider, 1985.

———. "Die mittelalterliche Kalendarillustration." In *Mitteilungen des Instituts für österreichische Geschichtsforschung*, 10 Band. Verlag Wagnerschen Universität: Innsbruck, 1889. 1–74.

———. "The Modern Cult of Monuments: Its Character and Its Origin." *Oppositions* 25 (Fall 1982): 21–51. Translated by Kurt W. Forster and Diane Ghirardo.

———. *Ein orientalischer Teppiche vom Jahre 1202 n. Chr.: Die ältesten orientalischen Teppiche*. Berlin: Siemens, 1895.

———. *Problems of Style: Foundations for a History of Ornament*. Translated by Evelyn Kain. Princeton, NJ: Princeton University Press, 1992.

———. Review of *Alexander Colin und seine Werke, 1562–1612*, by David R. v. Schönherr. In *Mitteilungen des Instituts für österreichische Geschichtsforschung*. 8 Band. Innsbruck: Verlag Wagnerschen Universität, 1887. 343–44.

———. Review of *Studien zur Geschichte der Miniaturmalerei in Oesterreich*. In *Mitteilungen des Instituts für österreichische Geschichtsforschung*. 8 Band. Innsbruck: Verlag Wagnerschen Universität, 1887. 662–63.

———. *Spätrömische Kunstindustrie*. Darmstadt: Wissenschaftliche Buchgesellschaft, 1973.

———. *Stilfragen: Grundlegungen zu einer Geschichte der Ornamentik*. Berlin: Richard Carl Schmidt, 1923.

———. *Volkskunst, Hausfleiß, und Hausindustrie*. Reproduction of Berlin, 1894 edition. Mittenwald: Mäander Kunstverlag, 1978.

———. "Vorwort" to *Kusejr ʿAmra*. Vol. 1, by Alois Musil. Vienna: K. K. Hof- und Staatsdruckerei, 1907.

Richards, E. G. *Mapping Time: The Calendar and its History*. Oxford: Oxford University Press, 1998.

Richardson, William J. *Heidegger: Through Phenomenology to Thought*. The Hague: Nijhoff, 1974.

Rosenauer, Artur. "Moriz Thausing und die Wiener Schule der Kunstgeschichte." In *Wiener Jahrbuch für Kunstgeschichte*. Band 36. Vienna: Heinrich Böhlau, 1983.

Rosenmund, Richard. *Die Fortschritte der Diplomatik seit Mabillon vornehmlich in Deutschland-Österreich*. Munich: R. Oldenbourg, 1897.

Roth, Michael. "Performing History: Modern Contextualism in Carl Schorske's Fin-de-Siècle Vienna." *American Historical Review* 99, no. 3 (1994): 729–45.

Ryan, Judith. *The Vanishing Subject: Early Psychology and Literary Modernism*. Chicago: University of Chicago Press, 1991.

Sältzer, Rolf, ed. *German Essays on History*. New York: Continuum, 1991.

Santifaller, Leo. *Das Institut für österreichische Geschichtsforschung*. Vienna:

Universum, 1949.

Sauerländer, Willibald. "Alois Riegl und die Entstehung der autonomen Kunstgeschichte am Fin de Siècle." In *Fin de Siècle: Zu Literatur und Kunst der Jahrhundertwende*. Frankfurt am Main: Vittorio Klostermann, 1977.

Scarrocchia, Sandro. *Studi su Alois Riegl*. Emilia-Romagna: Nuova Alfa Editoriale, 1986.

Schiff, Gert, ed. *German Essays on Art History*. New York: Continuum, 1988.

Schlosser, Julius von. "Franz Wickhoff." In *Neue Österreichische Biographie*. 8 Band. Vienna: Amalthea, 1935, 190–98.

———. "Die Wiener Schule der Kunstgeschichte." In *Mitteilungen des österreichischen Instituts für Geschichtsforschung*, Ergänzungs-Band 13, Heft 2. Innsbruck: Wagner, 1934.

Schnabel, Franz. *Deutsche Geschichte im Neunzehnten Jahrhundert*. Herder: Freiburg, 1934.

Schorske, Carl E. *Fin-de-Siècle Vienna: Politics and Culture*. New York: Vintage Books, 1981.

———. *Thinking with History: Explorations in the Passage to Modernism*. Princeton, NJ: Princeton University Press, 1998.

Schwartz, Vanessa R. "Walter Benjamin for Historians." *American Historical Review* 106, no. 5 (2001): 1721–43.

Seiterich, Eugen. *Die Gottesbeweise bei Franz Brentano*. Freiburg im Breisgau: Herder, 1936.

Semper, Gottfried. *Der Stil in den technischen und tektonischen Künsten*. Mittenwald: Mäander, 1977.

Shedel, James. *Art and Society: The New Art Movement in Vienna, 1897–1914*. Palo Alto, CA: SPOSS Inc., 1981.

Sheehan, James J. *Museums in the German Art World: From the End of the Old Regime to the Rise of Modernism*. Oxford: Oxford University Press, 2000.

Sherover, Charles M. *The Human Experience of Time: The Development of Its Philosophic Meaning*. New York: New York University Press, 1975.

Sickel, Theodor. *Acta Regum et Imperatorum Karolinorum Digesta et Enarrata: Die Urkunden der Karolinger*. Vienna: Carl Gerold's Sohn, 1867.

———. *Beiträge zur Diplomatik*. Nachdruck der Ausgabe Wien 1861–1882. Hildesheim: Georg Olms Verlag, 1975.

———. *Denkwürdigkeiten aus der Werdezeit eines deutschen Geschichtsforschers*. Edited by Wilhelm Erben. Munich: R. Oldenbourg, 1926.

———. "Das k.k. Institut für österreichische Geschichtsforschung." *Mitteilungen des österreichischen Instituts für Geschichtsforschung*. Innsbruck: Universitäts-Verlag Wagner, 1880. 1–18.

———. "Die Lunarbuchstaben in den Kalendarien des Mittelalters." In *Sitzungsberichte der philosophisch-historischen Classe*. Band 38. Vienna: K.

K. Hof- und Staatsdruckerei, 1862. 153–201.
———. *Das Privilegium Otto I für die Römische Kirche vom Jahre 962.* Innsbruck: Verlag der Wagnerschen Universitätsbuchhandlung, 1883.
———. *Römische Erinnerungen.* Edited by Leo Santifaller. Vienna: Universum, 1947.
———. *Zur Geschichte des Consils von Trient.* Vienna: Carl Gerold's Sohn, 1870.
Simons, Peter. *Parts: A Study in Ontology.* Oxford: Clarendon Press, 1987.
Sked, Alan. *The Decline and Fall of the Habsburg Empire, 1815–1918.* London: Longman, 1989.
Smith, Barry. *Austrian Philosophy: The Legacy of Franz Brentano.* Chicago: Open Court, 1994.
Solá-Morales, Ignasi de. "Toward a Modern Museum: From Riegl to Giedion." *Oppositions* 25 (Fall 1982): 69–77.
Sotriffer, Kristian, ed. *Das Groessere Oesterreich: Geistiges und Soziales Leben von 1880 bis zur Gegenwart.* Vienna: Tusch, 1982.
Spiegelberg, Herbert. *The Context of the Phenomenological Movement.* The Hague: Nijhoff, 1981.
———. *The Phenomenological Movement.* The Hague: Nijhoff, 1976.
Springer, Anton. "Moriz Thausing." In *Repertorium für Kunstwissenschaft.* 8 Band. Vienna: Gerold, 1885, 142–47.
Srbik, Heinrich Ritter von. *Deutsche Einheit: Idee und Wirklichkeit vom Heiligen Reich bis Königgrätz.* Munich: F. Bruckmann, 1935.
———. *Geist und Geschichte vom deutschen Humanismus bis zur Gegenwart.* Munich: F. Bruckmann, 1951.
Srdzenicki, Jan. *Franz Brentano's Analysis of Truth.* The Hague: Nijhoff, 1965.
Stadler, Friedrich, ed. *Scientific Philosophy: Origins and Development.* Boston: Kluwer Academic Pubs., 1993.
———. *Vom Positivismus zur "Wissenschaftlichen Weltauffassung."* Vienna: Löcker Verlag, 1982.
Steinberg, Michael. *The Meaning of the Salzburg Festival.* Ithaca: Cornell University Press, 1990.
Steinberg, Michael, ed. *Walter Benjamin and the Demands of History.* Ithaca: Cornell University Press, 1996.
Stern, Fritz, ed. *The Varieties of History from Voltaire to the Present.* New York: Vintage, 1973.
Streisand, Joachim, ed. *Die deutsche Geschichtswissenschaft vom Beginn des 19. Jahrhunderts bis zur Reichseinigung von oben.* Berlin: Akademie-Verlag, 1963.
Strobl, Alice. "Zu den Fakultätsbildern von Gustav Klimt." *Albertina Studien* 2 (1964).

Talbot, Daniel, ed. *Film: An Anthology*. Berkeley: University of California Press, 1959.

Tapie, Victor L. *The Rise and Fall of the Habsburg Monarchy*. Translated by Stephen Hardman. New York: Praeger, 1971.

Taylor, A.J.P. *The Habsburg Monarchy, 1809–1918: A History of the Austrian Empire and Austria-Hungary*. Chicago: University of Chicago Press, 1948.

Thausing, Moritz. *Dürer: Geschichte seines Lebens und seiner Kunst*. Leipzig: Seeman Verlag, 1876.

———. *Wiener Kunstbriefe*. Leipzig: Seemann, 1884.

Tietze, H. "Alois Riegl." In *Neue Österreichische Biographie, 1815–1919*. Band 8. Vienna: Amalthea, 1935, 142–48.

Vaterländische Blätter für den österreichischen Kaiserstaat. Journal. Vienna: Anton Strauß Verlag, 1808–1820.

Venturi, Lionello. "Robert Zimmermann et les origines de la science de l'art." In *Deuxième Congrès international d'esthètique et de science de l'art*. Paris: Librarie Felix Alcan, 1937.

Vergo, Peter. *Art in Vienna, 1898–1918: Klimt, Kokoschka, Schiele and Their Contemporaries*. London: Phaidon, 1975.

Voltelini, Hans. "Albert Jäger." In *Neue Österreichische Biographie, 1815–1918*, Band 5. Vienna: Amalthea, 1928.

Weiner, Marc A. *Arthur Schnitzler and the Crisis of Musical Culture*. Heidelberg: Carl Winter, 1986.

Werle, Josef. *Franz Brentano und die Zukunft der Philosophie: Studien zur Wissenschaftsgeschichte und Wissenschaftssystematik im 19. Jahrhundert*. Amsterdam: Rodopi, 1989.

White, Hayden. *The Content of the Form: Narrative Discourse and Historical Representation*. Baltimore, MD: Johns Hopkins University Press, 1987.

———. *Metahistory: The Historical Imagination in Nineteenth-Century Europe*. Baltimore, MD: Johns Hopkins University Press, 1973.

Wickhoff, Franz (dedicated to). *Beiträge zur Kunstgeschichte* von einem Kreise von Freunden und Schülern. Vienna: Schroll, 1903.

Wickhoff, Franz. *Römische Kunst: Der Wiener Genesis*. Berlin: Meyer & Jessen, 1912. Translated by S. Arthur Strong. New York: MacMillan, 1900.

———. "Ueber die historische Einheitlichkeit der gesammten Kunstentwicklung." In *Festgaben zu Ehren Max Büdinger's von seinen Freunden und Schülern*. Innsbruck: Wagnerschen Universitäts-Buchhandlung, 1898. 461–69.

Wiesing, Lambert. *Die Sichtbarkeit des Bildes: Geschichte und Perspektiven der formalen Ästhetik*. Reinbek bei Hamburg: Rowohlts, 1997.

Williams, Raymond. *Keywords: A Vocabulary of Culture and Society*. Rev. ed.

New York: Oxford, 1983.

Wind, Edgar. *Art and Anarchy.* London: Faber & Faber, 1963.

Winter, Eduard. *Der böhmische Vormärz in Briefen B. Bolzanos an F. Prihonsky, 1824–48.* East Berlin: Akademie Verlag, 1956.

———. *Franz Brentanos Ringen um eine neue Gottessicht.* Brünn: Verlag Rudolf M. Rohrer, 1941.

———. *Wissenschaft und Religion im Vormärz: Der Briefwechsel Bernard Bolzanos mit Michael Josef Fesl, 1822–1848.* Berlin: Akademie Verlag, 1965.

Wistrich, Robert S., ed. *Austrians and Jews in the Twentieth Century: From Franz Joseph to Waldheim.* London: St. Martins Press, 1992.

Wittgenstein, Ludwig. *Tractatus Logico-Philosophicus.* Translated by C. K. Ogden. London: Routledge, 1981.

Wolin, Richard. *Walter Benjamin: An Aesthetic of Redemption.* New York: Columbia University Press, 1982.

Wood, Christopher S., ed. *The Vienna School Reader: Politics and Art Historical Method in the 1930s.* New York: Zone, 2000.

Woodfield, Richard, ed. *Framing Formalism: Riegl's Work.* Amsterdam: Gordon & Breach, 2001.

Worringer, Wilhelm. *Abstraction and Empathy: A Contribution to the Psychology of Style.* Translated by Michael Bullock. London: Routledge and Kegan Paul Ltd., 1953.

Zaunschirm, Thomas. *Distanz-Dialektik in der modernen Kunst: Bausteine einer Paragone-Philosophie.* Vienna: Verlag des Verbandes der wissenschaftliche Gesellschaften Österreichs, 1983.

Zerner, Henry. "Alois Riegl: Art, Value, and Historicism." *Daedalus* 105, no. 1 (Winter 1976): 177–88.

Zimmermann, Robert. *Aesthetik.* Vienna: Wilhelm Bräumüller, 1858, 1865.

———. *Leibnitz' Monadologie.* Vienna: Bräumüller und Seidel, 1847.

———. *Leibnitz und Herbart: eine Vergleichung ihrer Monadologien.* Vienna: Wilhelm Bräumüller, 1849.

———. *Philosophische Propaedeutik für Obergymnasien.* In Österreichische Akademie der Wissenschaften Philosophisch-Historische Klasse Sitzungsberichte. Band 299. Vienna: Verlag der Österreichischen Akademie der Wissenschaft, 1975.

———. *Studien und Kritiken zur Philosophie und Aesthetik.* Vienna: Wilhem Bräumüller, 1870.

———. "Ueber den Einfluss der Tonlehre auf Herbart's Philosophie." In *Sitzungsberichte der Philosophisch-historischen Classe der Kaiserlichen Akademie der Wissenschaft.* Vienna. 73, heft 1–3, 1873.

———. "Wissenschaft und Literatur." In *Wien, 1848–1888.* Vienna: Konegan

Verlag, 1888.

Ziolkowski, Theodore. *Virgil and the Moderns.* Princeton, NJ: Princeton University Press, 1993.

Zohn, Harry. *Austriaca and Judaica: Essays and Translations.* New York: Peter Lang, 1995.

Zweig, Stefan. *The World of Yesterday.* Lincoln: University of Nebraska Press, 1943.

Index

www.ingramcontent.com/pod-product-compliance
Lightning Source LLC
LaVergne TN
LVHW040159080826
844660LV00001B/45

* 9 7 8 0 8 1 4 3 3 2 0 8 5 *